TV & TEENS

Experts Look at the Issues

Action for Children's Television

EDITED BY MEG SCHWARZ

ADDISON–WESLEY PUBLISHING COMPANY
Reading, Massachusetts · Menlo Park, California
London · Amsterdam · Don Mills, Ontario · Sydney

Library of Congress Cataloging in Publication Data
Main entry under title:

TV & teens.

   Bibliography: p.
   Includes index.
   1. Television and youth—United States—Addresses,
essays, lectures.   I. Schwarz, Meg.   II. Action for
Children's Television.   III. TV and teens.
IV. Title: T.V. & teens.
HQ799.2.T4T83   305.2'3   81-22856
ISBN 0-201-10295-1   AACR2

ISBN 0-201-10295-1 hc

   BCDEFGHIJ-DO-85432

Second Printing, October 1982

Contents

3 Role Models

4 The World of Work

5 Sex and Sexuality

6 Youth in Crisis

7 Radio

8 Advertising & the Teen Market

FOREWORD

by Robert Coles

Youth, as I have heard many high school students say over and over again, is a time of apprenticeship—when a boy or girl learns how to qualify as a grownup member of this or that nation. Television is a means by which powerful influences make their presence felt repeatedly, insistently, persuasively. No wonder youth and television together inspire the attentive thoughtfulness of the following pages—the two "phenomena" are a pair of twentieth-century windows inviting in what they reveal when opened: us as people all too involved with an assortment of hustlers, mischief workers, or plain fools.

On the other hand, there are honorable and decent sides to our national life; and certainly, youth can be a time not only of drugs and alcohol, illegitimate pregnancy, and destructive delinquency, but idealism, introspection, strenuous and unflagging devotion to certain aspirations. In these essays we are offered the full range of our humanity: adolescence as a wonderfully exciting time, when so very much is examined, tested, and yes, achieved; adolescence as a period of special vulnerability, with waywardness of one kind or another a distinct possibility; and television as a powerful edifying as well as entertaining source, but, too, television as a quite vulgar, opportunistic, even extortionate instrument, owned and run by those who care about nothing but the god Mammon, and to devil with anyone or anything in the way of that pursuit.

This book about the impact of television on American adolescents turns out to be quite something else: a broad look at a particular culture—its assumptions, values, ideals, and unfortunately, its blind spots and exploitative excesses. The authors range wide and deep, but are not intent on foolish or irrelevant fishing expeditions. They understand that a particular part of the life cycle and a particular medium of communication are a response to certain social and economic imperatives constantly at work among all of us.

These essays, in their sum, remind us that what is at stake, as we contemplate the uses and purposes of television, is no less than our self-respect. Are we a nation willing indifferently to surrender our own children to the manipulative dominance of a given industry, and those who use it for their own reasons? Are we to yield our critical intelligence to the dictates of insidiously compelling technology? What do we owe our youth, beyond food, shelter, clothing, and the luxuries an affluent society has turned into necessities—one of which, the holy tube, shines upon us implacably, greedily, a secular god of sorts, determined in its own manner to exert its sway over our hearts, if not our minds? These are only some of the questions one asks upon reading the essays that follow—a welcome contribution to our lives as (one hopes and prays) responsible American citizens, who (if we only knew it) are the owners of all television, because it is *our* air, *our* "waves," *our* channels which those various others (network personnel, advertisers, and on and on) claim as theirs and use, these days, with such provocative self-assurance.

INTRODUCTION*

The American adolescent, aged ten to fifteen, watches approximately twenty-three hours of television per week. Increasingly, young people are turning to television for answers, allowing television programs to guide their choices in relation to education, sexuality, careers, health, and personal relationships. Television frequently supplants the family, schools, and the labor force as the major socializing institution for the young adolescent. Nonetheless, these young adolescents have been underserved and underrepresented—if not ignored—on television.

Erik Erikson states that an adolescent's prime danger is identity confusion. For the most part, television ignores the adolescent's search for self-identity. Most of us believe that the Fonzies or J.J.s of commercial television neither portray a true composite picture of the young teenager nor provide realistic role models for this group of children. The search for self–identity is also impeded by the profusion of supermen and superwomen who race across the screen, performing humanly impossible feats in a way that causes young people to feel inadequate. The result is a lowered self-esteem, which sets the stage for the ingestion of mindless commercials showing all the latest methods for becoming beautiful, smart, and popular by eating and drinking particular products and engaging in exciting activities while dressing in just the right clothes.

A great many parents of adolescents are frustrated by the strong influence these television role models have on their youngsters. The experts in *TV & Teens* provide ammunition and sound advice for parents on a wide range of topics. A nutritionist discusses how television commercials affect the eating habits of teens and enumerates reasonable steps parents can take to help ensure that adolescent nutritional needs are met. A psychologist writes about the reasons for adolescent suicide, offers insights into the early detection of those who are at risk and makes suggestions for what friends and relatives can do to prevent this tragedy. Many of the essays include suggestions about particular television programs that can be especially useful for family viewing in order to promote discussions about values and ethics.

* ACT would like to acknowledge Maureen Harmonay's contribution to this book.

Teachers and others who deal with adolescents on a basic level are concerned about the racism, sexism, and ageism that constantly surface on television and prevent the development of healthy attitudes in teens. Some programs, according to these experts, could be used for classroom discussion to offset what is often acceptance caused by frequent exposure to unsound ideas.

TV producers should bear in mind that, because television has become a major arbiter of values and identity for this age group, they have some level of responsibility to assist young adolescents' physical, mental, and social development. To explore television's potential to help young viewers and to foster more and better programming for the ten- to fifteen-year-old adolescent, Action for Children's Television (ACT) went to educators, developmental psychologists, medical and health practitioners, researchers, and producers of teenage programming for answers to key questions such as: What are the facts about adolescence in our society? How can television help young adolescents in their search for identity? What are some things to remember when producing for young teens?

The essays in this book offer comprehensive research on adolescents' needs, examine what teenagers are currently learning from television, and suggest some creative programming ideas that could better meet the requirements of this young audience.

To dispel the myths and misconceptions of adolescence, child development experts and health care professionals present in Chapter One a portrait of young teenagers, outlining their emotional and social characteristics, behavior patterns, and health concerns. One of the most important influences on teens during this period is their normal —but often painful—physical growth and development.

Chapter Two outlines several different television program formats —soap operas, specials, series, sports, news, humor, and shows produced by teenagers themselves—and examines how each type of program should be designed for the teenage audience.

The authors in Chapter Three look at the role models currently presented on television and offer suggestions on how more positive models could be presented to young teenagers. A case study of the PBS program "Freestyle" by producer Norton Wright examines how the series offered young people models of male and female behavior that transcend the common stereotypes; Wright also analyzes his program's success in changing young viewers' attitudes about the roles open to them. Other essays look at the teenage role models that television offers to young blacks, Hispanics, Asians, and other minority groups.

Joan Lipsitz, president of the Center for Early Adolescence in

Carrboro, North Carolina, has said that the media "present insulting stereotypes of adolescents that would be unacceptable were they applied to racial or ethnic groups." There is a cruel, continuous discrepancy between the behavioral models offered by current programming and the adolescent's perception of the social reality in which she or he must operate. The authors offer practical suggestions about how these images could be changed to boost the self-concepts of minority young people and influence the attitudes of white teenagers to their non-white peers.

Teenagers are often asked to make decisions that will affect their ultimate career choices, yet they suffer from a lack of exposure to career training and career opportunities. The authors in Chapter Four describe the attitudes and expectations of young teenagers as they contemplate their futures, examine the characterization of people in various jobs on television shows that teenagers watch, and pose some ideas about how television could provide sufficient career information to teens in entertaining ways.

It is impossible to talk about this age group without acknowledging that many of their most pressing questions and concerns relate to sex. Chapter Five addresses sexuality and the young adolescent: how sexuality is presented to young viewers and what they might be learning about their own sexuality from television; the alarming facts about teenage pregnancy and how some programs have tried to be responsive to this growing problem; and the controversy over advertising contraceptives on television.

While the book as a whole deals with day-to-day adolescent development, Chapter Six takes a special look at some of the serious problems that teenagers can encounter. Three case studies by producers of dramatic and documentary specials reveal how programs about drug abuse, alcoholism, and teenage suicide can uncover some of the reasons so many young people have turned to these outlets to cope with the challenges of growing up. Each essay discusses how television can encourage young viewers to seek help with their problems. An article by producer Daniel Wilson chronicles the events that led to the scheduling of a significant special on teenage alcoholism. In this essay Wilson gives a frank inside view of the problems producers often face in getting a sensitive program of this sort on the air. Another author addresses the problem of rising juvenile crime rates and analyzes the link between juvenile crime and violent television programming.

It would be an oversight in a book about broadcasting and teenagers not to talk about radio. In Chapter Seven Michael Hirsh describes one way a popular top-40 major-market teenage radio station conducts a successful public service campaign that addresses the concerns of its young audience.

The last chapter examines television advertising geared to teens—the kinds of products targeted to them, the manner in which they are marketed, and the sex-role stereotypes in television ads and how they affect young teenagers' self-perceptions.

Under the best of circumstances, adolescence is a difficult period of growth and change—one that few of us would choose to relive. The U.S. statistics are frightening: the teenage runaway rate has doubled since 1970; young people are starting to drink at the age of twelve; over a million teenage girls get pregnant each year; teenagers have the highest rate of poor nutrition among any age group; suicide is the second leading cause of death among teens. These startling facts suggest a population in dire need of attention. Yet the young adolescent, the ten- to fifteen-year-old, is an almost invisible person, caught in a void between childhood and adulthood. Young teenagers are overlooked or ignored in research, in services, and in television. *TV & Teens* offers some of the resources necessary to correct this destructive imbalance.

—*Meg Schwarz*
Action for Children's Television

1 The Young Adolescent

Confidence

What's Confidence?
Confidence is a feeling that
you're sure of yourself
That you know you're going to be
something
That you know you're a-okay
That you're cute.
But I don't have this so
I'm broken up.
I don't even know what to be
I want to have confidence in me
But I don't know how.   I hope one
of these days I'll find my
confidence.

Miriam Lasanta, age 12
Brooklyn, New York

Themes and Variations of Adolescence

BEATRIX HAMBURG

COMING OF AGE in America has been such a lengthy process that adolescence now includes three distinct developmental states. Yet among the many myths about adolescence, the common distortion is to lump all adolescents together and to think in terms of "the adolescent" or "teenager" regardless of whether the person is junior high, high school, or college age. Failure to appreciate that there are distinct stages of adolescent development has imposed heavy burdens on young adolescents because the role expectations and the imagery of popular stereotypes derive from late adolescence. Early adolescents have very little in common with late adolescents. Each stage has its own characteristic developmental tasks, biological and psychological resources, and coping possibilities. Late adolescents are at the threshold of trying to succeed in the adult world. Mid-adolescents (high school age) have no new challenges. It is a time of consolidation and beginning to look to the future. Early adolescents are still moving, erratically, in and out of the world of childhood and groping for guidelines to define their new status.[1]

Early adolescence probably is the most stressful of all developmental transitions. James Tanner has stated that "for the majority of young persons, the years from twelve to sixteen are the most eventful ones of their lives so far as their growth and development is con-

* Beatrix Hamburg, M.D., is associate professor of psychiatry, Harvard Medical School and Children's Hospital Medical Center, and an editorial advisor for the *Journal of Adolescence*.

cerned. Admittedly during fetal life and the first year or two after birth developments occurred still faster . . . but the subject was not the fascinated, charmed or horrified spectator that watches the developments, or lack of developments, of adolescence."[2]

Throughout adolescence appear the recurrent themes of identity, autonomy, achievement, and intimacy. As young people move through the stages of adolescence, they meet the successive challenges of these tasks with ever-increasing physical and intellectual maturity and can build on the learning experience of prior periods. The ultimate success in negotiating these life tasks and setting patterns for adult functioning is crucially linked to the success with which the young adolescent copes with the earliest stage of adolescent development. Failure to cope with the stresses of early adolescence has immediate consequences as well. It has become painfully clear that severe problems such as drug abuse, alcoholism, inappropriate pregnancy, and suicide now show the most rapidly rising rates in these youngest adolescents.[3]

There are three sets of new preemptive demands for the young adolescent. First are the challenges posed by the biological changes of puberty. The individual must cope with the flagrant and undeniable impact of change in body configuration. An adolescent may perceive, at times erroneously, that his or her emerging size and shape is the physique that will be characteristic throughout adult life. This concern over body image is pervasive. Young adolescents have deep concerns about their physical attractiveness and often feel vulnerable to real or imagined assaults on bodily integrity. At the same time, they have relatively little information about the wide range of normalcy or the timetables for physical changes. Adolescents also present baffling changes of mood and temperament that may result partially from direct effects of the gonadal hormones but are interpreted as a response to interpersonal stress.

Second, there are the challenges posed by the entry into a new social system—junior high school. With this transition, the student relinquishes the former security of membership in one stable classroom and is faced with the task of negotiating six or seven changes of teachers and classes each day with no group support. This raises threats of failure in the face of vastly greater requirements for autonomy. There are greater academic demands and therefore concerns about achievement. Finally, there is uncertainty about the ability to make new friendships in this rather intimidating new context.

The third set of challenges derives from the sudden entry into a new role status. The admission into junior high school has become a convenient marker for the conferring of adolescent status and is the badge of entry into the teen culture. In a dimly perceived way, the early adolescent urgently feels in need of a new set of behaviors, values, and reference persons. Parents also view the junior high school student as entering a new world. They expect to treat their child differently and try to think of him or her now as an adolescent. Since the adolescent stereotype usually refers to the period of late adolescence, parental attitudes and behaviors tend to derive from this model, and parents may fail to provide their child with enough support and guidance in the mistaken belief that independence must be granted.

Each of these sets of challenges is formidable in its own right, and each represents the sharpest possible discontinuity with the past. In none of these areas can the young person draw on prior experience as a guide or coping resource. Additional stress is engendered by the fact that these challenges are superimposed. Even for the most competent individuals, early adolescence is a period of great stress, impoverished coping skills, and consequent high vulnerability. There is also the potential for much growth.

Adolescence is indeed a difficult time, but a careful review of the data on adolescent turmoil reveals that the extent and inevitability of turbulence have been greatly exaggerated. It is another myth of adolescence. This myth provides a climate of negative expectations that heightens the normal anxieties and tensions that pervade this complex transitional period.

It is now generally agreed that young adolescents are far more concrete in their thinking than was previously recognized.[4] Formal operational thinking does not become characteristic until after age fifteen or sixteen. Early adolescence is a time in which thinking is characterized by egocentrism and major deficits in ability to process information with objectivity. Young adolescents' sense of time is predominantly one of here and now with little real appreciation of the future. They are also prone to overgeneralizing from immediate experience. This can result in distorted social perceptions, particularly with regard to peer behavior or attitudes.

Because there are no clear guidelines for early adolescent behaviors, the ambiguity of the new social role leads even the soundest adolescent to develop feelings of being an outsider, a marginal person of questionable worth. In the face of these anxieties, young adolescents are unusually susceptible to outside influences and insecure about their own personal values and judgments. As a response to uncertainty, they vacillate and experiment with many roles and styles of behaving. At all times, there is a constant scanning for models and mentors from whom they can learn. Some of the most significant of these are popular figures from television, radio, and movies.

Identity

According to Erik Erikson, identity is the integration of the sum total of physical, psychosocial, intellectual, and ethical facets of self-concept.[5] It is a late-stage process, possible only after an advanced stage of cognitive development is reached and after considerable life experience on which to base judgments. Young adolescents focus chiefly on the aspect of identity that relates to body image. They are just starting to learn about their preferences, talents, and values from role experimentation and imitation of models. For them, identity issues are very much an open process. Early adolescence is an unusually favorable time for revising prior negative self-images, discovering new abilities, or reaffirming a sense of worth.

The media could be helpful in many ways. Young adolescents need sound information about the range of normalcy in the timing and events of body changes. Depicting the social dilemmas that relate to physical changes at puberty would be meaningful. Adolescents' deep concerns about their bodies too often have been belittled or ridiculed. They need to have responsible adults take their concerns seriously and explain their physical changes in ways that support their self-esteem.

In their search for identity, adolescents need constructive examples of individual differences, role rehearsals, and experimentations. They also need realistic portrayals of the experiments that will fail. For example, one cannot experiment with becoming a teenage mother. Parenthood is one of the most permanent commitments that can be made, and the lifelong consequences for parent and child when this occurs too early are grim.

Autonomy

Traditionally, autonomy is described as attaining independence of, or rebelling against, parents. Autonomy would be better described as the achievement of mature, interdependent relationships. Most young adolescents of ten to fifteen years of age will continue to live at home for many more years. Therefore the issue of true autonomy is not linked to a valid change in life situation. In moving toward independent functioning, the actual task of the young adolescent is to renegotiate the relationship with his or her parents. The relative ease or difficulty in moving away from childish independence and subordination to more responsible and independent status hinges on prior and continuing parental interactions. If the parents provide realistic, age-graded opportunities for responsible independence, the task is made easier. However, even in the best of circumstances, limit setting in early adolescence is the major source of strife between parents and adolescents, particularly as their children vacillate between irresponsible childishness and unexpectedly mature behavior.

The pseudoindependence of young adolescents is often characterized by a challenging and abrasive interpersonal style. Their use of arguments and an adversary stance, however, may represent a form of information gathering. If the significant adults can react without rancor, they are usually rewarded, after some delay, by finding that the young adolescent has incorporated these ideas and values. But many parents are hurt by this new adversary behavior of their children and lapse into a self-protective retreat when they feel attacked or rebuffed. These are the ingredients of the generation gap. With the distancing of parent and child, there is often a relaxation of the demands previously made upon the child, and a lessening, rather than a more appropriate increase, of the responsibilities expected of him or her. Some parents may lose touch with the activities and friends of their children in the name of privacy.

Young adolescents who lack firm parental guidance and availability of the parent as a model and coping resource more urgently need to seek peer support and adopt the badges of conformity. This uncritical allegiance to the peer group may be useful in allaying immediate anxieties, but it has serious limitations. At best, the peer group at this stage is usually too shallow and rigid to afford the necessary resources for growth and development. When the peer group is organized around drugs or acting-out behaviors, there is potential for considerable damage.

There is a need for public understanding of the different stages of adolescence and, in particular, information on the importance of parental interest, guidance, and support for young adolescents. Rather than accepting the notion of the generation gap as characteristic or even, somehow, growth promoting, parents need to carry out appropriate parental functions and learn about effective communication with their youngsters.

Achievement

Entry into junior high school catapults young adolescents into a drastic and demanding change in the format of school experience. They find themselves in large institutions with a succession of different teachers and classmates each day. The academic demands, both in quantity and difficulty, show sharp increases. There are nonacademic anxieties about feeling lost in the system, being laughed at, pushed around, pressured, or isolated from friends. Typically there is a drop in academic performance in junior high school, shown to be related to motivation rather than to intelligence.[6] Many urban schools are vandalized and covered with graffiti in apparent protest and rejection by the students. Models of modified junior high schools and middle schools that succeed in creating a learning environment and positive social experience need to be sought and publicized. Television could play a role in giving visibility to such models.

New avenues for achievement through nonacademic channels need to be highlighted. Young adolescents can develop a sense of self-worth through participation in needed community activities, such as tutoring, helping the elderly, working in hospitals, carrying out recycling projects, or cleaning up a neighborhood to make a play area. The potential for encouraging constructive youth participation has been sadly neglected.[7] It could enhance the desire to achieve and link academic exercises to meaningful demands of the community and world of work. It could offer girls the chance to explore jobs and roles previously believed to be restricted to males, and vice-versa, which would help to transcend sex-role stereotypes. It would also serve to enlarge the scope of their experience with adults of all ages as sources of information, friendship, and support. Youth participation may be the only way to lay a foundation of positive achievement motivation for some of the youngsters who have limited academic abilities or specific learning disabilities. The goal would be to maximize the likelihood that all young adolescents can begin to develop realistic expectations of future work and career choices.

Intimacy

In the past decade there has been a steep upsurge in rates of sexual activity, and the age of initiation has moved steadily downward. In 1970 the modal ages for starting sexual activity were between eighteen and nineteen years of age. Currently they are between fifteen and sixteen years of age.[8] Now more than ever young adolescents are confused about the distinctions among love, intimacy, and sexuality. This is vividly illustrated by a fifteen-year-old who explained her involvement in sexual activities by stating, "It's a good way to get acquainted." Ten years ago, when an eighteen- or nineteen-year-old initiated sexual activity, she or he typically stated that "it was because we care about each other very much" or "we are engaged," indications of mutuality and a sense of commitment. While this partly reflects a change in societal attitudes, the difference chiefly reflects the greater ability of the older adolescent to achieve and to value a truly intimate relationship.

Young adolescents are in the initial stages of learning to establish close friendship ties with members of both sexes. They are uncertain about what to say or do, how much to posture, how much to confide. Much of the power of peer pressure at this age derives from an almost desperate eagerness for acceptance and a sense of belonging. Many of the young adolescents who engage in sexual relations are actually seeking friendship and approval. Sexual activity is not a good way for them to get acquainted. It adds yet another layer of embarrassment, awkwardness, and anxiety about how one must appear to the other person. Under these adverse circumstances, sexual activity is often a negative rather than a positive experience for both partners.

Recently the media and movies have glamorized the sexiness of early adolescents and portrayed them in a variety of roles of explicit sexuality. *Time* magazine referred to "Hollywood's Whiz Kids" in this context in an admiring article.[9] A *New York* magazine cover showed the current top fashion models; they were all twelve to fifteen years old.[10] These images are reinforced on television, both in advertisements and in programming. Young adolescents pay selective attention to these messages. They would be better served by presentations that help them sort out issues of friendship, intimacy, and sexuality. They need to learn basic social skills for communicating with others and techniques for resisting negative peer pressures. They have a great deal to learn about equity and responsibility in close relationships, especially in sexual relationships.

Adolescent stereotypes obscure an understanding of the real needs of adolescents. Parents, teachers, media persons, and others who influence the lives of young adolescents rarely understand this age group. Without the benefit of a consistent, informed approach, many young people have fared badly. Although the casualty rate is still fairly low, it is not trivial. At a time when the health and well-being of most other sectors of the population now show satisfying gains, for young adolescents, rising rates of behaviors that have immediate and long-term negative consequences continue to rise.

Young adolescents are a target audience most susceptible to influence by adolescent stereotypes. These caricatures contribute to shaping their behaviors. Television could be of great service in enabling young adolescents to learn about the realities of adolescent experiences. They need presentations of the true nature and extent of peer behaviors that are salient for them. The media could help them to be aware of their tendency to amplify perceptions and to draw conclusions based on limited personal experiences. They need to see issues through the eyes of a range of thoughtful peers. They need to look beyond the adolescent stereotypes.

Their willingness to experiment and their receptiveness to new ideas and approaches can lead to problems for young adolescents. These attributes, however, also present an opportunity to engage their attention and harness their energies in constructive activities that foster their development and promote mastery of the tasks and challenges of this critical period of development.

References

1. Beatrix A. Hamburg, "Early Adolescence: A Specific and Stressful Stage of the Life Cycle," in *Coping and Adaptation*, ed. G. Coelho, D. Hamburg, and J. Adams (New York: Basic Books, 1974), pp. 101-124.

2. James M. Tanner, "Sequence, Tempo and Individual Variation in the Growth and Development of Boys and Girls Aged Twelve to Sixteen," *Daedalus* (Fall 1971): 907–930.

3. Sarah S. Brown, "The Health Needs of Adolescents," in U.S. Department of Health, Education and Welfare, *Healthy People: The Surgeon General's Report on Health Promotion and Disease Prevention. Background Papers*, DHEW (PHS) Publication No. 79-55071A (Washington, D.C.: Government Printing Office, 1979), pp. 333–364.

4. David Elkind, "Recent Research on Cognitive Development in Adolescence," in *Adolescents' Development and Education: A Janus Knot*, ed. R. L. Mosher (Berkeley, Calif.: McCutchan Publishing Co., 1979), pp. 40–48.

5. Erik H. Erikson, *Identity and the Life Cycle: Psychological Issues* (New York: International University Press, 1959).

6. Jerome Kagan, "A Conception of Early Adolescence," *Daedalus* (Fall 1971): 997–1012.

7. National Commission on Resources for Youth, *New Roles for Youth* (New York: Citation Press, 1974).

8. Melvin Zelnik and John Kantner, "Sexual Activity, Contraceptive Use and Pregnancy Among Metropolitan-Area Teenagers: 1971–1979," *Family Planning Perspectives* 12 (September–October 1980): 230–237.

9. J. Skow, "Hollywood's Whiz Kids," *Time*, August 13, 1979, pp. 64–70.

10. Mel Juffe and Anthony Haden-Guest, "Pretty Babies," *New York*, September 29, 1980, pp. 32–37.

Promoting Teen Health Care

KAREN HEIN

UNTIL RECENTLY it was assumed that adolescence is the healthiest period of life. It is true that mortality rates are low during this decade and that teenagers do not see physicians regularly, but adolescence is not necessarily a healthy period of life. Barriers to obtaining health care and the lack of appreciation of teenagers' special needs have resulted in a gap between the health needs of American youth and adequate resources to serve them.

Three factors contribute to the misconception that adolescents are healthy and require little medical intervention. First, adults often design health services for adolescents without polling the views of the consumers. Surveys of youth have shown that adults and teenagers view health concerns very differently.[1] Second, medical problems are defined as those conditions that have a readily available medical treatment or a known associated mortality rate. Many of the conditions that afflict adolescents (scoliosis and hypertension, for example) cause no apparent discomfort during adolescence but have their impact later in life.[2] Third, teenagers frequently have to overcome a series of barriers to reach existing health services. Consent, confidentiality, and expensive fees frequently discourage young people from seeking health care.

* Karen Hein, M.D., is assistant professor of pediatrics, College of Physicians and Surgeons, Columbia University, where she also serves as director of the Division of Adolescent Medicine.

PUBLIC HEALTH SERVICE
OFFICE ON SMOKING & HEALTH
ROCKVILLE, MD 20857

1. BROOKE: There's this guy who I thought was really terrific. I mean, well, self-assured.

2. And I really like that in a person. Anyway, one night I saw him at this party, and I got up the nerve to say, "hello."

3. And then, he takes out a cigarette! Blows my whole image of him.

4. I mean, I know I make some people nervous...but I thought he had it together.

5. VO: Smoking. It's a dead give-away.

6. BROOKE: I think people who smoke are real losers.

Brooke Shields speaks out against smoking in this public service announcement made by the Public Health Service Office on Smoking and Health and distributed by the American Lung Association.

Feeling awkward at their class Valentine's Day dance, Marcy (Jenny Feeback) and Wally (Michael Palmer) try to make the best of the situation in "I'm Soooo Ugly!," a Multimedia Young People's Special.

Dr. Lee Salk talks to his guests about how young people who live with chronic illness deal with their problems and the people in their lives on PBS's "Feelings." Photo courtesy of S.C. ETV.

Unmet Health Needs

American teenagers are a medically underserved group. Nearly one in four youngsters aged sixteen to seventeen had inadequate access to medical care in 1974. The rate for twelve- to fifteen-year-olds was nearly 22 percent. Although 90 percent of children under twelve have a regular source of health care, only 15 percent of sixteen- and seventeen-year-olds have a regular physician.[3]

Within the group of approximately 40 million American teenagers, there are subgroups where the gap between existing health services and needs is especially large. Urban and rural youth and minority group members are least likely to have health maintenance throughout adolescence. When a group of inner-city youths aged twelve to fifteen were asked about their health concerns, eight medical conditions not receiving medical care were listed for each condition already under care.[4]

Institutionalized or transient youths (those not currently living at home) compose another group of teenagers with special health needs.[5] The life-styles of these young people place them at a high risk for many illnesses. Forty-seven percent of youths screened upon admission to a detention center were found to have a medical problem. Polls conducted by the National Center for Health Statistics for American teenagers do not include this sizable group. It is estimated that a half-million youngsters are detained or placed in juvenile court-related facilities and that there are more than 1 million runaway youngsters per year. The type of institution that houses young people may change in the coming years, but their health needs will not.[6]

It is useful to divide medical conditions occurring during adolescence into three categories (see table, page 12). These three clusters of conditions and illnesses highlight the special relationship between the adolescent stage of development and health. In addition, teenagers with chronic handicapping conditions have special needs. These conditions include a broad spectrum of disorders of the central nervous system, musculoskeletal problems, cosmetic disorders, and persistent learning disabilities. The handicapped population has increased need for primary care and hospital services and more frequent examinations. Psychological and social assistance for these youths is frequently necessary. The impact of a chronic condition on the process of physical and psychological adolescent development is often profound.

What Young People Should Know about Health Care

The Supreme Court has stated that "neither the 14th Amendment nor the Bill of Rights is for adults alone."[7] The Court has extended

MEDICAL CONDITIONS OCCURRING DURING ADOLESCENCE

Problems Primary to Adolescence	Problems Made Worse by Adolescence	Problems with Origins during Adolescence
Scoliosis	Tuberculosis	Obesity
Slipped epiphysis	Automotive accidents	Alcoholism
Acne	Unwed pregnancy	Duodenal ulcer
Sports injuries	Suicidal tendencies	Hypercholesterotemia
Mononucleosis	Diabetes	Labile hypertension
Body-image distortions	Inflammatory bowel disease	Irritable colon syndrome
Drug abuse		
Venereal diseases	Menstrual dysfunction	Migraine
Goiter	Dental caries	Marital conflicts
Sexual dysfunction	Abortion	
Delinquency	Gynecomastia	
Tumors	Mental retardation	
Anorexia nervosa		
Hepatitis		
Primary amenorrhea		
School-learning problems		
Truancy		

Source: M. I. Cohen, I. F. Litt, S. K. Schonberg, A. J. Sheehy, F. Daum and K. Hein, "Perspectives on Adolescent Medicine: Concepts and Program Design," *Acta Paediatrica Scandinavica Supplement* 25 (1977): 9–16. Reprinted with permission.

these rights to include a minor's right to obtain sex-related health care and emergency care (except for abortions) and has defined many instances in which a minor can be considered emancipated for purposes of giving consent for a special type of health care. In the last few years, the concept of the mature minor has evolved in which a minor who initiates his or her own health care and demonstrates the ability to understand the nature and potential consequence of a given health plan may give consent for care without parental consent or knowledge.

Many medical schools and residency training programs now include concepts of adolescent growth, development, and disease as part of the curriculum so that physicians being trained now will have a different approach to their adolescent patients.[8] Specifically, the American Academy of Pediatrics has recently redefined the role of the pediatrician to extend care to patients through the age of twenty-one. Similarly, family practitioners, internists, psychiatrists, obstetrician-gynecologists, and others will be more familiar with the special needs of teenagers. Some physicians have been willing to help establish health care for adolescents outside the traditional formats of private practice or hospital-based services. They work with other health professionals (nurses, nurse practitioners, social workers, psychologists, and community organizers) to establish a health focus in places where teenagers tend to gather.

If teenagers do not have periodic contact with a health professional to assess these conditions, they may be harboring unnecessary concern about their bodies. Or if an adolescent has one of the many asymptomatic conditions that are easily detected and treated during adolescence, he or she may not become aware of its existence until the health consequence is more serious, prolonged, or difficult to treat. Therefore, it is important for teenagers to seek a sensitive, knowledgeable health care provider for health maintenance and care throughout adolescence.

What Can Broadcasters Do?

Many health education programs, whether they employ mass media or not, have been shown to influence knowledge but not necessarily to change teenage attitudes or behavior.[9] The following suggestions are offered to aid broadcasters in planning programs to further the understanding of health maintenance and care.

1. Disseminate information about the legal rights of minors to seek and obtain health care. Information about the current status of federal, state, and local statutes should be disseminated, and guidelines should be designed.
2. Encourage consumerism in the adolescent population. Once teenagers are aware of their right to health care, they should know about the elements of the medical history, physical examination, and laboratory tests that are appropriate for their age group.
3. Use mass media to advertise products such as condoms, diaphragms, and acne preparations that are known to be safe and effective for teenagers.
4. Use fewer stereotypes in depicting health providers and interactions between patients and health providers.
5. Take advantage of the curiosity that teenagers have about their growing, changing bodies to educate them about the need for health-promoting periodic self-examinations.
6. Refrain from a judgmental approach to health issues. Present facts

without prejudice to allow the adolescent to synthesize the information into the context of family, friends, and community. Refrain from scare tactics; they do not work with teenagers and will alienate them.

7. Television broadcasting can be used to encourage young people to seek out local community resources for health maintenance and care. By including a statement about fees, consent, and confidentiality, some of the barriers to obtaining care may be reduced.

References

1. R. Sorenson, *Adolescent Sexuality in Contemporary America* (New York: World Publisher, 1973).

2. H. Millar, *Approaches to Adolescent Health Care in the 1970's*, DHEW Publication No. (HSA) 75-5014. (Washington, D.C.: Government Printing Office, 1975).

3. P. Budetti, P. McManus, S. Stenmark, and L. LeRoy, *Child Health Professionals: Supply, Training and Practice, Prepared for the Select Panel for the Promotion of Child Health, 1980* (in press).

4. A. F. Brunswick, and E. Josephson, "Adolescent Health in Harlem," *American Journal of Public Health* (Supplement) (October 1972).

5. K. Hein, M. I. Cohen, I. F. Litt, S. K. Schonberg, M. Meyer, A. Marks, and A. J. Sheehy, "Juvenile Detention: Another Boundary Issue for Physicians," *Pediatrics* 66 (1980): 239–245.

6. M. Kramer, *Psychiatric Services and the Changing Institutional Scene, 1950–1985 (NIMH)*, DHEW Publication No. (ADM) 77-443 (Washington, D.C.: Government Printing Office, 1977).

7. E. W. Paul and H. F. Pilpel, "Teenagers and Pregnancy: The Law in 1979," *Family Planning Perspectives* 11 (1979): 297–302.

8. *The Task Force on Pediatric Education Report: The Future of Pediatric Education* (Evanston, Ill.: 1979).

9. K. Hein, "Impact of Mass Media on Adolescent Sexual Behavior," *American Journal of Disabled Children* 134 (1980): 133–134.

Shaping Up

The Teenage Diet

JOHANNA DWYER

YEARS AGO, Birdseye, in a brilliant series of advertisements for its frozen vegetables, urged customers to pay more attention to the "quiet corner" in their dinner plates and to fill them up with Birdseye vegetables. That campaign is a good example of how one company did well by promoting good nutrition; it sold more of its branded product, and many parents around the country found that their children were a little more venturesome in eating vegetables than they had been before. Since youngsters' intakes of certain nutrients found in many fruits and vegetables (such as vitamins A and C and calcium) are often low and many children are disinterested in eating vegetables, this change was nutritionally desirable.

The correlation between foods advertised to teenagers on radio and television and their dietary needs is often not so perfect, however. For this reason nutritionists feel that they have struck out when it comes to the role of television and radio in nutrition education.

The basis of good nutrition for any group of human beings is to get enough (but not too much) energy (or calories) and protective nutrients such as protein, vitamins, and minerals. All of this must be achieved at a reasonable cost, taking food preferences into account.

Food guides for teenagers are designed to meet their overall nutritional needs and are divided into five general food groups. The first

* Johanna Dwyer, D.Sc., is associate professor at Tufts Medical School and director of the Frances Stern Nutrition Center of Tufts-New England Medical Center.

four groups are high in protective nutrients as well as calories: milk and milk products; fruits and vegetables; meat, poultry, fish, eggs, and protein-rich beans; and breads and cereals. The fifth group of sweets, fats, and desserts consists largely of calories and little else. Teenagers have elevated needs for almost all of the protective nutrients, but only in the growing years of adolescence are their needs for calories elevated. The types of foods advertised in the media tend to emphasize higher-cost, brand-name products that are high in calories and low in the protective nutrients. The foods that are advertised are not necessarily bad, but they are not representative of the nutritional recommendations for a balanced diet. Nutrient-rich foods, on the other hand, are rarely advertised.

The second problem with TV and radio commercials for food is that they usually stress eating more of a particular food. From a nutritional standpoint, eating less or substituting one food for another is often more appropriate. The U.S. Dietary Guidelines of the two major government agencies concerned with food suggest moderation in intake of calories, total fat, saturated fat, simple sugars, salt, and alcohol for most Americans. Many of the advertised foods are high in these substances.

The third problem with the media is that its attempts to correct its nutritional balance by public service advertising or programming are few in number, so vague in content as to be almost meaningless, or presented at hours when many people are asleep or tending to their work.

Thus we are at an impasse; balanced nutritional content is the quiet corner on the broadcasters' programming plate. Children and teenagers spend several hours a day watching television or listening to the radio and food advertisements are frequently presented. Virtually all of the information relating to food encourages them to eat and is designed to sell products, not to promote wise nutritional choices and health practices. The nutrition education job is left to parents (assuming they can get a word in edgewise) and the schools, which are already taxed with solving or ameliorating a myriad of other problems.

What can be done? Attempts to infuse more balance into paid television commercials are unlikely to do the job, although some enlightened advertisers have presented their products in a more complete context lately. More promising is the use of better public-service advertising during prime time and better programming.

With suitable timing and frequency, there is good reason to suspect that well-designed nutritional messages can motivate young people to make appropriate choices and to balance their nutritional intake. The lack of success of public service announcements to date can be attributed to a number of problems: the use of poorly designed material produced by amateurs or second-rate professionals on low budgets, infrequent airing at odd hours when the target group is not watching, and poor follow-up in homes, schools, or other settings in which teenagers spend much of their time. In order to improve this means of nutrition education, nutrition experts must join with mass communications experts to get sensible, action-oriented messages across. The food advertisements currently presented on television and radio need to be balanced with messages whose primary purpose is promoting good nutrition.

Nutritional Needs and Growth

Teenagers are old enough to keep track of their growth in height and weight by graphing them every six months on a growth chart that a doctor can supply. It is easier to explain how their nutrient needs change if they actually see how rapidly their bodies are changing.

Enormous increases in nutritional needs occur during adolescence. Nutrient needs vary because of the different demands of the various phases of adolescent growth. In general, nutritional needs are especially high during pubescence, the period of sexual development that ends with the emergence of the capacity for sexual reproduction and usually occurs at ages ten to twelve in girls and thirteen to fifteen in boys. During later adolescence, nutrient needs stay high because new tissues and functions resulting from growth must be maintained.

Adopting Healthy Dietary Habits

The first step in adopting healthy dietary habits is to make sure that energy needs are met. Most teenagers' appetites will see to it that they get enough calories, so this is usually not a problem. Second, it is important to ensure that intakes of protective nutrients are satisfactory. At least four servings of milk and milk products, fruits and vegetables, and breads and cereals and at least two servings of meat, fish, poultry, eggs, or dried beans should be eaten each day. These quantities are higher than those needed by children or older adults because of adolescents' especially high needs for growth.

Third, teenagers need to be aware of their increased needs for iron and how to make food choices that provide it. During the early teenage years, growth of lean tissues increases the need for iron. In later adolescence, iron needs stay high to compensate for losses such as those occurring with menstruation in girls (or, more rarely, with adolescent pregnancies). Good sources of iron include red meat, poultry, eggs, whole grain, and enriched and fortified cereals. Animal foods and citrus fruits should also be stressed because they enhance assimilation of iron in the diet.

Another nutrient teenagers need to be careful to include in their diets is calcium. Needs for calcium rise because of the rapid growth in the skeleton and in other calcium-rich lean tissues during the adolescent spurt, and the increased need continues to be high in later adolescence. This is especially important for girls, who lose calcium during pregnancy and lactation later in life.

Fourth, teenagers need help in moderating their intake of foods high in energy and low in protective nutrients, such as fats, sweets, and alcohol. At least a quarter, and often much more, of the total energy intakes of adolescents consists of high-calorie foods that are low in vitamins and minerals. It is important to make sure that the four basic food group needs are met before foods of this type are emphasized. Otherwise it is easy to fill up on the high-energy, low-protective nutrient foods.

Finally, there are other groups of teenagers with special needs, including those who are pregnant and those with chronic diseases. These young people need guidance that is best given by a physician.

Food for Teenage Life-styles

Teenagers today place a great deal of emphasis on the need for independence, the importance of being in control of their own lives, and physical fitness and well-being. At the same time they tend to reject authority, favor the emotional over the rational, and feel most comfortable with informal life-styles. It is important to help adolescents see that these aspirations can be achieved with eating practices that also foster a healthy life. Parents can help to do this in several ways.

First, they should accept adolescent preferences for frequent snacks and minimeals. This can be done without becoming short-order cooks, letting teenagers abandon the few meals the family eats together, or having the diet go to pot. There is no reason why frequent snacks cannot be included in nutritious diets. Problems arise when choices of snacks are poor or mealtime intakes are not adjusted with the result that overall intakes are excessive. Many teenagers need to know how to choose snacks and fast foods wisely. The snack choices of teenagers today are relatively low in protective nutrients and higher in carbo-hydrate than regular meals and contribute from a fifth to a third of total energy intake. Parents can help teenagers by making suitable foods available at home for both meals and snacks. High-calorie, low-nutrient foods should be downplayed, as should foods high in total fat, saturated fat, sugar, and sodium.

A second step is to adjust meals to conform, within reason, to adolescent snacking patterns and life-styles. The key here is to provide the teenager with both freedom and responsibility in the realm of eating. If teenagers do not wish to eat at regular meal times, they can take a good share of the responsibility in preparing their food and cleaning up afterward. Parents can help by providing nutritious ingredients for the adolescent's self-prepared meals.

Third, parents can learn to ignore the sometimes odd or unconventional meals teenagers often eat. The full meal of pizza, ice cream, and pancakes eaten rapidly in a crowded drugstore at 10 A.M. may offend an adult's sense of aesthetics, but none of these odd habits has any effects on adolescent health or nutritional status.

Some common eating habits among teenagers, however, do make it more difficult for them to maintain good nutritional status and should be avoided. For example, extreme versions of vegetarian diets, especially when they are coupled with other limitations such as use of only "organic" or health foods, may limit nutrient intakes.

Reliance on vitamin pills to ensure nutritional adequacy does not make sense, and teenagers who place their faith in them need to understand why this is the case. Vitamin pills are frequently forgotten and often do not contain necessary minerals such as iron, calcium, and zinc that are in short supply. Finally, vitamin pills do nothing to correct dietary excesses of total and saturated fat, sugar, cholesterol, and sodium, which also may be present in adolescent diets. Large doses of vitamin or mineral supplements for acne, hyperactivity, or other similar problems do not work and may be dangerous.

Alcohol should be avoided entirely until late adolescence and used only sparingly, if at all, after that. Alcohol is both a food and a drug, and alcohol abuse is dangerous. Disordered nutrition as well as serious social and physical problems (including fatal automobile accidents) are often associated with teenage drinking and with the use of other drugs (including appetite suppressants).

Adolescents and Weight

Many teenage girls have unrealistic images about how slim their bodies should be. Teenage boys may also have unrealistic expectations. All teenagers need to receive help in understanding the changes in weight and body composition that occur during adolescence so that they are aware of the elements amenable to change and can set their minds at rest about other physical changes.

A second step is to provide support and positive role models to encourage teenagers to take responsibility for maintaining healthy dietary habits and weight levels. Example is more potent than preaching. Family food supplies and eating practices play a large role for good or ill in the development of teenagers' views about food.

Obesity is best prevented by having teenagers keep track of their weight, adopt moderation in their dietary habits, and lead physically active lives. Parents can help by providing positive psychological support for their efforts. It is easier to take action before obesity has become pronounced than it is to try to remedy it once it occurs because no known treatment is totally effective. For adolescents, moderation in the intake of high calorie snacks and desserts, the use of foods as rewards, and the emphasis on food to relieve emotional stress is particularly important. Since the energy expenditures of many teenagers are lower than recommended levels because of the sedentary lives they lead, an emphasis on high levels of physical activity and exercise is important and also makes it possible to eat more food without gaining weight. High energy outputs resulting from a physically active life may also help to decrease risks for certain chronic degenerative diseases such as diabetes and some forms of heart disease.

Adolescents who need to reduce their weight can be helped in several ways. Expert advice from a physician is necessary to make sure that the teenager needs and wants to lose weight. Harmful eating habits can often be identified if the teenager keeps a record of what is eaten and the calorie value of each item for a few weeks. Most obese teenagers also need help finding alternatives to eating in order to achieve emotional release. Reorienting their coping skills to non-food activities or to better expression of their problems is helpful. Finally, teenagers need help in learning to recognize and avoid ineffective fad diets and to eschew very low-calorie crash diets (under 800 calories) and unsupervised protein fasts, which may be dangerous when not supervised by a physician.

Nutrition Education

Adolescents sometimes need assistance in distinguishing between promotional material for marketing purposes and nutrition education efforts for health purposes. More balanced presentations of nutrition information over the mass media would be helpful. Radio and television have not yet realized their potential for nutrition education and health promotion. Better public service advertisements and more frequent airing of them at reasonable times when program content is likely to appeal to teenage audiences would help to fulfill the media's responsibility to society. Better programming dealing with nutrition-related issues would also be helpful.

During the late 1960s, the media, especially television, played a major role in reorienting government programs to cope more effectively with poverty-related malnutrition. During the 1980s, perhaps television should play a larger role in motivating and educating its audiences to combat the problems of poor nutrition and obesity, which often begin in childhood and adolescence.

Resources, Chapter One

ABC. "*Afterschool Special,*" "Where Do Teenagers Come From?" March 5, 1980. In this sixty-minute sequel to "My Mom's Having a Baby," Dr. Lendon Smith points out to three bewildered young teenagers the physiological and sociological changes they are going through. Produced by DePatie-Freleng Enterprises.

————. "The Best Little Girl in the World." May 4, 1981. A two-hour drama about a victim of anorexia nervosa. Seventeen-year-old Casey, who seems to be happy and successful, is unable to cope and nearly starves herself to death.

Adolescence. An international quarterly devoted to the psychological and educational aspects of the second decade of human life. Libra Publishers, P.O. Box 165, 391 Willets Road, Roslyn Heights, N.Y. 11577.

Agency for Instructional Television (AIT). "On the Level, 1980–1981." A classroom video series of twelve fifteen-minute programs for high school students focusing on their emotional and social growth. Each program dramatizes a common teenage concern, such as accepting feelings, self-understanding, career aspirations, and dealing with conflict. Includes teachers' guide. Special audio adaptations also available. AIT, Box A, Bloomington, Ind. 47402.

"*Am I Normal?*" A twenty-five minute film about a thirteen-year-old boy's quest to discover the truth about the pubertal changes he is experiencing. Available from Momentum Media, 7 Harvard Square, Brookline, Mass. 02146.

Axelson, Julien M., and Del Campo, Diana S. "Improving Teenagers' Nutrition Knowledge Through the Mass Media." *Journal of Nutrition Education* 10 (January–March 1978): 30–33.

Borio, Maria D., et al. *Family Life Theatre and Youth Health Services: A Blending of the Arts, Medicine, and Education in the Pursuit of Adolescent Care.* New York: New York Medical College, 1980.

Character. A monthly publication to address current public and private policies toward youth. 1245 West Westgate Terrace, Chicago, Ill. 60607.

Cherry, Florence. "The Need for Adolescent Health Care." *Human Ecology Forum* 11 (Winter 1981): 21–24.

Early Adolescence: Perspectives and Recommendations to the National Science Foundation. Washington, D.C.: Government Printing Office, 1978.

Friedenberg, Edgar Zodiag. *Coming of Age in America.* New York: Random House, 1965.

Gallagher, J. R., Heald, F. P., and Garell, D. C. *Medical Care for the Adolescent.* Appleton, N.J.: Century Crofts, 1976.

Gilberg, Arnold L. "Adolescence: The Interface of Neurophysiology and Cultural Determinants." *American Journal of Psychoanalysis* 38 (Spring 1978): 87–90.

Gordon, Sol, and Roger, Conant. *YOU! The Teenage Survival Book.* Fayetteville, N.Y.: Strawberry Hill Book, Time Books, 1975.

Green, Morris. "Adolescent Health Care." *Children Today* 8 (September–October 1979): 8–11.

Hauser, Stuart T. "Ego Development and Interpersonal Style in Adolescence." *Journal of Youth and Adolescence* 7 (December 1978): 333–352.

Hill, John P. "Social Cognition and Social Relations in Early Adolescence." *International Journal of Behavioral Development* (1978): 1–36.

Kagan, Jerome, and Coles, Robert. *Twelve to Sixteen: Early Adolescence.* New York: W. W. Norton, 1972.

Kanopka, Gisela. "Requirements for Healthy Development of Adolescent Youth." *Adolescence* 8:31 (Fall 1973): 291–316.

Kavanaugh, Dorriet. *Listen to Us!* New York: Workman Publishing, 1978.

Kett, Joseph F. *Rites of Passage: Adolescence in America, 1790 to the Present.* New York: Basic Books, 1977.

KQED-TV, San Francisco. "Up and Coming." A dramatic series of fifteen thirty-minute programs about three black teenagers' attempts to explore their identities and their independence within the context of a strong and united family.

Lambert, B. G., et al. *Adolescence: Transition from Childhood to Maturity.* Monterey, Calif.: Brooks/Cole Publishing Company, 1972.

Lipsitz, Joan Scheff. "Adolescent Development: Myths and Realities." *Children Today* 8 (September–October 1979): 2–7.

————. *Growing Up Forgotten.* Lexington, Mass.: D. C. Heath, 1977.

————, ed. *Barriers: A New Look at the Needs of Young Adolescents.* New York: Ford Foundation, 1979.

Lopez, R. I., ed. *Adolescent Medicine, Topics.* Volume 1. New York: Spectrum Publications, 1976.

Thornburg, Hershel D., ed. *Contemporary Adolescence: Readings.* Belmont Calif.: Brooks/Cole Publishing Company, 1971.

Time Life Multimedia. *The Teenage Years,* "Sara's Summer of the Swans." A thirty-three minute drama about a skinny fourteen-year-old girl with braces who lacks self-confidence and isolates herself until her younger brother runs away and she is forced to reevaluate her self-image. Based on the book of the same title by Betsy Byars. Produced by Martin Tahse.

White, Kathleen M., and Speisman, Joseph C. *Adolescence.* Monterey, Calif.: Brooks/Cole Publishing Company, 1977.

Wynne, Edward A. "Facts about the Character of Young Americans." *Character* 1 (November 1979): 1–7.

Youth: Transition to Adulthood. Report on the Panel on Youth of the President's Science Advisory Committee. Chicago: University of Chicago Press, 1974.

Organizations

American Academy of Pediatrics, Adolescent Health Division; P.O. Box 1034, 1801 Hinman Avenue, Evanston, Ill. 60204.

American Library Association, Young Adult Services Division, 50 East Huron Street, Chicago, Ill. 60211.

American Society for Adolescent Psychiatry (ASAP), 24 Green Valley Road, Wallingford, Pa. 19086.

Boys' Clubs of America, 771 First Avenue, New York, N.Y. 10017.

Boys Town Center for the Study of Youth Development, Boys Town, Neb. 68010.

Center for Early Adolescence, Suite 223, Carr Mill Mall, Carrboro, N.C. 27510.

Child Welfare League of America, Inc., 67 Irving Place, New York, N.Y. 10003.

Girls' Clubs of America, Inc., 205 Lexington Avenue, New York, N.Y. 10016.

Girls Town of the Florence Crittenden League, Inc., 307 East 12th Street, New York, N.Y. 10003.

Health Sciences Communications Association, P.O. Box 79, Millbrae, Calif. 94030.

Media Center for Children, 3 West 29th Street, 11th Floor, New York, N.Y. 10001.

National Education Association, 1201 16th Street, N.W., Washington, D.C. 20036.

National Network of Youth Advisory Boards, Inc., P.O. Box 402036, Ocean View Branch, Miami Beach, Fla. 33140.

Society for Adolescent Medicine, P.O. Box 3462, Granada Hills, Calif. 91344.

University of Maryland Hospital, Division of Adolescent Nutrition, University of Maryland, Baltimore, Md. 21201.

Young Adult Fiction

Hinton, S. E. *Tex*. New York: Delacorte, 1979. Story of a young boy's passage from adolescence to young adulthood, a transition complicated by his irresponsibility.

Meyer, Carolyn. *C. C. Poindexter*. New York: Atheneum, 1978. A bright, cynical, six-foot fifteen-year-old girl tries to cope with her new "adulthood."

O'Neal, Zibby. *Language of Goldfish*. New York: Viking, 1980. A talented thirteen-year-old girl has difficulty growing up in the shadow of her popular, beautiful older sister.

Oppenheimer, Joan. *Working on It*. New York: Harcourt Brace Jovanovich, 1980. A shy, self-conscious teenager feels that being fifteen "is the pits" until she takes a drama class and rises to stardom, at least in the eyes of a special boy.

Paterson, Katherine. *Bridge to Terabithia*. New York: Gollancz, 1978. A young boy and girl make a pact of friendship and secrecy in which they retreat when the stresses of growing up seem too hard to bear.

2 TV as Entertainment and Information

I'VE WATCHED TELEVISION, MAN, when I was so low, you know, and all I wanted was some dude to get up there on that screen and move. Dude didn't even have to talk, you know what I'm saying? I just wanted someone up there. Talk, walk, move around, he could stand on his head for all I care, long as he didn't go away. Didn't make no difference if it was a commercial or the best show.

Then other times, I'll get in this mood where I want to see folks get knocked around. I know while they're doing it they're only messing around, but that don't make no difference, I want action. I know who's going to win. Kojak ain't going to lose. Baretta ain't going to lose. Old Rockford, he always gets beat up, but in the end he's going to win. I like that guy Columbo too. Peter Falk. That's his name. Guy's out of his mind. Funny guy. He could be your friend. Folks on TV get to be, like, friends. So you wait to see your friends, and then hope they club hell out of some dummy, if that's the way you're feeling.

Fourteen-year-old Michael

You Win Some, You Lose Some

TV Sports for Teens

DAVID KLATELL

EVEN A CASUAL OBSERVER of adolescent athletes will notice the imitative behaviors inherent in much of their play. Famous athletes such as O. J. Simpson, Pélé, Nadia Comaneci, Jimmy Connors, and Julius Erving are frequently mimicked down to their manner of walking, grunting, or dunking. These erstwhile adolescent mimes are working from secondhand material at best because the overwhelming majority have never seen their subject in person—all impressions were garnered through television. It is not even uncommon to hear these young athletes imitate television announcers and do their own play by play of a schoolyard contest. It is a little like starring in your own movie, and it is a seductive, wonderful illusion.

Television sports play a powerful role in shaping the opinions of youngsters about sports, competition, role models, and participation. It is not difficult to perceive the reasons. Adolescents are of the age and inclination to be physically active and involved in athletics; they watch a great deal of television; televised sports programs are aired at night and on weekends when young viewers are at home; and the program formats emphasize fast-paced visuals, accentuated sound, dramatic confrontations, and popular personalities.

There is an unmistakable aura of glamor surrounding all the participants in a sports telecast—athletes and announcers alike. The

* David A. Klatell is chairman of the journalism department, School of Public Communication, Boston University, where he also serves as director of the Institute in Broadcast Sports. He is the author of *Television, Sports and Society*.

images of success, power, and money (much of it injected into sports by television itself) are not lost on young viewers and often stimulate the desire to imitate. One must scrutinize, therefore, the role models and images being imitated.

Roone Arledge, the acknowledged master of television sports marketing and promotion, is generally credited with the famous phrase, "the thrill of victory and the agony of defeat . . . the drama of athletic competition," which seems to capture television's interest in sports. For many years, we have accepted this promotional phrase as though it were the definition of sports in this country; we have made television's emphasis our own. As a result, television's wholehearted endorsement of this and similar definitions has done much to damage the integral linkage of sports and sport.

I am concerned that television's definition of sports has diminished our appreciation of sport. Most television events emphasize competition rather than participation, excellence and achievement rather than effort, and organized, regulated contests rather than less structured individual pursuits. The net result has been an alarming tendency of viewers to dismiss as unworthy of attention or imitation those events or athletes concentrating on effort and participation rather than professional excellence.

Young viewers adopt role models through a curious culmination of conscious and unconscious decisions and are influenced by many factors including peer pressure; publicity and promotion of athletes; social factors such as race, religion, and sex; and their own physical abilities. A cursory check of television sports programming quickly reveals the most common role models.

Television sports are overwhelmingly male events. The vast majority of athletes, announcers, producers, directors, and executives are male. In many events, the only females prominently displayed are cheerleaders mugging for sideline cameras. In general, women athletes are restricted to tennis, swimming, some golf, and gymnastics. Interestingly women's gymnastics in the United States is a virtual creation of television, a result of the exploits of Olga Korbut and Nadia Comaneci in Olympic telecasts.

Unlike many other television formats, sports programming is heavily populated by minority males. Black athletes are among the best-known, highest paid, and most respected athletes. However, as Harry Edwards of San Jose University points out, the image of a few fabulously successful black athletes may be a trap for the hundreds of thousands of black or other minority youngsters who seize on achievement in sports as their only hope for success in society.

Edwards notes that only the tiniest fraction of youngsters have the ability to become great athletes; many others would be better served by role models in education, business, or other fields within the world of sports. Although not necessarily television's fault, we rarely see black coaches, trainers, executives, officials, or announcers.

For some adolescents—particularly those of modest physical abilities—seeing an endless series of athletes so proficient in their skills may be so discouraging as to deter, rather than encourage, participation. Youngsters who are slow, skinny, short, clumsy, small, fat, or hesitant should see role models too.

At the same time, the level of skills demonstrated on television may lead other adolescents to the pursuit of activities that can only be practiced by a small number of extraordinary people. Programs such as "The World's Strongest Men," "Survival of the Fittest," stunt-man competitions, and Evil Knievel's motorcycle and rocket-bike exploits are interesting glimpses of obsessions but hardly suitable for the vast majority of adolescent viewers. In a number of cases, youngsters have been hurt or even killed while imitating particular stunts, despite the television warnings not to do so.

Even in legitimate sports such as football, ice hockey, and tennis, dangerous or obsessive behavior can be learned from television. Many parents and high school coaches have remarked on the upsurge in violence, hostility, and rule breaking among youngsters in local sports down to the peewee level. It often seems that they are imitating the roughest, toughest, most contentious players instead of the most skilled. Perhaps it is because television tends to focus on—and replay —winning and losing, personal competition and confrontation, dramatic moments, highly charged emotions, and distinctive personalities. These are the elemental building blocks for almost all types of television entertainment formats, and sports are just that—entertainment.

It is believed that to abandon these elements would cost the broadcaster considerable audience share and therefore the revenues that are television's lifeblood. What, then, can be done to emphasize the positive influences of television sports on young audiences while reducing some of those that are less attractive? Any changes must be made within the context of competitive commercial broadcasting and cable television; I offer a few suggestions.

1. Deemphasize the thrill of victory and the agony of defeat. Emphasize the thrill of participation, comradeship, self-fulfillment, learning, and growing. Emphasize that while defeat or failure can indeed be agonizing, they can also be instructive and valuable.

2. Reduce the dramatic nature of some personality conflicts and

athletic competitions. There is no need for Olga Korbut to be portrayed as "defeated" or implicitly unworthy of imitation simply because some other gymnasts caught up to and eventually surpassed her. The rise of one athlete should not necessarily dictate the fall of another.

3. Increase the instructional content of programs. This does not need to be done in a heavy-handed teaching style. It can be accomplished more subtly through the imaginative use of camera placement and shot selection to show techniques not often highlighted in broadcasts, through the announcer's discussion of the hows and whys of athletic participation and performance, and through formats designed with more thought given to adolescent viewers.

4. Integrate sports into other entertainment formats such as the after-school specials, situation comedies, and family dramas in which adolescents are featured characters. Raise some relevant sports issues in these scripts where they will reach young people and their parents without offending the diehard sports fan who wants to watch a game as it is traditionally presented.

5. Feature more women prominently. The recent upsurge in athletic participation by women makes marketing sports programming to them sensible and potentially lucrative. As full implementation of federally mandated Title IX funding equalizes the opportunities for sports participation, coaching, and training for girls, it will provide a growing source of new sports viewers and consumers.

6. Show minorities in roles other than that of the great athlete. Deemphasize the notion that all black athletes have come from wretched backgrounds and that they can achieve success only through sports. Remind the audience that many black athletes are successful businessmen in the off-season and that they have other skills, interests, and accomplishments. Show black coaches, trainers, officials, and executives where they exist and note their disproportionately small numbers when appropriate.

7. Place more ordinary, everyday, achievable sports on the air, such as jogging, racquetball, soccer, and bicycle racing. Feature participants possessing more typical skills instead of paid professionals or college all-stars. Place these segments in magazine formats such as "CBS Sports Spectacular," "ABC's Wide World of Sports," and "NBC Sports World," which are sold to sponsors without reference to specific events and which afford the opportunity to experiment with audience preferences and interests with a minimized risk.

8. Made-for-TV events such as "Battle of the Network Stars" and "Challenge of the Sexes" should emphasize events that are

commonly practiced by the general public. Although the overall competition is an artifice, the events themselves should be real and the participants should perform to the best of their abilities.

Cable television and the new electronic media offer almost limitless opportunities to adopt many of these recommendations and to significantly alter the presentation of television sports. The Entertainment and Sports Programming Network's round-the-clock presentation of sports demands the inclusion of less professional sports and more down-to-earth participants as role models.

The smaller, specialized audiences attracted to individual cable television channels may also afford the opportunity to produce more instructional programming; programming geared to minorities, women, and previously unserved audiences; and coverage of sports and sport previously deemed too unpopular with mass audiences.

Television sports will remain a popular viewing choice, particularly among adolescents, due to the attractive nature of the programming and the unique combination of sports and the television, promotion, and marketing industries. We should take care that the lessons young viewers learn will be constructive for them, for the healthy and necessary role of sports in society, and for the appreciation of sport.

Christopher Glenn, host of CBS's "30 Minutes," talks with the winner of the first National Scholastic Surfing Association competition. Photo courtesy of CBS News.

These young racers are being filmed for "Time Out," a local sports program for young people produced by Chambers and Asher, Inc. in cooperation with WSB-TV, Atlanta.

TV News for Teens

JOEL HELLER

ONCE, after a miraculous surgical procedure, a man who had been blind since birth was asked what it was like to see for the first time in his life. His response was that he was totally overwhelmed by all the new information that was now suddenly flooding his brain. Through the deft strokes of the surgeon's knife, life for him had taken on a new complexity. Added to his normal senses of hearing and touch were the strange new sensations of color, form, movement, and depth. It was a steady stream of unexplained and bewildering data, which he thought would take considerable time to sort out and understand. The gift of sight had thrust upon him a new and unknown language of light and shadow.

To a normal child, the introduction to the world through the images of television represents a similar confusing experience. Television is a new language of sight and sound that carries, in rapid-fire succession, a wide variety of messages and impressions about the real and imaginary worlds that television portrays. At first, there are no clear lines separating one world from the other. The child calls out to the nearest interpreter for clarification: "Daddy, did that man really die?" "No, that was only a story. It's only make believe." And once again, when what seems like a similar message repeats itself: "Mommy, did that man really die?" "I'm afraid so dear, you're watching the news." And so for a child, the gradual decoding of life as seen on TV begins with one of the first lessons: news

* Joel Heller is executive producer of "30 Minutes" and "In the News" for CBS.

carries messages that are real and unsettling. As they get older, children begin to understand that this real world they see on TV is full of problems, people, and events over which they have little influence but which must be understood so they can survive in today's society. They also learn at an early age they can control these difficult television challenges by turning the dial to another station.

Television news and public affairs broadcasters have a special responsibility to help bring some order and understanding to the constant barrage of information to which the young are exposed. But there are certain major problems in presenting these programs to young people.

First, it is important to gain the acceptance of young people for news and public affairs broadcasts. With children, as it is with adults, informational programs have traditionally taken a back seat in viewership. Programs that remind us of our responsibilities, other people's hardships, problems that have no ready solutions, diseases with no cures, and programs that present ideas without exciting visuals are regarded by adults as "avoidable" and by children as "another day of school." To a child there is probably the attitude there is time for all this "when I grow up." Both adult and young audiences prefer the escapism programming that television has so artfully mastered.

In order to entice young viewers to the set for information, many broadcasters have devised programs that use show-business techniques to make their material attractive. They keep their programs moving at a very rapid pace on the theory that all young people have an attention span as short as a preschooler's, so they push the "Sesame Street" syndrome to higher age limits. In the long run, however, this snappy type of visually entertaining production with its emphasis on pace rather than content provides only the most superficial information. Furthermore, young people quickly see through the artifice. They realize they are being fed informational "medicine" along with the sugar. Although many critics applaud these expensive efforts, the history of these broadcasts attracting young people is quite poor.

Another method often used by broadcasters in their belief that children must be treated as children is to create a world of fantastic characters to deliver information. Rather than have the information come in a straightforward manner from one person to another, they rely on talking dogs, robots, computers, and even vegetables to deliver serious messages. A talking carrot extols the virtue of his goodness and then asks the child to stay healthy by eating friendly characters just like himself. These cute gimmicks sometimes end up being so entertaining that they fail to pass on much information at all. The advertising world is full of examples of failed campaigns in which commercials were extremely popular but did not sell the sponsor's product. The message was lost in the show-biz pizzazz. Perhaps the time has come when along with decrying sugar-coated foods, we should begin to feel the same way about our presentation of information.

This does not mean I'm advocating dull and boring broadcasts because we have gone too far toward entertainment in trying to reach young people with information. It is still possible to present information and attract viewers with honest enthusiasm for the material, but the material must be relevant to the audience's needs. Preteens are more interested in facts than they are in the more subtle issues. As young people enter their teenage years, they begin to become more interested in the political process, in movements, in changes in the social order. Their own life experiences make them a little more attuned to find shades in human behavior. Broadcasters can now begin to deal less in programs with the presentation of either pure fact or pure fun and deal more with the complexities of the social order as it affects adolescents. Programs for adolescents should deal with their issues directly and, above all, honestly. Teens should be treated as though they were already adults.

One major way we try to establish a line of honest communication with young people in "30 Minutes" is to use experienced adult journalists as on-the-air hosts. We have found that it is better to use an adult to present the broadcast rather than a young person speaking to other young people. Although youthful enthusiasm can be charming, a fourteen-year-old talking about teen problems does not ring true unless that young person is talking about his personal experiences.

No matter what we do, specialized informational programs produced for young people will probably never have great popular appeal. As the teen years begin, young people regard the TV set as a minor source of their entertainment and an unimportant source of their information unless some event or some school assignment draws them to it. However, we can improve our news and public affairs programming for young people by making sure that what we do broadcast is relevant to their real needs. Among those needs are information about their future, their acceptance by the opposite sex, their use of drugs, and their advanced education. We can also improve existing news and public affairs programming so adults as well as children will have a better grasp of world events.

Much of what is now broadcast on news and public affairs programming assumes that the audience has been following the story. After a while, news broadcasts in particular tend to develop a shorthand language to refer to continuing events. The newscast's short time on the air does not permit a daily recap of a running story, so the daily changes in information are merely piled on top of what is assumed an audience has already seen and understood from the day a story started. Television news in its headline format does not have the time to explain ideas to the fullest. Yet it is ideas and the workings of the human mind that are really the most important news of the day. The world still vibrates with the ideas of Marx, Gandhi, and Christ but the Action News footage of the Alamo has long since been forgotten. We have yet to develop an effective way of presenting ideas both to adults and to young people on television. Both audiences suffer for it.

If they ever come into being, the long-sought-after expanded network newscasts would be well served by using some of their additional time to explain why things happen or what has happened previously. Young people as well as adults would be served by this added information. Ironically, television presents background information very well when broadcasting long events such as political conventions, elections, and inaugurations. To guard against dead air time, mountains of background material are prepared as fillers. Many times this filler provides some of the most useful information offered.

Broadcasters can best serve the needs of young audiences by recognizing their feelings. They need to be treated as already mature, lacking mainly the life experiences necessary to understand fully what is happening to them and the world. Broadcasters can provide information to help them by keeping information relevant to their needs and by understanding that not everyone is already an expert on the story about to be told.

Although the viewing audience has not been blind since birth, its introduction to the real world through the light and shadow images of television needs to be carefully sorted out and explained. Otherwise the potential of this powerful language can be forever lost in the confusion of those who can see but who do not understand.

Specials and Mini Series

SQUIRE D. RUSHNELL

IN THE EARLY 1970s, the ABC television network inaugurated a series of bimonthly, high-quality specials designed for young adolescents and aired in the afternoon hours—the "ABC Afterschool Specials."

Young people of junior high age had been neglected by almost all television programming: they were too old for Saturday morning programming and too young for prime-time efforts. Moreover, eleven- to fourteen-year-olds go through one of the most complicated periods of their lives. To an early adolescent, almost every problem is magnified several times: not only do feet seem bigger, chests flatter, and pimples more prominent, but the anxieties of parental divorce, peer pressure, and other societal distresses seem more perplexing.

Targeting for this age group served two purposes: it filled a definite void of meaningful television programming for teens and preteens and the problems and issues of adolescence provided the network with dramatic story conflicts from which strong scripts could emerge —dramas that would appeal to the target audience, as well as parents, grandparents, and even elementary school-aged youngsters.

The network's intent was to create a series of specials for young people that would be unique in American television, specials that would fill audience needs and interests and at the same time provide the network with competitive programming.

* Squire D. Rushnell is vice president, "Good Morning America" and Children's Television, ABC Entertainment.

"Rookie of the Year," an early "ABC Afterschool Special" program produced by Danny Wilson and starring Jodie Foster, is a story about a young girl who sought to break the female sex barriers in little league baseball. It became the prototype for all "ABC After-school Specials."

The writer's guideline for the series, which network executives distribute to all producers and interested parties, states that the goal of the "ABC Afterschool Specials" is "to employ high-style drama, comedy and animation, deliberately steering away from documentary techniques, which have proven neither successful as an attraction for/ children nor effective in getting our message across. Our prime target audience is the often-neglected, usually fickle, but extremely important kids eight to fourteen years old. Telecast but twice a month at a highly competitive time in the afternoon, it is imperative that they are compelling enough to capture and retain that audience's attention, while presenting a rewarding, explicit bottom line."

Although the costs of producing such high-quality hour-long programming continued to escalate at a pace beyond that of revenues from advertising, thereby never quite breaking even, the "ABC Afterschool Specials" attracted significant audience levels. In the 1979–1980 season, for example, fourteen telecasts averaged an 8.4 rating and a 23 percent share of the viewing audience. By comparison, network programs preceding the specials averaged ratings from 4.7 to 5.9 and 15 to 19 percent of the audience. The "ABC Afterschool Specials" have been successful in reaching not only youngsters but also their parents. On the average, 13 percent of the viewers were teenagers, 17 percent were of elementary and junior high school age, and 61 percent of the viewers were over eighteen.

During the first eight seasons, the series tackled such subjects as teenage alcoholism, the ill effects of marijuana, unwed pregnancy, young runaways, and the handicaps of blindness, retardation, juvenile rheumatoid arthritis, and teenage paraplegia. In addition, the "ABC Afterschool Specials" dealt with the problems of parental divorce, child abuse, deafness, and strict parents, always told from the youngsters' point of view.

In 1977, DePatie-Freleng produced "My Mom's Having a Baby," an "Afterschool Special" that explained the facts of life. It was the highest-rated daytime special in network history. Two seasons later, a sequel, "Where Do Teenagers Come From?" helped young adolescents understand the perplexities of puberty.

A few seasons after the "ABC Afterschool Specials" went on the air, NBC launched a similar program form, "NBC Special Treats," and CBS began the "CBS Library Series"; both are late-afternoon miniseries designed for young people. The Capitol Cities Stations created similar specials that dramatized the problems of young adolescents. Meredith Broadcasting Company, in association with the Avco stations, has designed for their stations and for subsequent syndication several programs in "The Young People's Specials" series. These half-hour programs focus on the issues teenagers face and on the life-styles of young people in history, including the young Indian girl Sacajawea, who led Lewis and Clark, and a black youngster sold in slavery during the pre–Civil War period.

In 1975, ABC launched the "ABC Weekend Specials," half-hour dramas based on books or short stories, telecast at noon on Saturdays. ABC hoped to encourage reading through dramatization of such works as O'Henry's "Ransom of Red Chief," Edgar Allen Poe's "The Gold Bug," and Robert Newton Peck's charming series of books about "Soup." Like the "ABC Afterschool Specials," this series of weekly telecasts is aimed at the eight- to fourteen-year-old. To encourage reading further, the network sends monthly posters proclaiming, "Read the Book, See the Program," to junior high school libraries throughout the country.

Targeting to a young teenage constituency can be risky. Not only does this age group consist of a smaller segment of the population than other age groups, but teenagers are notoriously busy with school and social activities, keeping their weekly viewing below the levels of other age groups. The secret to success in this area, it would seem, is to create programming that attracts teenagers and is also appealing to adults and elementary school-aged children. To achieve such a goal, producers must respect their young audiences and relate the story lines and topics of programs to the teenage viewers' own experience and interest level.

Daytime Drama for Teens

No Soap

ARNOLD J. FRIEDMAN

THREE AND A HALF soap operas for teenage audiences, with teenage actors in dominant roles, were launched with great fanfare in 1980, but by now it is likely these soaps are all washed up.

The "half" soap was the first to go. In February 1980, it died aborning after one brief outing on the CBS television network. Called "Sign On," it was designed by the Children's Television Workshop (CTW) as a daytime series for youngsters eight to fifteen years old. One segment of the series was a ten-minute continuing drama. If successful, "Sign On" would have been the first daily network program for youngsters to be developed since the 1950s, and television would have had its first teenage soap opera.

Called "Welcome to Twin Oaks," the soap segment centered around a divorced career woman and her teenage daughter who are trying to adjust to life in a new town. What was distinctive about the series, including the soap, was its attitude and tone. According to David Connell, vice-president for production of CTW and executive producer of "Sign On," it was not condescending, as some other children's programs tend to be. "CTW has never underestimated the level of sophistication of contemporary youngsters when it comes to TV viewing," he said. What it had overestimated, apparently, was the level of support for and commitment to provide social children's programming. "Welcome to Twin Oaks" received only a modest welcome and no funding at all. It was dropped.

* Arnold J. Friedman is a contributing editor for *Back Stage*, *TV World*, and *Business Screen*.

In the meantime, six of the leading companies and many of the best people in the television industry were producing and pitching the three full-fledged teenage soap operas. In March 1981, pilot episodes were screened at the National Association of Television Program Executives (NATPE) annual conference in New York City.

Some orders were taken but not enough to justify production of the series. A general rule used by distribution companies is that markets representing 65 percent, or at least 55 percent, of the homes using television in the United States must order a syndicated show for it to succeed, even to survive. None of the companies got nearly that kind of response.

Alan Sloan, a prolific and successful producer, attributes this station reluctance at least in part to the pioneering aspect of the concept. He was referring to the way programming executives hang back when something new and therefore unproved is proposed.

Sloan's Los Angeles–based company was producing one of the teenage soaps, "Worlds Apart," in association with Meredith Broadcasting, which had originally planned to premiere the series on its five TV stations in September. By mid-May it had been decided to push back the fall start of the series until more stations linked up.

Another serial, "The Halls of Haywood High," was also deleted from September schedules. It was a coproduction of Viacom Enterprises, which would syndicate the property, and Scholastic Production, which would supply the material from a highly regarded magazine serial of the same name appearing in *Senior Scholastic* from 1975 to 1978.

At the time the series was announced in July 1980, Viacom vice-president for program development Robert Goldfarb commented, "The timing for this project could not be better. The FCC encourages stations to devote more time to such programs. Teens and parents alike want accurate, truthful depictions of today's teen and adult life-styles. As a result, stations who know what viewers will watch are looking more than ever before for quality productions with strong dramatic themes, targeted for young people and their parents." Despite the propitious timing, however, Viacom did not line up enough stations either.

The soap that had been developed most aggressively during this time was Post-Newsweek Productions' "Young Lives." After disappointing sales following the NATPE conference, the company's program production and distribution vice-president, Tay Voye, decided to inaugurate a unique marketing strategy in an effort to pull the project out. He literally gave the pilot week away. Five half-hour programs for "stripping" Monday to Friday were made available to stations in the top twenty-five markets at no cost, and the stations also got to keep all the commercial time for local sale. In addition, Post-Newsweek paid the cost of on-air promotion and *TV Guide* layouts (but not the space) for a test of the property in the market-place in July "sweeps," a period when the Nielsen and Arbitron services survey the stations and report ratings would indicate how much audiences wanted to see the series. The level of homes using television is low in July, so this test alone was not expected to sway reluctant buyers completely.

Why were stations so reluctant to program the teenage serials, especially when the adult dramas had already begun to program for that market? Charting an increase in teenage viewing, the networks had introduced teen elements into the adult drama story lines in order to accommodate the growing audience of adolescents. ABC's "General Hospital" is the most successful soap and best example of this trend. Producer Gloria Monty has acknowledged that she "went after the kids," and in 1980 the soap showed a 29 percent increase in young viewers. Allen Potter, who produces "The Guiding Light" for CBS, was quoted in *People* magazine saying, "Most of the serials are going for a younger look and we're no exception." On the other hand, teenagers have always comprised the smallest television-viewing audience, a fact reconfirmed by the A. C. Nielsen 1981 report on national audience demographics, which showed for the first time that females watched a little less than males.

Another survey, compiled by the editors of *The Media Book*, reported that for every hundred homes tuned to weekday serials, ninety-five women over eighteen are watching, but only seven viewers in those one hundred homes are in their teens. Probably the reason is that they are not in their homes, and advertisers know this, as do the station executives who sell them time on their program schedules. But they also know that in 1980 there were 27,446,000 Americans between thirteen and nineteen with a disposable income of $39.1 billion. These youngsters have many common consumer aims, including high-priced items like $40 and $50 designer jeans. Girls thirteen, fourteen, and fifteen years old tend to spend like their older sisters. So although teens watch television less than any other demographic group measured, they still comprise a good market. That it was cost-effective to reach this market on television was something advertisers seemed to have resolved at the time the teen soaps went into production. Each of the production companies evidently received enough indication of support to proceed.

In the end, however, the stations did not buy. Inertia had a lot to do with the sales resistance, and so did the traditionally tentative character of most station managers and station groups. Alan Sloan ("Worlds Apart") noted that soaps had always been provided to stations by their parent networks; local stations had never bought and sold them on their own. No one had done it. The concept was new and therefore risky.

Also at this time, broadcasters were beginning to feel pressure from New Right groups, specifically the Moral Majority and the Coalition for Better TV, which wanted to rid television of programs they considered offensive by boycotting their advertisers. At the NATPE convention, broadcasters received telegrams from the Church of Christ in Tennessee, urging them to boycott "Young Lives." Cal Thomas, communications vice-president of the Moral Majority told broadcasters, "I think a lot of people are concerned about TV's portrayal of youthful sex, adultery, and American life in general. Television is not representing American life as it is."

Creator and executive producer of "Young Lives," Ken Livesay acknowledged later that the fuss made by pressure groups did not help. "Stations are conservative," he said. "They're reluctant to jump into something that might cause them problems." Ironically, Livesay had conceived "Young Lives" to accomplish exactly what Thomas claimed television needed: an accurate representation of American life. The show, he said, dealt in a responsible, nonexploitative manner with problems identified by child psychologists. Story lines were to explore such teenage worries as peer pressure, romance, drug abuse, identity, loneliness, and parental relations, through the eyes of both the young characters and their parents and teachers.

Post-Newsweek believed that through the powerful and popular medium of daily serial drama, the series would not only entertain but also provide realistic examples of human problems people face in today's complex society. "To me this is an idea whose time has come," Livesay said. "The audience is there, the emotions are there, and quite frankly, the need is there. Our problem, as with any new idea, is to make sure it is done right."

All three teams producing teen soaps hired experienced writers, directors, and producers who had worked with children's programming and soap opera formats. They were drafted from all over the industry and backed with consultants.

"Halls of Haywood High" had writers' guidelines and a pilot written by a former teacher and author of five young adult bestsellers. "Worlds Apart" had an entire team of psychiatrists, psychologists, and educators reviewing its scripts. "Young Lives" had both a psychological and medical consultant. Professionals were working earnestly to produce important programs meant to be taken seriously and have positive impact.

In addition to the academic stature of the personnel on the inside, there was an impressive coterie of scholars on the outside, anticipating the trio of teenage soaps with high hopes. I talked to two of them at New Jersey's Monmouth College at a seminar, "Teenagers and Soap Operas."

Mary Cassata, director of the State University of New York's Project Daytime, a comprehensive research endeavor that monitors daytime television, has said that "teenagers get a set of gratifications from the soaps that are probably different in degree from those of other age groups." Under her direction, the project is developing content analyses and perceptual studies of soap operas. Asked what impact soaps have on these teens, Cassata said, "It's my contention that the soaps socialize teenagers, supplying them with information on how to behave—what is proper and what isn't." Adolescents, she said, have specific needs: peer group acceptance, freedom, the need for understanding by their parents and older adults, the need for understanding themselves in terms of the physical and psychological changes that they are experiencing. "I believe a lot of teaching goes on on television," she said, "although teaching is not the primary purpose of these programs. Still, entertainment seems to do it best because it does get around the most critical barrier of all: getting the viewer's attention."

Cassata has taught courses in what are generally known as continuing daily dramas. She finds that her college students have been watching soaps since high school, and sometimes earlier. "One of the regrets I hear expressed often among my college students concerns facing up to the pursuit of employment. It's equated with a time that will interfere with their soap viewing. They hate the thought of having to wean themselves away from the soaps."

Laura Singer, fellow and past president of the American Association for Marriage and Family Therapy and a fellow and faculty member of the American Institute for Psychotherapy and Psychoanalysis, agrees with Cassata's contention that soaps socialize teenagers. "Adolescents need to stretch; they want to know about the next level," she said; "they need role models. If a teenager told you precisely what was happening inside, you might hear something like this: 'I used to be taken care of. Everything was done for me. Now I'm between wanting to be independent . . . and not knowing how. I'm expected to make some decisions for myself. I need to know how to handle it. My feelings are unclear. My peers are familiar. I see *them* every day. They're just as mixed up as I am. What do they know? We're all faking it. I need to know about making it.' "

Singer is familiar with the parameters of television drama, having hosted "Living Together," an award-winning series on marital therapy. She has also coauthored a book, *Sex Education on Film*. I asked her if a teenager could really learn how to succeed in the grown-up world from a teenage soap opera. Teens would relate if they were not preached at, she said, if they were not lectured: "They get enough of that. But if their needs and fears and frustrations could be presented squarely on these programs they could benefit."

Singer was somewhat apprehensive that wrong information might be relayed by the scripts or even by the actors whose body language and attitudes could convey clear messages to teen viewers. When asked if teens can be reached in any useful way on programs that last only a half-hour, she said, "Sure. One fresh concept per segment will do it, if it's honestly portrayed. Kids know."

Harry Francis, vice-president of operations for Meredith Corporation's Broadcasting Group, said that "Worlds Apart" had always intended to take "a tough, gutsy approach to teenage problems, including sex, self-identity, and, most importantly, healthy parent-child relationships." And the other producer-distributor joint ventures had organized impressive resources in order to develop prosocial commercial programming for teenagers and their families.

Yet the stations were not picking them up. Was it possible the producers were meeting a need that was not there? Did teenagers and their families want teenage soaps? Singer had said that teenagers wanted to look ahead to the next level. I recalled a young lady at the Monmouth seminar who said frankly that she did not want to see stories about herself and her peers. Other adolescents I spoke with assured me they knew enough about the way they were; what they needed to know about was the way they will be. My daughter reminded me, patiently, that she had been watching "adult" programming as long as either of us could remember. "Teenage" programming had the sound of, well, of teenage programming.

Awareness of this attitude may have influenced Alan Sloan to change the name of the Meredith soap from "Julie's World" to "Worlds Apart," which has the ring of a soap. No matter how he turned the world, however, it still was not in orbit the last time we spoke. "Originally there was too much concentration on Julie, who is only one of the characters in the series," said Sloan. "Now the serial spans preschool, teen, and adult story lines, which are for all the family. They ask the question: are they worlds apart?"

I asked the question myself. "Are they?"

"No!" said Sloan. "That's the point. They have many problems in common. If we had only teens on the serial, we wouldn't have a chance. Role models will be available on the series. Teens want to know where they'll be when they're a few years older, and how to get there."

They may have to continue finding out from the adult soaps. Whether teenage daytime drama will come into being as age-specific programming is still unresolved. What does seem certain is that youthful characters will continue to play prominent, sometimes dominant, roles on afternoon soap operas.

A shy boy (Ronnie Scribner) learns that color and age differences have no meaning among friends in "A Home Run for Love," an ABC Afterschool Special. Photo courtesy of ABC, copyright © 1978, 1979, 1980, 1981 by American Broadcasting Companies, Inc.

For the past several years, teens have spent countless afternoons tuned into the stormy and improbable love life of Luke and Laura on ABC's "General Hospital." Photo courtesy of ABC, copyright © 1978, 1979, 1980, 1981 by American Broadcasting Companies, Inc.

Humor

An Interview with Norman Lear

ACT: At ACT's conference on children, television, and health, you said that more people absorb information when it is couched in humor. What about the young adolescent audience, the ten- to fifteen-year-olds? Teenagers often reject information that is fed to them by adult authorities. Can humor be an effective tool for communicating messages to this audience?

Lear: We live in a most complex time when problems for adolescents are as complex as they are for any other group in society, and the answers are equally complex. There is so much competition in the marketplace of ideas to reach the minds of people, young and old, with answers to those problems. Youngsters and their families are surely feeling the economic crunch now, so that I imagine dinner table conversation for today's teenager is much as it was for me growing up in the depression. All the talk around the dinner table has something to do with money: what the family can afford and what the family cannot afford. And particularly in the case of adolescents, who spend much of their time in school, there are so many ideas being thrown at them all the time that they are leading emotionally crowded lives. So with the constant bombardment of information reaching for the minds of these young people, to reach

* Norman Lear is president of Tandem TAT Productions, which has produced "All in the Family," "Maude," and "One Day at a Time."

45

them viscerally through laughter is one of the sure ways of getting in.

There is something spiritual and certainly something emotional about laughter. People laugh with their bellies and experience with their emotions. There's a sort of spiritual umbilical cord between the theatrical piece and the adolescent viewer, and through the cord of emotion and laughter, there is plenty of room for the message, the thought, the idea. It's a wonderful channel through which to pass the information, and it arrives because it arrives viscerally.

ACT: Are there different types of humor that might be more effective for adolescents? What can you do for adolescent viewers that you can't do for children or you might not want to do for adults?

Lear: Very little television that one might prepare for adults wouldn't be right for adolescents too. I think adolescents are deeply concerned, when they're asked to be, with the problems of society, and they are very interested when their interest is elicited. And I think it's a pretty good idea to try to get young people to think about the problems of the moment because that's going to help them think about the problems of the future, when they will be the problem solvers. "All in the Family" was very popular with adolescents. It wasn't intended for them, but it seems to me that as a writer you write for everybody. There is such a thing as a children's story, obviously, but if you're writing about people and about families, you're writing with the hope that everybody will read it.

ACT: Teenagers are extremely self-conscious about their bodies and unsure of themselves and the way they relate to their peers and to adults. They always worry that they are too tall or too short, or developing too soon or too late, have acne or braces, and are clumsy and awkward. Can TV humor help young people cope with these feelings by helping them laugh at themselves? Can this help boost their self-confidence, or is there a point at which this kind of mockery becomes cruel?

Lear: I think that being able to laugh at oneself is essential. I don't know how one achieves emotional health without the ability to laugh at oneself. Anything that will help youngsters learn to laugh at themselves and not take themselves altogether seriously has to be a positive thing.

I'm always fond in moments of crisis of saying, "Hold on, there are one billion people in China who don't know this is happening, so how important can it be?" I think it's terribly important to have some understanding of where one is in the cosmos and of the relative importance of any individual moment. I think that's healthy.

There is great community in laughter. Adolescents need a sense of community. If you stand in the back of the theater and watch an audience laugh, you see them all as one—a whole audience rearing back and then sailing forward in a large guffaw. So often in the back of an audience I've watched this go on; it's almost as if the audience were being conducted. What is locking them all together is the laughing, the community of laughter. It's not unlike singing in church. There's a feeling of oneness, and I think adolescents need that sense of family and community as all other groups do.

ACT: Are there any kinds of humor that may be hurtful or destructive for this audience?

Lear: At some point it's possible for humor to become so hostile and angry that it diminishes the feeling of community. Twenty years ago there were still ugly women jokes and ugly wife jokes; we don't hear them so much anymore. That's the kind of put-down that is destructive. But I would hate to see a nation so afraid in its humor of all kinds of infirmities and all kinds of minorities that it never dared in humor to venture into these areas. That wouldn't be healthy because everything ought to be right for humor.

ACT: How about sexual humor: innuendos, double-entendres, "sex with a titter." Much of the humor in today's sitcoms suggests a flippant attitude toward sex. What effect do you think this might have on twelve-, thirteen-, or fifteen-year-olds who are trying to deal with their own sexuality?

Lear: I think that kind of humor is noxious. But I also think that the American public has a way of fending off after a while what is noxious to them. People try it and then it bores them; the wheel turns full circle and something else is going on. I think more harm is done by paying too much attention to it. It's a cycle—like the western, it will come and it will go and then it will come again.

ACT: How can teenage sexuality be approached in a positive way and still be entertaining to young audiences?

Lear: Dealing with the problems of human sexuality well and constructively is where television should be. We have dealt with all
kinds of problems of human sexuality over the years through "All
in the Family," "Maude," and "One Day at a Time." The networks
always tried to stop programs that dealt with sexuality. In an episode in the very first year of "All in the Family," Mike was study-
ing for finals, and there was so much at stake for him and his future
that he had not been able to make love to Gloria for some weeks.
He did not know that it was this enormous anxiety that was causing
his problem, and in the beginning Gloria did not know either. The
question of how to handle that, how to discuss it and how to turn
somewhere for help, made for an extremely controversial but valuable exploration of that kind of problem. That was one of the times
that the network said they simply did not want to air the program.
We said that we would not make another episode until that one
went on the air. In the end, they put it on the air, and of course
there was no public outcry, people did not march on CBS in protest,
and that episode went out across the country to various counselors
and rabbis and ministers who worked with problems of sexuality in
families.

   As a parent of two daughters, I went through everything that was
shown on "One Day at a Time." I was always able to say to the network, "Don't tell me this is inappropriate because I've just gone
through it at home. These problems are real."

ACT: In the early days of television, the issues of adolescence were
portrayed as: "Why am I flat-chested?" "My best friend doesn't
like me anymore," and "Is he going to call me tonight?" But now
television focuses on different issues: "My best friend tried com-
mitting suicide," "My brother's a heroin addict," and "I think I'm
pregnant." While these dramatic issues, when sensitively handled,
are important and valuable, there seems to be a danger of showing
adolescents as being pathological and crisis ridden. The normal
everyday experiences that all teenagers go through are almost being
overlooked.

Lear: We have seen a concentration of those kinds of episodes recently, especially during sweeps weeks. They proliferate so because
the name of the game is ratings, and drugs and suicide and other
crises make for ratings in the network's minds. So they exploit those
issues. The smaller problems are no less important. They're real
problems for kids.

ACT: You have a reputation for getting a message across to people in a way that really reaches them. Why do you think that so few others are doing this?

Lear: I've never had a compulsion to send a message in the dramas with which I've been involved. I have always thought that our first and biggest obligation was to entertain. In the case of the shows that were strictly comedy, that obligation was not just to make people laugh but to knock them off their chairs from laughing and to be just as full emotionally, as funny, warm, and tender as we could possibly be.

Then as a thoughtful adult raising a family of my own and reading the newspapers each day, it was just impossible for me not to deal with what was happening in life. My every instinct drove me in that direction. I quickly realized that audiences laughed harder when they cared. The desire to make people laugh and the desire to involve them in an issue went hand in glove. The substance and the laughter became part of the same thrust.

ACT: If you could get one important point across to young adolescents, what would it be?

Lear: I would want kids to know that life is not about winning and losing; life is about succeeding at the level of one's best. I would like them to know that the current message in the media and the government that says if you're not a winner, you're a loser, that if you're not in the top five or if you're not number one you're not succeeding, is a fallacy. Success is only a question of how much you make with what you're given in life. Success must not be measured in long-term achievements; it must be measured day by day, almost hour by hour, in short-term achievements. So they must remember to feel good about each small achievement, each small instance in which they connect with another person. I would like them to learn to pat themselves on the back and say, "good job," at each small success and then move on to the next moment. The good feeling, the sense of elation that comes from having connected with another human being—it is these moments that add up to a successful life.

It's a hard message to get out to kids today because most of what is happening in our society mitigates against it. But I would try to help them realize that all work is proud work, and that if you like what you're doing and concentrate on what you're doing, you should be proud—even if it's not grand—because that's what life is full of.

TV for Teens by Teens

MARGIE NICHOLSON

THERE IS a real excitement and immediacy in having young people write, produce, and host their own television programs. Television is not just a medium for getting a message from the adult world to youth but also a vehicle for youth to use in communicating with adults and with each other. Today's youth have grown up with television. They intuitively know and understand the medium. They are also experts in the problems and feelings of youth. Are teenagers capable of producing a broadcast-quality television program? Yes. Would anyone want to watch it? Again, yes, Nielsen and Arbitron will, as usual, have the final word. Broadcasters are beginning to work with young people to develop television programming by teens for teens. Pilot projects are currently being developed and implemented in schools, cable systems, and broadcast stations around the country.

Training youth in television production has come about mainly due to the development and proliferation of small-format, low-cost video equipment. This equipment is portable, light weight, and extremely easy to operate. The quality continues to improve and the price keeps coming down. Children and teens are now being exposed to television technology at home and at school at an early age. They are not afraid of the new technology, and they are careful and conscientious in using it.

* Margie Nicholson is director of community programming for U.S. Cable Corporation and a member of the Board of Directors of the National Federation of Local Cable Programmers.

Nearly every school system has adventuresome teachers who realize that the television equipment stored in the audiovisual room can be used for more than just off-air taping and playback of educational programs. They are putting that equipment in the hands of their students and teaching them how to use and understand television. Students work on their own productions and show them to their class, their school, and in some cases to the entire community through the local cable television system.

The expansion of cable television, and particularly the establishment of community cable television access centers, has been another major impetus in the development of programming by and for youth. Cable television access enthusiasts believe that everyone should have access to the equipment and time to express their views on the local cable television system. In many communities, they have established centers where young people can have low- or no-cost access to studios and remote equipment, training classes, and a viewing audience of cable television subscribers.

At home, in school, and in community cable television access centers, youth are being given the opportunity to experiment with new ways to express themselves and to communicate with each other through the medium of television. This experimentation starts at a very young age. In Monona, Wisconsin, third-, fourth-, and fifth-grade students learn television viewing skills, television aesthetics, and television production during a thirteen-week Saturday morning class at the library. When these students reach high school, they can join the Creative Video Club (CVC). CVC members produce Monona City Council and School Board meetings for the local cable television access channel. They also produce school news programs, talk shows, drama, and school and community sports events. Similar activities are taking place in other schools, libraries, and cable systems around the country.

In Sun Prairie, Wisconsin, the community has taken the process one step further. The Sun Prairie cable television ordinance requires that one cable television channel be reserved exclusively for programming selected and produced by nine- to thirteen-year-olds in Sun Prairie. Since its inception in 1978, hundreds of Sun Prairie youth have auditioned for the opportunity to plan, produce, and appear on their own television channel, KIDS 4. Equipment and training are provided by Viking CATV, the Sun Prairie Cable Commission, and community volunteers, but the youngsters do their own production work, including research, writing, camera, audio, and on-air performing. Even with the support of the community and the local cable systems, plus grants from local businesses, the National Endowment for the Humanities, and the National Telecommunications Information Agency, KIDS 4 is continually seeking new funding for its activities.

The KIDS 4 production team has produced and cablecast programs on everything from careers to clowns to cooking. They have broadcast tours of local amusement parks, researched and reported on Sun Prairie history, and interviewed visiting celebrities. When Chip Carter visited Sun Prairie in 1979, a thirteen-year-old KIDS 4 producer took the initiative of calling the White House to set up an interview for the KIDS 4 news team. The local newspaper provides regular coverage of KIDS 4 activities and program schedules.

To expand their activities and their audience, KIDS 4 is developing a cooperative project with the local ABC affiliate, WKOW-TV in Madison. The KIDS 4 production team will work with a WKOW director to produce a half-hour special introducing Madison-area youth to local art galleries and museums. KIDS 4 will use their own production equipment for the special, WKOW will provide post-production assistance and facilities, and the Wisconsin Arts Board and the Dane County Cultural Affairs Commission will provide funds for videotape, transportation, adult coaching and supervision, and publicity.

This type of cooperative effort between a children's television project, a broadcast station, and local arts institutions will benefit everyone involved. The KIDS 4 crew will learn from the experience of working with broadcast professionals; WKOW will air an innovative and exciting community service program for area youth; and the arts institutions will introduce a new audience to their activities.

Another Madison broadcaster is initiating television programming by and for youth. Seventeen-year-old Andy Garcia is talking with NBC affiliate WMTV about producing a program with his high school class about teenage alcoholism. Garcia developed his television production skills at the Madison Community Access Center (MCAC), whose facilities include studio, editing, and portable equipment. Hundreds of Madisonians of all ages have graduated from their regular television production training classes.

Andy Garcia has worked on so many studio and remote productions at MCAC that university communication arts students read his resumé with envy. Yet Garcia feels that he is not an unusual teenager. "I'm in a mass media class at high school," he says, "and there's a lot of talent there. It's just that there's no accessibility to equipment." Garcia and his class are working on a script about alcoholism from a teenage point of view and will produce the program with WMTV equipment and assistance. Susan Harris at the Wisconsin Association on Alcoholism and Other Drug Abuse fully supports Garcia's efforts. She believes that a teen-produced television program will be a creative and credible way to develop awareness and understanding of alcoholism and drug abuse among teenagers.

The students at Clemente High School in Chicago have produced a film on gang violence, "Too Late for Me," which was shown nationally on CBS in March 1980. Clemente is a new school in a primarily Latino and Polish neighborhood that is often disrupted by gang violence. No gangs are allowed in school; gang members come to school because they want to learn. One of the things they learn is television and film production. Clemente provides the space, television equipment, staff producers, and an engineer. The students and staff take it from there.

According to staff producer Claudia Crask, "Too Late for Me" began as a summer Comprehensive Education Training Act (CETA) project. Students were paid for their work through the CETA program and gained experience and professional working credentials. Several Clemente graduates who had gone on to professional work came back to help on the film for the summer. "We had a mix of kids," says Crask, "but most of them had previous experience in our high school production classes. You can't take all inexperienced kids and shoot a professional film in one summer."

Raising the funds necessary to produce a professional 16-mm film was a long, slow, and arduous process. There was little support or interest from local broadcasters because, Crask believes, they did not understand the project. Instead Crask found support from the business community. Local businesses, including Ogilvy and Mather, All State Insurance, Behrends, Standard Oil, Sears, and Allied Film Processing Lab, provided funds, discount prices, and other support.

A national publicity campaign was mounted when the film was completed. It was run on WTTW in Chicago, but there was no other reaction from local broadcasters. Finally, at an awards ceremony in New York, Crask was able to contact CBS producer Joel Heller, who arranged to have "Too Late for Me" shown on the CBS network within a month.

The students are delighted with the national publicity and encouragement they have received for the film and are now working on two more film projects: a drama about a Latino male trying to succeed in the media world and a program about venereal disease. Clemente student Rich Quinones said that "when the people in New York

[CBS] saw "Too Late for Me," they were surprised. They had done a show on venereal disease but didn't like it, so they called us to ask if we would work on it. They wanted the teenager's point of view."

The program on venereal disease will be produced by teens for teens. It will deal primarily with attitudes and will not be overloaded with medical information and advice from adult experts. Teens are often suspicious about advice and messages from adults. "Adults tell teenagers that marijuana will make them junkies," says Crask. "Then they try marijuana and they aren't junkies. So they don't believe it when they are warned about heroin." One way of eliminating teen suspicion about adult messages is to put the responsibility for the television message in the hands of the teens themselves.

Broadcasters and adults may be apprehensive about allowing teens to work with the equipment and technology to produce television programming, but young people have shown over and over again that they are careful and responsible users of television equipment. If teenagers are given the support and opportunity to run their programs on broadcast television, adults may be afraid of what teens are going to say. "Teens speaking for teens is a traumatic experience for many adults," says Crask, "but these young people are incisive; they can go right to the heart of a problem and get the answers."

What can a broadcaster do to help develop programming by teens for teens? Broadcaster responsibility does not begin and end with supplying air time. Innovative broadcasters can work with local schools, community cable groups, and youth organizations to help stimulate and support the growth of television by teens for teens. They can help with publicity, training, equipment loan, postproduction work, and fund raising. Above all, they can listen and respond with cooperation and concern when approached by teens and teen representatives. Teenagers have a lot to offer: enthusiasm, wonder, energy, and hope. If adults can offer them the means to communicate through the medium of television, they might learn a lot from and about teenagers.

When young Alex (Glenn Scarpelli) gets his first call from a girl, his private conversation stimulates everyone's curiosity on CBS's "One Day at a Time." Photo courtesy of T.A.T. Communications Company/CBS.

Continental Cablevision of New Hampshire has received national attention for "I Like Kids Creating," a program designed and produced by fifth and sixth graders. Here, one of the teams films an interview. Photo by Don Cline.

Teens and Cable

New Opportunities

DONALD R. SMITH

TO MOST PEOPLE, cable television is a wire running from a pole to the house or apartment. It provides a better television picture in weak reception areas, movies without commercials, and more sports programming than anyone could wish. But cable can provide much more. In some communities, cable delivers a twenty-four hour international news network or allows subscribers to vote on local issues by punching buttons with a home console. In other cities and towns, cable provides live coverage of local council meetings, police and fire alarm systems, access to the local library's card catalog, and twenty-four-hour request programming on as many as six channels.

Cable has become more than a television antenna system. It has become a community resource, and local governments, social service agencies, and cultural, informational, and educational institutions are learning to use that resource. To use cable television effectively, however, communities must define their cable system's potential and develop systematic utilization strategies. For parents, educators, librarians, children, and teenagers, cable television offers an incredible range of services—but only if local communities are organized to require, establish, and support them.

As existing cable television systems expand their carriage capabilities and as new systems are built, more television channels will become available for children's and teenagers' programming. On the

* Donald R. Smith, Ph.D., is president of the National Federation of Local Cable Programmers.

local level, programmers in the schools, libraries, and youth centers can begin developing programs to meet the specific entertainment, educational, informational, and cultural needs of the community's young people. For example, the local community cable programming center might acquire a nationally produced film on fire safety for school-age children. This program could be cablecast to classrooms during the school day and to homes in the evenings and on weekends when parents could be encouraged to watch with their children. A local follow-up program could be produced with the area's fire department. This program would allow local fire service personnel to define problems and techniques unique to that community. They might show the fire-reporting methods used in area schools and public buildings or community emergency evacuation routes and procedures. Junior high school students in the hills surrounding Los Angeles could learn how to prevent, report, and escape brush fires; students in Chicago, how to prevent, report, and escape from an apartment building fire.

Cable television programming can also be used to develop an awareness of local culture and history, as well as to involve young people in the actual production of videotapes. The local channels can be used to showcase school programs such as choir performances, school sports, and dramatic productions. These programs are popular with parents, visiting relatives, and performers alike. Allowing young people to produce their own programs has several benefits. It demystifies television by allowing young viewers to perceive and analyze the techniques that go into any production. They begin to develop sophisticated critical viewing of both the technical aspects and the narrative content of television programming. It also gives them a chance to explore their communities through the use of a creative medium. Six teenagers on a video field trip to a historic museum, fire station, or county fair will explore those sites and activities in depth. In addition, they will develop an appreciation for the amount of planning, work, and skill that goes into producing television documentaries.

Producing their own programs gives teenagers a creative outlet for their talents and abilities. Their creativity is stimulated by the potential of a television audience, no matter how small, and the excitement generated through working on the television programs carries over into other activities.

One of the most exciting capabilities of cable television is request programming. Every cabled community in the country should have a channel or channels dedicated to requests—a channel whose programming viewers could control. All that is needed is a central library system of videotapes, a videotape player, and access to the cable system. Local communities could use their resources to acquire high-quality films and videotapes for young people. Parents and their children could plan television viewing around their activities, not around network programming schedules. Schools and youth centers could request programs to fit their routines, programs that literally change with the weather.

To develop local film and videotape libraries and the community access facilities to produce cable programming for young people requires substantial initial and continued funding. If a community is in the process of granting a cable franchise, in refranchising, or in mid-franchise, a citizens' advisory board or telecommunications council must be formed to make sure that in acquiring the franchise, the cable company allocates leased access channels for community use, provides funding for community access facilities, and agrees to provide continued funding for community access programming.

A special task force on programming for children and teenagers should be established by the cable advisory board to ensure that the franchise agreement includes a diversity of commercial-free programming services to children and teenagers designed for each age level. The narrow segmentation that cable offers affords a unique opportunity for producers to develop programming specifically targeted to meet the needs and interests of teenagers. The task force can also establish a method of supplying the community access centers with films and videotapes for young people and can help develop production guidelines for local programming.

In communities where cable franchises have recently been awarded or will not be renegotiated in the near future, citizens interested in getting high-quality cable programming for children and teenagers must find out if the cable operator is required to provide channels for community programming. If an access channel already exists, citizens, including teenagers, can work to help acquire and develop programming for young people. The older twelve-channel systems may have no local capability, but the operator, searching for a public relations tool leading to the variable renegotiation of a franchise with more channels, could be convinced to provide channels for local use. In most cities and towns, the local governing body regulates the rates that cable companies charge subscribers. When the cable company seeks a rate increase, the community can legitimately ask for additional community services, including allocation of channels, facilities, and funding.

Cable companies know that community programming is good business, but for most, broadcast television with its commercials and cartoons and sitcoms is the only model they have to follow. It is up to local groups of parents, educators, librarians, and young people to develop viable community cable programming centers that they operate and control. Cable television can be an extremely valuable resource if every community learns to use it.

Resources, Chapter Two

ABC. *Making the News.* August 1979. A project designed for high school students and teachers to explore and better understand television news.

CBS. *Going Places.* November 6, 1979. A junior edition of Charles Kuralt's *On the Road.* To show teenage viewers the people and places that make our country great.

CBS. *30 Minutes,* Saturdays, 1:30–2:00 p.m. A weekly half-hour news program for young people focusing on issues relevant to its young audience.

Comstock, George. *The State of the Art of Television Research and the Young Adolescent.* Syracuse: S. I. Newhouse School of Public Communications, 1972.

Elliot, William R. and Slater, Dan. "Exposure, Experience and Perceived TV Reality for Adolescents." *Journalism Quarterly* 57:3 (Autumn 1980): 409–414, 431.

Indiana University Audio-Visual Center. *News.* 1977. A series of five programs to tell the story of people who gather and present the news on television, in the newspapers, on radio, and in magazines. Available for rental or purchase from Indiana University, Audio-visual Center, Bloomington, Ind. 47405.

Levine, G. F. "Learned Helplessness and the Evening News." *Journal of Communication* 27:4 (1977): 100–105.

Levy, M. R. "Experiencing Television News." *Journal of Communication* 27:4 (1977): 112–117.

Nickelodian. *Livewire.* A daily, one-hour magazine program for teenagers, which features a wide variety of information and entertainment. A service of the Warner Amex Satellite Entertainment Company.

O'Connor, John J. "30 Minutes: The Growing Pains of a New Program for Teen-Agers." *New York Times,* January 7, 1979, sec. 2, p. 25.

Prisuta, Robert H. "The Adolescent and Television News: A Viewer Profile." *Journalism Quarterly* 56:2 (Summer 1979): 277–282.

Smith, David M. "Some Uses of Mass Media by 14 Year Olds." *Journal of Broadcasting* 16:1 (Winter 1971–1972): 37–50.

Television/Radio Age Seminar. "New Forms Emerging for Syndicated Shows." *Television/Radio Age,* January 17, 1977, pp. 23–27, 56–64.

Young Adult Fiction

Pfeffer, Susan Beth. *Starring Peter and Leigh.* Story of a teenage soap opera actress who leaves acting to become a "normal" teenager. New York: Delacorte: 1978.

3 Role Models

Reflection

When I look
into the mirror,
I sometimes wish
I could really see
myself
and know
who I am
what I want
why I do
the things I do.
Instead, I see
a girl looking back
who's just as puzzled as I am.

Jodie Arey
Camden-Rockport High School

Teenage Stereotypes

RICHARD PECK

A WRITER OF BOOKS for and about adolescents is bound to be of two minds regarding television. For years writers have suspected that television robs them of readers, but in recent seasons it has given a number of books readers they would never otherwise have had. Mysteriously, the young make a rush for the paperback on the morning after the television airing. Therefore, the authors of such novels-turned-television programs as *Summer of My German Soldier*, *Are You in the House Alone?*, *Mom, the Wolfman and Me*, *Lisa Bright and Dark*, and a number of others have reason to be grudgingly grateful.

It has taken television an astonishingly long time to catch its first glimpse of adolescents, despite the fact that they are faithful viewers and have a large, expendable, unearned income. Ours is a society in which children enjoy a higher standard of living than their own parents. But it is a rare teenager who sees much of himself on a television screen, and teenagers rarely look for anything else. This generation has been spared the coming of age of Ricky and David Nelson and the teenaged offspring, both grim and prim, of the Father Who Knew Best.

In more modern times the young have been invited to see themselves either as supporting players meant to bolster adult starring roles in such programs as "Welcome Back, Kotter" and "One Day at

* Richard Peck is the author of numerous young adult novels, including *Secrets of the Shopping Mall*, *Father Figure*, and *Close Enough to Touch*.

a Time," or they have been portrayed as the victims of dour social and psychological problems: narcotic, sexual, racial. The television camera shifts from a season of adolescent alcoholism to another of teenaged runaways. The young are either played for laughs, kept subordinate to adult roles, or cast as victims—three states they are anxious to avoid in their own lives.

Television limps along in pursuit of the relevant, but the relevant issues of adults rarely compare with those of the young. Why has no one thought to ask the young themselves? They can be very verbal about television. It has a far greater hold on them than school, and it has taught them to be critics of other people's performances.

They are not, however, very forthcoming on the newest season of serial shows, nor are they much caught up in specials. They're not looking for anything new. They prefer the same fare over and over, whether they're reading through every volume of Nancy Drew for the second time or watching with limitless patience "Happy Days" every afternoon of their lives. They read and view not for sensation but for ritual, and the reinforcement of reruns is often more meaningful than the novelty of a special.

Television often exercises more effective control over its teenaged characters than American parents exercise over their own children. In the early days, Ricky and David were adjuncts to Ozzie and Harriet, already durable performers. Surely things must have gotten out of hand when one of Gabe Kaplan's supporting sweathogs became John Travolta. Perhaps a reason that the young never seem to mention "One Day at a Time" is that Bonnie Franklin as the mother of two (fatherless) young daughters is still given center stage and, in her bumbling contemporary way, still seems to know best. Adolescents do not welcome parental control on or off the screen. They are trying to put all that behind them, and in our society they succeed early.

We seem now to be on the threshold of a new era when adolescent characters are creeping into the daytime soap operas. While it is true that teenagers will cut school to watch daytime television, they are not likely to approve of actresses impersonating teenaged vixens who are alienating married men from their wives. The young are markedly judgmental about other people's standards, and they are shocking prudes. They have an innate moral code for others to abide by that would make any rating system pale. They like to look up to characters with whom they wish to ally themselves. They don't want to become clowns, addicts, greaseballs, or Lolitas.

Teenagers are not as anxious to grow up and assume adult responsibilities as earlier young generations were. They want a great deal now, including advice. All of this has very little to do with adult situations or adult performers. The young have already won all their battles with adults—parents, teachers, the local police—and in this era they live a private life safe from prying eyes.

They want a great deal, but nothing so surprising: power, respect, freedom, and escape. Don't we all? But the young want all this on their own terms. It would seem that television has reached them only by inadvertence. An adult can readily generate an admiring conversation with a teenager about Starsky and Hutch and Erik Estrada. To the teenaged girl they are interesting older men. To the teenaged boy, they have a power and nobility, astride their motorcycles, that is worth aspiring toward. Teenagers even give an approving nod for the central figure of the rerun "Rockford Files"—that glibly world-weary adolescent trapped in an aging adult society.

But what about an authentic adolescent image worth befriending or becoming? It seems to come down to a single figure, now nearly immortal, in an enduring series: Radar in "M*A*S*H." Even when the Fonzes fade, "M*A*S*H" lasts, gathering up succeeding young generations. By now, they cannot remember a world without it, nor anything in it to criticize. Such success is worth a closer look.

"M*A*S*H" is clearly meant as adult fare, drawn from a long-ago movie the young were discouraged from seeing. It is even set in the midst of a war now rarely mentioned and hardly taught in school. And all of its stars are grossly overaged for their parts.

It is a story about disparate people trapped together in the isolation of war. Without meaning to, they provide a surrogate family for one another. There is considerable warmth in their snappy, snappish dialogue, leavened with moments of deeply felt, quiet, well-realized emotion and compassion—compassion for suffering, for loneliness, for each other.

They are family not only for one another but also for the young viewer, weary of his own. Colonel Potter, wry and understanding, is the grandfather unknown to the nuclear family. Hotlips, the female butt of all jokes, is overaged, oversexed, overloud—the teenager's pitiless image of a mother figure. Klinger, lurching through a battle zone in high heels and earrings, is not as audacious as he seems; he is the relentless rebel against the bureaucracy of elders who imprison him; he will never be free, but he will never give up.

And then there is Radar, clearly an adolescent in a world of adults less wise than he. Even his name suggests extraordinary perceptions. He is shorter than the rest, younger, the enlisted man in a hierarchy of officers. Best of all, he is the ideal blend of instinctive wisdom and innocence, virginal innocence. He is a very quiet little winner. He loves his mother, but he doesn't have to confront her. He is lovable, he is loved, and he tends to get his way.

There must be more direct approaches to the youthful viewer than Radar, though he's not a bad guidepost. Most viewers think they look far more like him—or Gary Coleman—than like Shaun Cassidy.

Glamor is television's long suit, and perhaps the young would not have it any other way. But they have been scarred by the endless reiteration of programming and commercials that promote the notion that only the beautiful deserve to be loved or even noticed.

In their reading, adolescents are highly receptive to messages and situations that are too subtly low key to be discovered by television. They much prefer a sweetly sad love story with a happy ending to any sort of sexual exploitation. They like stories of people of good character. But the young will not be preached to. They will not pay much attention to messages meant to revolutionize their psyches. They want instead stories that inspire them to survive in the world as it is: in their almighty peer groups, in their middle-class standards of propriety, in their unremitting need to be accepted. They do not want the boat rocked; they want to keep from falling overboard. And so they will be drawn to situations they can rise to: success stories about young people who manage to survive in their peer groups without losing all of their individuality; stories that pit the standards of the individual against the rules of the group. There are plenty of such stories that hold out a little light in the jungle of the present-day youth culture, if only television can change enough to find them.

Changing Male and Female Roles

CHARLES ATKIN

SINCE THE EARLIEST DAYS of television, men have outnumbered women in television programming by a wide margin. Unlike the fifty-fifty split in real life, there are about three times as many men as women in the video world. This disparity has not changed during the past decade, although women have attained a larger number of major rather than secondary roles, and certain types of programs—situation comedies, family dramas, and soap operas—have near parity of the sexes. On the other hand, crime-adventure shows and Saturday morning cartoons score well above the three-to-one ratio. Surprisingly, an analysis of public television programming showed that 85 percent of the characters were male, including more than 75 percent of the characters on the child-oriented "Sesame Street" and "Electric Company." One study discovered that three of four cartoon animal characters were male.

The characteristics of females who do appear on television are not typical of true population attributes. TV women tend to be younger (primarily mid-thirties or under, with very few elderly women), and more home bound (only one-third hold outside jobs). Occupationally TV women are underrepresented in higher-status professions (medicine, law, and business), and especially rare as criminals; furthermore, the range of female occupations on TV is far narrower than that for males.

* Charles Atkin, Ph.D., is professor of communications, Michigan Sate University. He has conducted several research projects analyzing the content and effects of TV entertainment, news, and advertising.

TV men and women can also be compared in terms of physical traits and behavior patterns. Research shows that TV males are relatively more rational, intelligent, powerful, stable, tolerant, aggressive, and task persistent. Females on TV tend to be more passive, warm, sociable, altruistic, sympathetic, humorous, emotional, dependent, and deferential than male characters. The social interactions between the sexes display a clear dominance by males in giving advice and orders, except when programs are set in the family context. Although these characteristics follow conventional societal differences between males and females, the TV portrayals are more aggressive and stereotyped than in contemporary reality.

There are few indications that the pattern of sex-role depictions has changed substantially over the past few years. With certain notable exceptions, such as female police officers or subordinate husbands, most of the portrayals of both sexes are still narrowly stereotyped along traditional image dimensions. Clearly the rate of change has not satisfied feminist media critics, who argue that TV programming has lagged behind the evolving role of women in society.

Rigid stereotyping is even more prevalent in TV commercials than in entertainment programming, as advertisers cater to what they perceive as the traditional males and females who constitute the bulk of the market. Although the sheer numbers of each sex are more equivalent in advertisements, males and females are assigned to highly predictable roles: women disproportionately appear in advertisements for domestic and personal grooming products, in those set in the home, and in roles as wives, mothers, or decorative sex objects. More than half of the women in this country hold jobs today, but very few women in television commercials are portrayed in occupations outside the home.

By contrast, men in TV advertisements are more often cast in business or outdoor settings. Men are shown in advertisements for automobiles, appliances, alcohol, and insurance. Studies plotting trends across the 1970s indicate that some gradual changes have occurred in reducing these stereotypes. But one distinct sex disparity remains unchanged: more than nine of ten off-camera voices that provide the authoritative information about the product are male.

The research on audience response to sex-role content is categorized in terms of character identification and long-term effects. Most of the research has focused on the acquisition of information and reactions such as occupational aspirations and sex-appropriate values, rather than actual behavior.

Concerning identification with TV performers, studies demonstrate that boys relate almost exclusively to male characters; they almost never want to emulate female stars (except for attractive female police officers or private detectives). Girls tend to identify with fewer characters and are more likely to select opposite-sex models than are boys. In one study, both boys and girls preferred to watch programs where performers displayed sex-typed activities rather than non-sextyped activities.

Research on the long-term effects of viewing TV entertainment is difficult to conduct because almost all young people are exposed to some degree to direct experience with actual sex-role models similar to the traditional characterizations on TV, and because TV offers relatively few nonsexist portrayals of male and female roles that might produce measurable effects. Nevertheless, some investigations have attempted to trace the impact of both the stereotyped and counterstereotyped presentations on TV. One pair of studies shows that elementary-age children who view the greatest amount of television (and presumably see the most traditional content) tend to hold the most traditional views on sex role measures. In one case, the heavier viewers made more stereotyped occupational aspiration choices. In the other study, the most frequent viewers gave sex-typed responses when choosing between activities usually associated with masculine and feminine roles in society.

A survey examining the influence of counterstereotypes in entertainment programs yielded findings of informational and attitudinal learning. The investigators focused on five regular female characters in nontypical roles: two police officers, a park ranger, a television producer, and a high school principal. Children in late elementary school who were familiar with each character were compared with those who were not. The former were more likely to perceive that real-life women held these occupational roles; for example, those familiar with the female police officer on "Police Woman" thought that 3.8 out of every 10 police officers were female, compared with an estimate of 3.0 among the control group respondents.

Viewers familiar with the female counterstereotyped characters were also more likely to feel that it was appropriate for women to hold the occupation in four of the five comparisons. For example, on a scale of occupational appropriateness ranging from 1 to 3, children familiar with the female ranger in "Sierra" gave a rating of 1.8, compared with 1.6 in the control group unaware of this character. Although the differences were small, the pattern is consistent in showing more liberated responses.

Several experiments have been designed to test the sex-role impact of TV advertising portrayals. One researcher looked at advertisements that intended to influence sex-role attitudes: commercials featuring beauty products using sex appeal or physical attractiveness themes. Teenage girls in the experimental group were shown fifteen such advertisements, and a control group was exposed to neutral commercials. When asked what characteristics a woman should have to be popular with men, the exposed girls were significantly more likely to cite sex appeal, youthful appearance, glamor, and a slim body.

Another study with elementary school children looked at a toy commercial that intended to broaden play preferences beyond traditional sex typing. Most active toys promoted on TV are aimed at the male market and feature boys playing with the product. To test the impact of a counterstereotypical use of a toy racing car set by girls, two versions of a standard advertisement were filmed: one depicted two young boys playing with the racing cars, and the other presented the same sequence of actions performed by two young girls. Half of the sample saw each version, inserted in a videotaped cartoon program. Those in the female-player condition who perceived that the characters were girls (due to selective perception, some mistakenly considered the players to be boys) were twice as likely to feel that girls should appropriately play with racing cars, and they were slightly more likely to indicate that they would like to play with the cars, compared to children in the boy-player treatment.

Finally, two experiments assessed incidental learning of occupational sex roles that occurred as a side effect in advertisements intended to sell a neutral product. In each case, the evidence indicates that exposure to females in nontraditional occupations serves to broaden conceptions of child viewers. The most interesting study manipulated the occupation portrayed by a woman in a standard testimonial-style advertisement selling eyeglasses to a general audience. The same middle-aged female endorser was featured in three alternative versions of the message. In one, she was presented in a courtroom environment dressed as a judge, the second version showed her at a console as a computer programmer, and the third version portrayed her as a TV repair technician in an equipment-cluttered shop. In each advertisement, the woman introduced herself and identified her occupation before discussing the product's usefulness in carrying out her job. Elementary school students viewing the judge version were strongly influenced; half thought that the judicial profession was appropriate for women, compared to one-quarter of the control group. Modest differences were found in the other two versions. In each case, the greatest impact occurred for older girls, demonstrating the potential power of just a single exposure to a message focusing on the product rather than the model's role and indicating the extent to which advertising may teach incidental lessons to young viewers.

The research suggests that male and female role portrayals do shape the attitudes of young viewers of programs and commercials. Since the predominant orientation of TV modeling is traditional sex typing, the impact is likely to be primarily conservative. To the extent that counterstereotypical models are depicted, however, TV can serve as a source of learning about the diversity of sex-role options in society. One effort at systematically broadening role models is the public television series "Freestyle." The success of that program in expanding career awareness of girls and reducing stereotypic conceptions shows the potential of television as a liberating force in the 1980s.

Male and Female Roles

A Case Study, "Freestyle"

NORTON WRIGHT

The Beginning: Goal-Development Seminars

THEY CAME from universities and schools across the nation to attend the first goal-development seminar in Long Beach, California, in September 1976. Twenty-two in number—career awareness experts, behavioral psychologists, researchers—they came to define the need for overcoming sexist and racist stereotyping in the career aspirations of youngsters and adults, and they were enthusiastic about the prospect of formulating a list of awareness goals that a soon-to-be-created national television series might reasonably be expected to achieve.

The project was called "Freestyle," a $4.2 million effort funded by the Department of Health, Education and Welfare's National Institute of Education (NIE). A team of Hollywood script writers also attended this two-day session, for it would eventually fall to them to turn the goals defined in this and subsequent seminars into an appealing television series that would show youngsters the range of accessible careers that they could realistically prepare for.

Writer Sue Milburn came with strong dramatic series credentials at the networks; Matt Robinson from "Sesame Street" brought a valuable black perspective; and Elaine Laron had written for "The Electric Company," and a number of network variety specials and was passionate in her advocacy of sex equity. Sandra Harmon brought the

---

* Norton Wright was executive producer of "Freestyle." Currently, he is director of family programming for Disney Television.

humor and wit of her work on the "Dick Cavett Show," and Sybil Adleman was a master of comedy sketches for Lily Tomlin.

During the course of the seminar, the participants helped to identify the needs and goals of the "Freestyle" project, which began to take shape in a range of outpourings from the advisers. Sometimes the messages were conceptual: sexist and racist stereotyping on the job, in the home, in the classroom, and on the playing field restricts the occupational choices and family roles open to women, men, girls, and boys. Sometimes they were factual: fifty percent of the female work force is involved in seven occupations, most of which tend to be low paying and without promising vistas of advancement: secretary, book-keeper, teacher, librarian, nurse, seamstress, housewife. Sometimes they were theatrical: the Cinderella myth says most young girls in America still expect Prince Charming to come along and spirit them off to the castle where they will live happily ever after. They don't realize that the prince may never come, or that if he does, he may not be as charming as imagined or may later abandon the castle and his princess, and she, having left her mechanical, mathematical, scientific, management, and athletic skills undeveloped, will have only a small range of menial jobs open to her as she strives for self-support.

And so in this and in two subsequent seminars in 1976 and 1977, the mandate of the "Freestyle" project was shaped. There would be a television series of thirteen half hours broadcast nationwide on the Public Broadcasting Service (PBS) and targeted to an audience of girls and boys aged nine to twelve—youngsters old enough to imagine what their future careers and lives might be like but young enough to be open to considering a range of nontraditional activities and behaviors.

Goals with Measurable Outcomes

The NIE called for the "Freestyle" project to develop a statement of goals so specific that the effectiveness of the TV series in achieving these goals could be measured. As a first step, a target audience sample would be pretested to determine its career knowledge and attitudes. Then that sample would watch the TV series, and finally the sample would be posttested to measure whatever cognitive and effective changes had taken place as a result of viewing.

The goals of "Freestyle" fall into two categories: nontraditional activities and nontraditional behaviors. The series encourages girls to try out preoccupational activities involving science, mathematics, mechanics, and physically rigorous home and athletic challenges. Boys are encouraged to explore activities involving child care, social and service duties, writing skills, and the arts.

Nontraditional behaviors presented as choices for girls are leadership, assertiveness, reasonable risk-taking, coping with failure and success, and cooperation. For boys, the choices for nontraditional behavior include being empathetic and caring, emotionally expressive, and accepting of female leadership.

The Pilots

The NIE allowed fifteen months to refine the goals statement, to develop and produce three half-hour pilots (each of a different format), and to test the effectiveness of each format on a national audience sample before selecting the final format for the series. Using Los Angeles public television station KCET as a production base and the research capabilities of the Annenberg School of Communications at the University of California, pilot development was well underway by March 1977.

The first pilot was a "Sesame Street"–styled variety show, with short, fast-paced modules of animation, live action film, and TV studio sketches, songs, and dances performed by a company of four young actors, who were cast to look like big brothers and sisters whose attitudes and behaviors our target audience could emulate.

Actor Mike Farrell, who plays Captain B.J. Hunnicutt on "M*A*S*H," hosted the half-hour pilot and proved to be both appealing and persuasive. His "M*A*S*H" image combines both traditional, he-man heroism with nontraditional sensitivity, and his real-life interests in sex equity and responsible parenting gave his performance the ring of credibility. When he attacked sexist and racist stereotyping and advocated that boys and girls make some gutsy, nontraditional behavioral choices, he was convincing. It was tough not to believe him.

The first pilot worked well enough on a cognitive level. It was clear, comprehensible, and on the nose in telling the target audience about the limiting effects of stereotyping, the broad range of preoccupational activities they could pursue, and nonstereotypical jobs they could realistically train for. But the research team headed by the dean of USC's Annenberg School of Communications, Frederick Williams, found in testing the pilot that it was short on emotional clout. The youngsters in the audience understood the messages presented and believed them to be true but did not feel emotionally moved to change their personal lives by adapting the attitudes and behaviors modeled. Clearly another format needed to be explored, one that would involve the heart as well as the mind of the audience.

Storytelling

Pat Seeley suggested storytelling as the basis for one of the "Freestyle" pilots. Although her main assignment was to oversee the goal-development effort contracted to the Office of the Superintendent of Los Angeles County Schools, her experience as a teacher prompted her to point out that youngsters could be emotionally caught up by stories, especially stories that related to the challenges youngsters encounter in their everyday lives.

Her interest in storytelling resulted in the production of a second pilot that was a sequence of six self-contained situation comedy and soap opera–styled stories in a half-hour program. The cast of characters in each story was designed to be realistic—no "Six Million Dollar Man" or "Bionic Woman" but rather a boy hero and his father coping with the absence of a working wife and mother and finding the fun of making a household on their own, or a girl heroine rejecting the Cinderella myth and asserting herself by taking on a summer job at an all-male car wash.

The story format was another step in the right direction, but the testing of this pilot revealed two drawbacks. Trying to explain and involve the audience emotionally in six nontraditional behaviors and activities in a single half-hour was too much. Formative research showed that many of the messages of this format went by too quickly to register on the audience. The range of careers and life skills the series was designed to address was immense, but the research findings showed that it was better to do a few things well than too many things inadequately. The messages of the individual episodes would have to be reduced in number and made more explicit.

A second weakness in the six-story format was that although comedy situations were fun and appealing to the young audiences, the comedy often confused the messages. If the character of a female welder was presented in a sketch with comic overtones, the audience could mistake the nonstereotypical model of a female welder for a joke. Similarly, if comic incongruity called for extreme role reversal (for example, a father getting a job as a cocktail waitress) again our young audience would feel that trying the nontraditional was foolish, and adults in the audience could be offended if such extreme role expansion was deliberately advocated.

Format for the Series

"Greasemonkey," the third and last pilot, became the basis of the "Freestyle" series. Like an afternoon special for young people on one of the commercial networks, one complete, self-contained story was told, and the emphasis was on drama. The plot dealt with a twelve-year-old girl who took a nontraditional summer job as a gas station attendant and fought her way up through a series of calamities until she eventually became a bonafide grease monkey and used her newly acquired mechanic's skills to repair a pregnant woman's car and save the lives of the woman and her baby.

The teleplay, scripted by adventure series writers Tom August and Helen August, was action packed. Numerous on-location filming sites and some twenty scenes in the first half-hour format made for an abundance of visuals. The fast-paced picturization of the drama's suspense and jeopardy would hold the target audience while the career awareness messages were conveyed.

Following the recommendation of the research team, only two goals were addressed in the "Greasemonkey" pilot: the behavioral goal of reasonable risk-taking, which encourages girls to accept new physical, intellectual, and emotional challenges where a good chance of success exists, and the activity goal of mechanical skills, which prompts girls to develop their understanding of machinery maintenance and repair and their skills with tools.

Addressing only two goals in each half-hour episode subsequently became the standard formula for the "Freestyle" series. If a nontraditional activity was emphasized in an episode, the episode was categorized as an activity show; if a nontraditional behavior was the focus of the drama, it was a behavior show. Of the two categories, activity shows proved more successful in achieving their goals than behavior shows.

The Series Premise

The "Freestyle" series is based on the adventures of a multiethnic group of six ten- to fourteen-year-old youngsters in a middle-class suburban environment who battle the limiting effects of sexist and racist stereotyping in the community, in school, at work, and at home. Their parents, for the most part, model nontraditional behaviors and careers. The Asian-American girl in the series has a mother with management skills who holds the job of a bank officer. The Chicano boy's father is a rough-and-tumble contractor but is also caring and empathetic. One Anglo girl has a very independent widowed mother who owns and manages a hardware store. The black youngster's parents run their own high-technology printing plant. The villains of the series are peers and adults who advocate only stereotypical behaviors and careers, and the series' ongoing heavy is the bigoted father of one of the Anglo boys in the cast. One or two of the six young principals are featured in each weekly episode of "Freestyle," and the rest of the principals play supporting roles.

To heighten the appeal for adult viewers and to broaden the series' audience, star talents such as Lois Nettleton, Larry Pressman, Mike Farrell, Greg Morris, and William Daniels are featured in guest star roles where they model nonstereotypical behavior that can be emulated by adults and youngsters alike.

The mix of plot lines in "Freestyle" is balanced to relate to girls, boys, and adults. One boy-oriented story deals with two boys who foul up their volunteer work at a home for the elderly until a nurturing occupational therapist, an ex-football star, shows them that caring requires them to empathize with the patients' feelings, to put themselves in their place, and understand the need of the elderly to do things on their own.

One adult-oriented story concerns the male bigot of the series who quarrels with his wife because she wants to take a job in a factory for personal satisfaction and additional family income. The disagreement continues until the husband is suddenly laid off from his job and sheepishly realizes that now his wife must work to support their family—and the higher paying her job, the better.

In a plot focusing on both racist and sexist stereotyping, a Chicano boy is reluctant to compete in his school's science contest because he thinks that Latinos are not supposed to be good at disciplined endeavors. He meets a girl who wants to join in the contest but feels that her participation would make her seem bookish. Together they fight their stereotypical fears, join the science contest as a team, and win. Scientific excellence is shown to be achievable by both, and both demonstrate independence from the pressure of their peers to stay out of the contest.

A typical girl-oriented plot tells the story of a shy girl who has a tough fight campaigning for class president against an all-boy slate of candidates until she gets the advice of her local council person, played by Lois Nettleton, and learns the importance of speaking up and organizing in seeking leadership posts.

Scripts, Production Values, and Techniques

To merit viewer attention, scripts and production values for "Freestyle" were fashioned to be competitive with those of commercial network programming. Hollywood writers of network series and motion pictures were contracted to script the series, among them Rod Peterson and Clair Whitaker of "The Waltons," Ron Rubin of "James at 16," Katharyn Powers of "The Fitzpatricks," and Sally Robinson of "Family."

Three days of cast rehearsals were allocated to each episode; a typical "Freestyle" shooting schedule at various locations ran five days. Shooting was accomplished using single camera technique with either 16-mm film or 1-inch videotape. Outstanding feature motion picture directors of photography were used, among them John Bailey of *Ordinary People* and Willie Kurant of *Harper Valley*. Editing was done on videotape using the CMX 50 and 300 process, and the resulting fine cuts were scored by feature film composers David Shire and Jim DiPasquale.

Cliff-hangers for the Classroom

Each half-hour episode of "Freestyle" designed for family viewing is also designed to be split into two individual quarter-hour segments for use in the school classroom. The classroom segments are shown on separate school days. To promote teacher-student discussion and activities, the first quarter-hour segment ends abruptly in the middle of a cliff-hanger scene with a printed question superimposed over a frozen frame. A question such as "Can Tess Rescue Ramon?" usually gets the classroom discussion off to a good, and sometimes heated, start. The concluding quarter-hour segment ends with a verbal review, delivered by the episode's guest star, of the activity or behavioral goal featured in that half-hour of "Freestyle."

Publications

In support of the "Freestyle" series, Science Research Associates (SRA) of Chicago designed and distributed a test sample of publications through PBS stations nationwide. A comic book in both English and Spanish versions reinforced the messages of the series for young people. A calendar for home use by parents presented "Freestyle" messages and historical features on nonstereotypical heroines and heroes. A teacher's guide facilitated classroom discussion of the series by giving teachers a synopsis of each of the thirteen episodes of "Freestyle" and by suggesting a range of episode-oriented questions, discussion topics, games, and activities.

Goal Achievement

A summary evaluation of the "Freestyle" series during its premier airing in the fall of 1978 was conducted by Jerome Johnston and a special team of researchers at the Institute for Social Research (ISR) at the University of Michigan. Audience data in the evaluation showed widespread acceptance of the series by PBS stations and their audiences, and teacher endorsement was equally strong. In seven test sites across the nation, a sample of 268 teachers used "Freestyle" with over 7,000 nine- to twelve-year-olds; 96 percent of the teachers recommended that "Freestyle" be used by other teachers.

The effectiveness of the series in achieving its stated goals was summarized in ISR's evaluation report:

> When implemented under conditions of heavy viewing and extensive classroom discussion, "Freestyle" showed the ability to change a large number of beliefs and attitudes regarding sex-appropriate childhood behavior, and adult job and family roles. It was less successful influencing the children's own interest in nontraditional endeavors. With the exception of girls in leadership roles, it was not effective in changing beliefs and attitudes regarding childhood behavioral skills. These are apparently too complex to be dealt with in a single television series and supporting classroom activities.

The evaluation pointed out that "Freestyle" was at its most effective when addressing goals in which nonstereotypical activities were modeled. The physical action of unfaked scenes (a girl playing flag football and catching a forward pass or a boy sculpting an aesthetically pleasing clay pot) showed viewers the range of real-life activities appropriate for girls and boys to explore.

Only in the area of stimulating interest in nontraditional careers did the activity shows show weakness. After watching an episode like "Greasemonkey," the audience sample did show a shift in its beliefs and attitudes, coming to recognize and approve of girls involved in mechanical tasks, but few girls expressed a desire to become a mechanic or an engineer. Perhaps a more romanticized presentation of a mechanic's duties using star-burst lenses and soaring music would have generated more interest in the jobs modeled, but the aim for this first series was to achieve credibility with the audience by not using production trickery to enhance the subject matter. In future projects of a similar nature, a more idealized and flamboyant presentation of nonstereotypical careers may prove more effective in piquing interest.

In the area of behavioral goals, in spite of each episode's focus on a single nonstereotypical behavior and scenes in which the specific behavior was verbally explained in detail, "Freestyle" fell short of its aims to teach and win approval for reasonable risk taking, assertiveness, and cooperation by girls. With the exception of girls in leadership roles, the nontraditional behaviors modeled by the serie's principals were either not clear enough or not persuasive enough to change the attitudes of the audience in favor of adopting those behaviors. Perhaps a TV series totaling only six and one-half hours in the total TV viewing experience of nine- to twelve-year-olds is too little time to teach and encourage the complexities of certain human behaviors. It is interesting to contemplate, however, what effect a steady diet of programs modeling prosocial behaviors would have on the young audiences. That experiment is for the future.

The evaluation of "Freestyle" clearly points out that the series is most effective and most influential when viewed and discussed by adults and youngsters who watch the series together. The success of this kind of family and classroom viewing appears to confirm that, as appealing and influential as television can be, nothing is so effective in shaping the life skills of youngsters as dedicated teachers and motivated parents.

The Future

In "Freestyle," TV talents, educators, and researchers combined their disciplines to achieve affective as well as cognitive goals. The success of the "Freestyle" storytelling format in affecting emotions, changing attitudes, and nurturing nonsexist, nonracist behavior can serve as an encouragement to others who are developing prosocial television programs, especially for young audiences.

In one of his research reports for "Freestyle," Frederick Williams noted, "It is difficult to find a twelve-year-old bigot." All those in the "Freestyle" project took heart from that thought. If youngsters can be reached early enough with the right kind of programming, television has the opportunity of telling them that they are inherently right, that their natural appetite to try everything, to fail and try again is okay. If that twelve-year-old can be encouraged to keep doing what she or he is already naturally doing and can be steeled to question the stereotypes of adult society, then all of us, young and old, will surely be the better for it.

Age Stereotypes

LYDIA BRAGGER

OLD PEOPLE are ugly, decrepit, stupid, forgetful, toothless, and sexless; after sixty-five they are ready to fall off the conveyor belt of life. This is the way the media has portrayed the old.

The Gray Panthers receive many complaints about the treatment of the old by the media. Because the media influence the attitudes and behavior patterns of persons of all ages, radio, television, newspapers, and magazines are largely responsible for the perpetuation of this stereotypical image of the old. It is important to change this image, which the Gray Panthers believe is the cause of negative attitudes and prejudices toward the elderly.

From the time children learn to read, their first books show old people walking with canes, sitting in rocking chairs looking off into space, being meddlesome, forgetful, helpless, and ill. In *The Upstairs Nana*, the great-grandmother in the story is either sick in bed or tied in a rocking chair so she will not fall off. I am a great-grandmother, and I cannot identify with this image, nor can many other grandmothers I know. We want children to get accurate portrayals of the old.

Many young people have very little contact with old people. The extended family in America is the exception rather than the rule. The only way many of the young know the old is by the way they

* Lydia Bragger is chairperson of the National Gray Panthers Media Watch Task Force. She is a long-time writer and producer of radio and television programming.

see them portrayed in the media. And the media's image is pervasive: every day old people are portrayed as stupid, comic figures.

The South Carolina drivers' handbook warns young drivers: "An older person, his mind perhaps dulled by age or preoccupied with memories of days gone by, may wander into the street without any thought of an oncoming vehicle." Is it any wonder that society treats old people the way that they do and that old people who believe these myths have so little regard for themselves?

A New York City radio station aired a commercial for a health food store that said, "It used to be that the clientele of our store were little old ladies in tennis shoes. But now we have the intelligent shoppers . . . young people are buying health foods." The Gray Panthers objected to the implication that old ladies were not intelligent. They received a letter of apology, and the commercial was taken off the air.

Many times the message is more subtle but no less offensive. In a yogurt commercial showing couples of all ages eating yogurt, young couples were shown eating raspberry yogurt, strawberry yogurt, and peach yogurt. Then the camera showed an old couple and zoomed in on their container of yogurt; the flavor was prune. The advertising media seem to focus on old people and prunes.

In the news there are instances of old people's problems shown without sensitivity, sensationalized out of proportion, and too often done in a manner that invites ridicule of older people instead of creating understanding. Even newscasters who are usually sensitive sometimes project society's image of the old. For instance, David Brinkley, speaking about a television program on old age that was about to be aired, said, "One ailment we all have in common—we're all growing old." Is growing old an ailment?

The media are all guilty of negative stereotyping of the old, but television is probably the most persuasive. It is said that television is a reflective medium, but while TV stereotypes may reflect the injustices of our society, at the same time they reinforce and perpetuate those injustices. TV legitimizes ideas. Ninety-eight percent of all homes in this country have TV sets. Americans—mainly the very young, the old, and the poor—tune in over six hours a day. That is close to 2,400 hours a year. Between the ages of two and sixty-five, the average person will watch nine full years of TV. I think we all recognize that there has never been a more powerful or effective medium of education, for good or for bad, than TV. And the Gray Panthers need the help of that powerful and effective medium to change the image of the old in society today. Television should explore on a regular basis the satisfaction of life after sixty, showing liveliness, intelligence, fruitful work, love, and sex, which do not end at some arbitrary point. TV must expand its limited view of human life and possibility.

"All in the Family" once aired a segment about two old people getting married in the Bunker home. The guests were residents of the home where Edith Bunker worked. The old people were shown in such a demeaning and insulting way that the Gray Panthers Media Watch complained by writing to the vice-president in charge of creative practices for Tandem TAT, asking her to take another look at that program. She replied, "Thank you for your letter, and we are concerned," and asked for the name of a Gray Panther on the West Coast who could screen "All in the Family" programs before they were produced to "tell us what we are doing wrong." After that a consultant worked on the program.

The image of old people on television is beginning to change. "A Family Upside Down," an NBC movie starring Helen Hayes and Fred Astaire, was a love story using two older people in the leading roles. Ten years ago this would not have been shown. Recently the Gray Panthers were consulted throughout the production of a "Lou Grant Show" segment that presented sensitive and realistic images of the old. A few years ago young performers were made up to look old, but now more older actors and actresses are being used to play characters their own age. Society is beginning to understand that persons over sixty are still capable of thinking, learning, and performing. *Morning's at Seven* is a sensitive Broadway play, and only two of the nine characters are under fifty. "The Last Tenant," shown on ABC in 1978, did not flatter old age but was realistic in its portrayal of an old man who burdens his children unnecessarily. This was a good teaching tool, useful for promoting discussion.

Commercials are also beginning to portray old people in positive and realistic ways. In the past, old people were shown only as experts on aches and pain remedies, laxatives, and fixatives for dentures—the elderly were the Geritol generation. Geritol commercials used to show only old people using their product. The Gray Panthers complained. Now we see persons of all ages taking Geritol. An earlier Country Time Lemonade commercial showed two old men playing checkers; one was asked a question by a younger man and his response was irrelevant due to his hearing loss. His deafness—something that anyone could suffer from—was made the brunt of a joke. The Gray Panthers were one of many that complained about this ageist commercial, and it has now been changed.

For the first time, an advertising agency called the Gray Panthers recently to look at a commercial that included an insulting image of an old woman. The commercial was still in the story-board form. The network had refused to run it, saying, "The Gray Panthers will be after us." I went to the agency and, after viewing the story-board, pressed for change. Eventually the frame with the old woman was dropped.

I am serving on the advisory committee for "Winslow House," a television series created by Christopher Sarson. This is a story of older and younger people living together and includes many comic situations done sensitively.

It is exciting to be old today and one of the pioneer generation. This is the first generation of old people to organize and fight for their rights. Because most old people are healthy, they feel that they have a greater responsibility to society. They want to be in the mainstream of life, where the action is. In a Harris Poll directed to older Americans, the response to a question regarding action and the old showed the majority of old people wanted to be involved in community and national affairs. When the elderly become activists, they not only improve their own lives but also become change agents for all of society.

Older people are functioning adults for the most part and want to be shown that way—as human beings taking an active part in society, interacting with all ages, and making the contributions they are able to make.

The television networks are quite responsive to concerns of the elderly. The image of the older person has improved, but there is still much more room for improvement. The bottom line is money; when the ratings go down, then the program content will change dramatically. Education is needed so that people will not watch stereotypical programs.

The Gray Panthers hope to strengthen people's awareness of the effect the media have on the roles and relationships of women, men, and children of all ages. Television, the most powerful communicator of our time, can become a creative, challenging, and responsible medium for counteracting ageism, for counteracting the oppression of people of all ages, instead of reinforcing and perpetuating that oppression. As they become more aware, people will refuse to watch the unrealistic image of the old now being portrayed.

Teenagers and the Elderly

A Case Study, "Rocking Chair Rebellion"

MARY ALICE DWYER AND
ELLEN RODMAN

THE YOUNG and the old have a great deal in common. Children must attend school. Older adults often face mandatory retirement. Children must reside in their parents' home. Older people frequently live out their days in nursing homes. Neither have a choice of alternative living arrangements. While young people experience a sense of helplessness and identity crisis as they wait to "live," the elderly experience a sense of hopelessness and identity crisis as they wait to die. Both age groups seem to lack chances for self-determination.

Because they often lack jobs and money too, they are economically dependent on others and feel powerless and alienated. People speak about them rather than to them. They feel ignorant but can learn from each other, they feel useless but need each other, and they feel isolated through unnatural segregation but crave interaction.

Because of these similarities, young and old have much to offer one another. But because of the numerous sterotyped and misleading images of old people, children do not always take advantage of opportunities to get to know the elderly with whom they come in contact, so both miss the chance to share experiences and to help one another.

* Mary Alice Dwyer, formerly vice president of children's programs for NBC, is currently vice president of programming, Hearst/ABC Video Services and "Daytime," the women's channel.

* Ellen Rodman, Ph.D., is director of Children's Informational Services, NBC, Inc.

According to Richard Peck, Radar (Gary Burghoff) from "M*A*S*H" is one of television's best teenage role models. Photo courtesy of CBS.

A teenage boy (Stephen Austin) with a talent for both ballet and basketball has to choose between the two in the face of his father's contempt for his dancing in "A Special Gift," an ABC Afterschool Special. Photo courtesy of ABC, copyright © 1978, 1979, 1980, 1981 by American Broadcasting Companies, Inc.

Denise (Denise Kumagai), a terrific pass receiver, talks to Marcus (Marc Jefferson) about the way the boys' flag football team is treating her in PBS's "Freestyle." Photo courtesy of KCET, Los Angeles.

The multi-racial Apples—Big Neck (Mykel T. Williamson), Glo (Kutee), D.C., Junior (Joey Camen), and Sandy (Elizabeth Daily)—make music and deal with problems on "The Righteous Apples." Photo by Jim Britt courtesy of Rainbow TV Works.

This multi-racial group of high school journalists deals with a variety of complicated social and personal problems on PBS's "The New Voice." Photo courtesy of WGBH, Boston.

A teenager (Cheryl Arutt) persuades the residents of an "old folks" home to start living on their own in "The Rocking Chair Rebellion," an NBC Special Treat. Photo courtesy of The National Broadcasting Company, Inc.

Bobba June (Amy Wright), an aspiring trombonist who works in a nursing home, gets a lesson from her idol in "Sunshine's On the Way," an NBC Special Treat. Photo courtesy of The National Broadcasting Company, Inc.

In an effort to dispel stereotypes of the elderly and to correct the distorted perceptions young people often hold about the elderly, two NBC Special Treat presentations effectively dramatized positive—albeit atypical—relationships between young and old. One of these Special Treats, "The Rocking Chair Rebellion," is based on the juvenile novel of the same name by Eth Clifford.[1] The principal characters are thirteen-year-old Opie Cross, her elderly neighbor, Simon Pepper, and Jessica Sherman and the other residents of the Maple Ridge Home for the Aged.

The story begins with Opie losing her summer job as a lifeguard because she is underage. Simultaneously, her neighbor, Mr. Pepper, learns that he must take up residence at the Maple Ridge Home because his widowed daughter, with whom he has been living, is moving away to be with her children. Both individuals—one young, one old—find themselves at opposite times in their lives with exactly the same problem: they are without direction and have overpowering feelings of helplessness and hopelessness.

Realistic, stereotypical reactions become evident when Opie rejects a friend's suggestion that she try volunteer work at Maple Ridge. Opie has no desire to spend her summer with old folks. Opie's mother reinforces her attitude, but her father has a much more positive feeling toward old people. Even Mr. Pepper emphasizes the stereotypical response as he tells Opie not to visit him; an old folks' home is no place for a young girl.

In spite of herself, Opie becomes involved in a search for Jessica Sherman who has typically wandered off again. When Opie catches up with Mrs. Sherman, the two discover they have something in common: people address them in a patronizing way and treat them like children. Little by little, Opie realizes that old folks are intelligent, creative, resourceful, and caring individuals from whom she can learn and to whose happiness she can contribute.

As Opie gets to know the residents of Maple Ridge, they get to know themselves better, especially Simon Pepper and Jessica Sherman, who develop a warm affection for one another, which piques Opie's curiosity. "Do old people make love?" she asks her father. Another myth about old people evaporates as Opie's father explains that sexual feelings have less to do with age than with feelings of caring and concern for another human being.

Youngsters need to establish their independence as they mature; some of the residents of Maple Ridge reclaim theirs, primarily through an inspiration of Opie. Many of them, including Mr. Pepper and Mrs. Sherman, know they would be much happier with the increased freedom and decreased regimentation that would be possible if they lived in their own home. And when Opie discovers a house for sale in the neighborhood, she suggests that six of the senior citizens pool their resources and make the move. But, again, the neighbors' stereotypical prejudices block the way. As one character says, "People want us out of the way. We remind them they'll all be old one day."

"Sunshine's on the Way" is the story of Bobba June, a fourteen-year-old aspiring trombonist; her idol, T. P. Jackson; and the other musicians who reside at the Sugar Hill Nursing Home where she works.[2] When we meet her, Bobba June does not share Opie's aversion to old people. She has been a paid employee in their residence long enough to have overcome those feelings, and she totally accepts them. In fact, she has organized a number of the residents into a band. Music is their common ground and age is irrelevant. Bobba needs these old people as much as they need Bobba because they understand her love of music more than her own family does.

After Bobba's idol, the famous trombonist T. P. Jackson, suffers a stroke that leaves him without the use of one arm, he arrives at the home where she is working. He is bitter and wallows in self-pity. Bobba and T. P. are both musicians. She needs a new horn and wants T. P. to teach her some "tricks," and he needs encouragement and a trick that will enable him to play the trombone with one hand.

The band is soon invited to appear on Johnny Carson's "Tonight" show, but Bobba's mother does not want her to go, and the nurses and doctors do not want the old folks to go. They are "too fragile," they are told. In reality, they have appeared as anything but fragile, and they find the incongruity very funny. Nurse Crellin's concern for the old folks' "regularity" is also funny. In both instances, humor weakens the stereotypes.

By interacting with old people, the young people in both productions see that homes for the aged need not be horrible and that old people are not feebleminded but feisty. They also learn that death is part of life: Opie, reluctant at first, helps Mrs. Sherman select a gravestone, and Bobba discusses death with T. P. at his deathbed.

As birthrates decline and life is prolonged, the proportion of old people in this society, which is preoccupied with youth, is growing. By the turn of the century, one of five Americans will be over fifty-five.

The number of crimes committed against old people by adolescents has also grown, in part because the old have been stripped of their self-respect, and the young do not respect those who do not respect themselves. In "The Rocking Chair Rebellion," Mrs. Sherman points out to Opie that we live in a "labeled" society that loses sight of individuals. As Opie explains to her parents, "She's a 'senior citizen' and I'm a 'teenager.' We've been sorted out and dumped into baskets marked potatoes or onions. No one is an individual anymore."

The next several decades may well be the age of the elders. Active role models like Ronald Reagan, George Burns, and Bette Davis are highly visible. Organizations like the Gray Panthers, involved with the concerns of older people, can keep the momentum going in the right direction. Projects like Foster Grandparents provide opportunities. Television can help dispel stereotypes of the elderly through shows that portray positive portraits of vigorous, eager-to-teach old people and caring, eager-to-learn young people.

References

1. NBC, "The Rocking Chair Rebellion," October 23, 1979, by Daniel Wilson Productions.

2. NBC, "Sunshine's on the Way," November 11, 1980, by Highgate Pictures, a division of Learning Corporation of America.

Minority Role Models

Hispanics

AIDA BARRERA AND FREDERICK P. CLOSE

MARTIN LUTHER KING had a dream: "Four little children will one day live in a nation where they will not be judged by the color of their skin but by the content of their character." We too have a dream: that our nation will no longer hinder but will encourage the development of the character of our young people such that they may lead rich, satisfying, productive lives.

If we were to make this dream a reality, what changes in our nation and in our young people's more immediate environment would we make? Initially we would try to provide what Aristotle called the "conditions of external prosperity" that even a virtuous person needs for happiness: decent housing, sound medical care, sufficient food and clothing, and freedom from worry about the availability of such necessities. We would like our young people to grow up in a society free of racial prejudice. We would want them to be able to find satisfying work. We would want them to have the skills to adapt to the exigencies of the future, to cope with the personal and professional difficulties they will surely encounter. And finally we would want them to be sufficiently educated to understand and fulfill their civic and moral duty, to sympathize with the suffering of others, to appreciate aesthetic and religious values, and to know the value of their history, their culture, and, ultimately, themselves.

* Aida Barrera is president of the Southwest Center for Educational Television. She is executive producer of "Carroscolendas" and "Checking It Out," two bilingual series for PBS.

* Frederick P. Close, Ph.D., is director of research for the Southwest Center for Educational Television.

No other society in human history has ever realized these conditions. And it is obvious that no amount of television programming —even the finest, most entertaining, and informed programming— can make our dream a reality. Television alone cannot eliminate racism, create full employment, pay medical bills, or tear down ghettoes. Other forces in society are better equipped to deal with these problems. But television does have a role to play. There are certain tasks for which it is uniquely suited, certain needs of young people, especially Hispanic young people, that television alone can address.

The problems of Hispanic-American youth are, on one hand, problems that they share with all young people and, on the other hand, problems that are unique to them as a racial, Spanish-speaking minority. All of them, especially those with darker skins, must confront racism. Many of them come from homes that are economically impoverished. They are more often unemployed than the majority culture: Mexican-American teens have a 60 percent unemployment rate; Cuban-American teens, a 62 percent rate. This problem is especially acute for Puerto Rican youth, of whom only 21 percent were working at any given time in 1977. Spanish-dominant youngsters are poorly educated and suffer special difficulties in English-only schools. Statistics all too clearly demonstrate what has happened to Hispanics in the school system. *The U.S. Commission on Civil Rights, Mexican American Education System, 1971-1974*, states that compared with the median of 12 school years completed for whites, the median is 8.1 years for Mexican-Americans and 8.16 for Puerto Rican-Americans; 40 percent of Mexican-Americans who enter first grade never complete high school.[1] The average Mexican-American drops out of school by seventh grade. Mexican-Americans account for more than 40 percent of the so-called mentally handicapped in California.[2]

These problems—racism, poverty, unemployment, poor education— are of such vast proportions and so multifaceted that it is unlikely television can serve as a central force in their alleviation. But there is a role for television to play in this effort.

Among the difficulties faced by Hispanic young people is low self-esteem, one of the most fundamental and invidious effects of racism. Low self-esteem underlies many difficulties in education, skills development, and lowered career aspirations that trap Hispanics in unemployment and poverty. It is here—in affecting people's perceptions of themselves and others—that television can be a powerful force.

Self-concept is defined as "an organization of images which a person has about himself in the world. These images develop over time from the reflected appraisals of others around him."[3] The importance of self-concept cannot be overstated. It will influence and be influenced by educational experiences, career aspirations, and the development of lifelong values, attitudes, and beliefs. A realistic self-image is crucial to an individual's ability to lead a happy and productive life. Educators now realize the importance of building a positive self-concept, and consequently, current developers of school curricula have attached as much importance to building self-esteem as to transmitting knowledge. In his book on the implications of bilingual education, Ricardo Carnejo states, "Motivation is the key to learning and a child's self-concept is the key to motivation."[4] Some researchers emphasize the importance of developing a positive self-concept in order for learning to take place, while others stress that a positive self-concept is necessary for children to grow into mature and functioning adults.[5]

The adolescent personality is particularly open to potential influence and change. During early adolescence, there is a loosening of the youngster's personality structure, and through interactions with significant others (those persons, groups, or institutions that play a major role in influencing an individual's identity formation) adolescents are likely to experience broad changes in values, attitudes, and beliefs about themselves and the world around them. According to psychologist R. A. Schmuck, the teenager is "at the crossroads of developing an identity."[6] Unfortunately, this openness to influence is not always beneficial, especially when teenagers are exposed to such pervasive elements in American society as racism, ethnic and sexual stereotyping, and other unwarranted negative views of themselves.

> Like at our school, most of them [whites] are prejudiced. . . . Like this white boy he goes, 'What we ought to do is we ought to vote on if we gonna let Mexicans and blacks sing in our choir. And the Mexicans and blacks jumped on him and beat him up. [Fourteen-year-old Mexican-American male]

Minority adolescents are continually bombarded with derogatory views of their racial or ethnic group. Most blacks, Hispanics, Jews, women, and other American out-group members have at least a few stories of personal encounters with racism and bigotry. But the overt forms of racism they are likely to describe are sometimes the easiest to defend against psychologically. Numerous subtle and often unconsciously received messages are delivered to young Americans daily, teaching them common stereotypes. One of the most pervasive of these messages is the superiority of the Anglo-American male.

In uncountable ways, majority and minority group members are shown that the Anglo-American male is the ideal. He holds the positions of power, wealth, and prestige. His history is glorified in the schools; his culture, values, and life-style is the model depicted in textbooks. He is more likely to play the lead roles in television, in the movies, and in real life. He is the employer, the landlord, the banker, the professional, the teacher. In comparison, the minority group member has few readily visible role models of comparable stature.

Because of the pervasiveness of this kind of racism in our society, the minority child does not acquire healthy self-esteem. Many studies of children's self-concept support the view that racism adversely influences psychological development.[7] This is not surprising, given the importance psychologists attach to the child's need to define his or her identity, a need that can only be fulfilled through the evaluation of the images they receive from their significant others. Psychologist Gloria Powell maintains that the way an individual "thinks and feels about himself is mediated through his perception of what others think and feel about him. Within a given culture and society an individual's self-perception is mediated via his status and role, which are acquired or assigned to him by the society."[8]

Self-esteem is also intimately bound up with a sense of enjoyment, pride, and interest in the varied aspects of one's heritage. Carl Jung demonstrated how deeply embedded the personal self is within the larger cultural self. Pride in the culture of one's particular heritage must come along with, not be isolated from, the images of one's personal future self. Affirmation of one is affirmation of the other. But for the Hispanic youth, that affirmation involves the Spanish language.

> In my first period class there's this guy who just came from New Mexico City, and he can't speak English that well. The teachers make him look dumber than he is . . . and guys will sit back there and they'll be talking about the guy and the guy will just be smiling. . . . They're not treated the same. [Fifteen-year-old black female]

> I'd rather want to speak Spanish, but I went through all twelve years of school [speaking] English, English. And back then if we were to speak Spanish in class they would get after you, send you to the principal and everything. But when I talk to my parents I get confused 'cause I'm so used to talking English, and my parents get mad. They say that's not the correct Spanish. And I feel bad 'cause I know more English than Spanish. My parents get mad. They go, "What do you think you are? Don't you know how to speak Spanish." And I go, "Well, you're the one who sent me to school here. It's your fault." [Eighteen-year-old Puerto Rican female]

Students may be told that their culture, people, and language are equal to that of any other, but failing to see anyone from their group in a position of power and prestige makes it difficult to believe in that equality. There is a shortage of positive Hispanic role models not only in schools (recent efforts in bilingual-bicultural education, however, have sought to remedy this situation) but also in high positions in the nation's leadership. This lack of successful role models in relation to the dominant society cannot help but be destructive to full political, social, and economic participation in that society.

The problems created by the low visibility of Hispanic role models are further compounded by another major socializing institution: television.

> Well, really, I don't see them on TV. Well, "I Love Lucy," you know, Ricky, he's a Puerto Rican. That's the only Mexican I see on TV. [Sixteen-year-old black male]

Those who have studied the kinds of images commercial television presents, especially its characterizations of minorities and women, generally find reflections of America's commonly held stereotypes. A report of the U.S. Commission of Civil Rights for August 1977 (*Window Dressing on the Set*) revealed that in 1973, in the thirty-five television series in which nonwhite characters appeared, the seven Hispanic characters pictured were an ex-con and ex-acrobat, a truck driver, a welfare worker, an auto parts salvager, and three unknowns. In the thirty-seven series listed in 1974 in which nonwhites appeared, the eight Hispanics were a messenger, a cowboy, a farmworker, an outlaw, a mechanic, a butcher, a lawyer, and an unknown.[9] Except for the outlaw, the jobs represented are not derogatory, they are honorable and necessary to society. Yet on television, the roles for Hispanics have been too few and their range too limited. Hispanic viewers are unlikely to picture themselves in professional roles unless these roles too are depicted more frequently on television.

A series of studies conducted by Melvin DeFleur and Lois DeFleur found that the images presented on television regarding occupational status were stereotyped according to traditionally held views of sex and minority roles. More importantly, the authors found that young viewers are more likely to trust television images as accurate than knowledge gained from personal experiences. Considering the strength of television as a teaching instrument and the kind of images the media transmitted, the researchers were justifiably concerned. They concluded that "TV provides children with much superficial and misleading information about the labor force of their society. From this they acquire stereotyped beliefs about the world of work. Given the deep significance of occupational roles for both the individual and his society, any learning source which distorts reality concerning this aspect of the social structure and the child's 'generalized other' may be laying the foundation for difficult personal and social problems."[10]

> They're usually dopers, punks, and bums [on TV]. I mean, they never show the ordinary average everyday Mexican teenager. [Sixteen-year-old Anglo-American male]

> I think that the shows that have Hispanics on them they're shown as being in the lower class, or not intelligent, where they're barely making it above water. . . . They're always being put down or they're shown as being unaware or ignorant about everything. [Seventeen-year-old Cuban-American female]

One aim of career guidance programs for which television is well suited is to aid students to visualize themselves in a chosen occupation. Career guidance can be more dynamic and vital when workers and their work can be observed directly within actual work settings.[11] Audience impact can be further influenced by the model's discussion of problems, failures, successes, sacrifices, and conflicts, especially if these encompass experiences that the viewer and subject share. Such similarities are important because the observer needs a model whom he or she sees as subjected to the same forces and to the same rewards as himself or herself. Similarities can indicate to observers that the same rewards that the model receives are available, or could be available, to the observers if they imitate the model's behavior.[12] Through a frank and informative presentation, viewers will be presented with a positive career model and will be better informed of how such a career is attainable and what one might expect from life should such a career choice be made.

The use of Hispanic role models on television demonstrates to young Hispanic viewers that they have a realistic hope of achieving what they aspire to. It is crucial that Hispanic viewers be presented with a realistic and factual discussion of how these role models have faced problems of poverty, racism, and cultural conflict to help the viewers identify their occurrence in their own lives and deal with them successfully. A realistic treatment of social obstacles must demonstrate that sometimes these obstacles can be overwhelming.

There is also a need to make clear to Hispanic young people that success is not always to be measured economically. A man can be a hero in his community, a good father, and not have very much money. A woman can accomplish great things and not be rich. There are many alternative avenues to success, and wealth is hardly the most important.

An effective role model is one whose conduct and actions an adolescent would respect and admire and, simultaneously, one who possesses a background that is similar to the viewer's. This is not to say that someone who has attained financial success should not be considered a possible role model. Studies of imitative behavior have shown that observers more readily imitate models of higher status and prestige.[13]

Young persons need to see not only successful models of adults from their own cultural group; they also need and desire to see models from their own age group. It is teenagers themselves whom young viewers want to see solve life-coping problems; teenagers themselves need to be seen opening new avenues of possibility. Richard Schmuck's work with adolescent peer groups led him to the discovery that those who suffer from low self-esteem are especially susceptible to the influence of their young friends. During adolescence, the power of peers to influence personality development can even reshape negative self-concepts developed through years of interactions with family members and at schools.[14]

Television can serve a valuable purpose by presenting to the American public, in dramas and documentaries, Hispanics who can serve as role models for Hispanic viewers. The cognitive and affective learning that is possible for these viewers, especially for young people in their crucial formative years, can lead to increased appreciation of their culture and greater sense of self-worth. Such television programming would also help to undermine the ignorance that feeds racism and stereotyping, improve interracial and interethnic cooperation, and build a more tolerant America.

> Ever since I have been . . . [in high school] the blacks be in one group, the whites be in one group and the Mexicans be in one group. [Sixteen-year-old black female]

> In school I don't want to really discriminate against them [Hispanics] but it's kinda like they're really snobs. They all stick together. In all the little groups, there's no white people in there and they don't associate with whites. They do with themselves and with the blacks. . . . Like they don't want to be around us, when we try to be friendly. . . . It's kind of ridiculous actually. You kinda have to discriminate against them sometimes, because . . . they're kinda hostile towards whites. [Sixteen-year-old Anglo-American female]

> We gotta prove to them [Anglos] that we're just as high as they are. [Fifteen-year-old Puerto Rican male]

I think in elementary [school] all they [Mexican-Americans] ever know is their own cultures, their own race and they're used to [it]. Like one big family, they're all together and they're used to what they do. But, then in sixth grade they just throw everyone together—whites, blacks, Mexicans, and they expect you to adjust. They think you're just a kinda big happy family. But you're not. They expect you to get along. But the cultures are different and you got to learn about different people's cultures. [Sixteen-year-old black female]

References

1. U.S. Commission on Civil Rights. *Mexican-American Education Study* (Washington, D.C.: Government Printing Office, 1971–1974).

2. Juan M. Alvarez, "Comparison of Academic Aspirations and Achievement in Bilingual Versus Monolingual Classrooms" (Ph.D. diss., University of Texas at Austin, 1975), pp. 2–3.

3. Walcott H. Beatty, "Emotion: The Missing Link in Education," in *Improving Educational Assessment and an Inventory of Measures of Affective Behavior* (Washington, D.C.: Association for Supervision and Curriculum Development, 1969), p. 76.

4. Ricardo J. Carnejo, *A Synthesis of Theories and Research on the Effects of Teaching in First and Second Languages: Implications for Bilingual Education* (Austin, Texas: National Educational Laboratory Publications, 1974), p. 5.

5. U.S. Commission on Civil Rights, *A Better Chance to Learn Bilingual, Bicultural Education* (Washington, D.C.: Government Printing Office, 1975), p. 31.

6. R. A. Schmuck, "Influence of the Peer Group," in *Psychology and Educational Practice*, ed. Gerald Lesser (Glenview, Ill.: Scott, Foresman, 1971), p. 510.

7. Gary W. Healey, "Self-Concept: A Comparison of Negro-, Anglo-, and Spanish-American Students across Ethnic, Sex and Socioeconomic Variables" (Ph.D. diss., New Mexico State University, 1969).

8. Gloria Johnson Powell, "Self-Concept in White and Black Children," in *Racism and Mental Health*, ed. C. Willie et al. (Pittsburgh: University of Pittsburgh Press, 1973), p. 300.

9. U.S. Commission on Civil Rights, *Window Dressing on the Set* (Washington, D.C.: Government Printing Office, August 1977).

10. Melvin DeFleur and Lois DeFleur, "The Relative Contribution of Television as a Learning Source for Children's Occupational Knowledge," *American Sociological Review* 32:5 (October 1967): 777–789.

11. Reyko Ruth Shiraishi, "Effects of a Bilingual/Bicultural Career Guidance Project on the Occupational Aspirations of Puerto Rican Adolescents" (Ph.D. diss., Boston University, 1975), p. 136.

12. Ibid., p. 23.

13. Ibid., p. 30.

14. Schmuck, "Influence," pp. 502–503.

Minority Role Models

Native Americans

JAMAKE HIGHWATER

WHEN I WAS about five years old, I used to watch a bird in the skies of southern Alberta in northern Montana where I was born on the Blackfeet Blood Reserve. I loved this bird; I would watch him for hours. He would glide effortlessly in that gigantic sky, or he would come down and light on the water and float there very majestically. Sometimes when I watched him he would creep into the grasses and waddle around not very gracefully. We called him *méksikatsi*, which in the Blackfeet language means "pink-colored feet"; méksikatsi and I became very good friends.

The bird had a very particular significance to me because I desperately wanted to be able to fly too. I felt very much as if I was the kind of person who had been born into a world where flight was impossible, and most of the things that I dreamed about or read about would not be possible for me but would be possible only for other people.

When I was ten years old, my life changed very drastically. I found myself adopted forcefully and against my parents' will; they were considered inadequate parents because they could not make enough money to support me, so I found myself in that terrible position that 60 percent of native Americans find themselves in: living in a city that they do not understand at all, not in another culture but between two cultures.

A teacher of the English language told me that méksikatsi was not

---

* Jamake Highwater is the author of *Journey to the Sky, Song of the Earth, Anpao, an American Indian Odyssey*, and *The Sun, He Dies*.

called "méksikatsi," even though that is what my people had called that bird for thousands of years. Méksikatsi, he said, was really "duck." I was very disappointed with English; I could not understand it. First of all, the bird didn't look like "duck," and when it made a noise it didn't sound like "duck," and I was even more confused when I found out that the meaning of the verb "to duck" came from the bird and not vice-versa.

This was the beginning of a very complex lesson for me that doesn't just happen to black, Chicano, Jewish, and Indian children, but to all children. We are born into a cultural preconception that we call reality and that we never question. We essentially know the world in terms of that cultural package or preconception, and we are so unaware of it that the most liberal of us go through life with a kind of ethnocentricity that automatically rules out all other ways of seeing the world.

As I came to understand English better, I understood that it made a great deal of sense, but I never forgot that méksikatsi made a different kind of sense. I realized that languages are not just different words for the same things but totally different concepts, totally different ways of experiencing and looking at the world. Television, of course, is one of the ways in which we look at the world and one of the major ways we teach people how to see.

As artists have always known, reality depends entirely on how you see things. I grew up in a place that was called a wilderness, but I could never understand how that amazing ecological park could be called "wilderness," something wild that needs to be harnessed. Nature is some sort of foe, some sort of adversary in the dominant culture's mentality. We are not part of nature in this society; we are created above it, outside of it, and feel that we must dominate and change it before we can be comfortable and safe within it. I grew up in a culture that considers us literally a part of the entire process that is called nature, to such an extent that when Black Elk called himself the brother of the bear, he was quite serious. In other words, Indians did not need Darwin to find out that they were part of nature.

I saw my first wilderness, as I recall, one August day when I got off a Greyhound bus in a city called New York. Now that struck me as being fairly wild and pretty much out of hand. But I did not understand how the term could be applied to the place where I was from.

Gradually, through the help of some very unusual teachers, I was able to find my way into two cultures rather than remain helplessly between two cultures. The earth is such an important symbol to most primal people that when we use European languages we tend to capitalize the E in much the way that the word God is capitalized by people of the dominant culture. You can imagine my distress when I was ten years old to find out that synonyms for the word *earth*—dirt and soil—were used to describe uncleanliness on the one hand and obscenity on the other. I could not possibly understand how something that could be dirty could have any kind of negative connotation. It would be like saying that the person is godly, so don't go near him, and I could not grasp how these ideas made their way into the English language.

I have the feeling when I watch television that one of the major problems in dealing with it as a viewer, and one of the major problems in dealing with it as a creator, is that we must fit our thoughts into a form that may be alien to our thoughts. It is just like when you want to tell someone about a dream you have had; you must change the dream in order to facilitate its being expressed in language. You cannot convey what happened so vividly in the dream by using the language of your culture. You begin to change your reality to suit the ways in which we traditionally express ourselves. Language not only permits us to be expressive but also predetermines what we are going to say and limits what we are able to say.

It is for that reason that the arts exist, and it is for that reason that poets created metaphors, so that they could imply things that cannot be explicitly said. What I am trying to suggest is that there are alternative worlds to the one of which we are so certain, and we must realize what Carlos Castenada said in his Don Juan books: there are separate realities. We must realize that so-called primitive art is not simply naturalistic art that has not yet achieved perfection but an alternative and valid form unto itself.

My mother once said something to me that impressed me a great deal: "Isn't it strange that in the dominant society men tend to give away everything that is best about being human to women and children?" They give away taste, responsiveness to color, the ability to cry and to feel emotion, intuition, inspiration—all of the things that do not fit into a linear construction of the world, a notion of certitude of that ultimate truth that lies behind all ideas.

If television could somehow open up rather than close the doors of perception, how many more brilliant people we might produce. If only we could suggest in the images we provide on that screen some of the thoughts and ideas of children that they will soon abandon because they will be taught not to think them or will be told that there is no way to think them using the accessible tools of their culture. Wouldn't it be nice to affirm children's ideas rather than to deny them?

My grandfather was watching a John Wayne movie on television one day (my father was a stunt man and died many times for Wayne), and we were waiting for a glimpse of Dad doing one of those fantastic falls off a horse, when Wayne said to another gentleman, "You're nothing but a dirty coyote." Well, my grandfather turned off the set right then because that was blasphemous to him. He said, "I won't allow swearing in this house," and I said, "He didn't mean that as swearing." And my grandfather said, "Why, if he hates this man, would he call him a 'coyote'?" The Coyote clan among the Blackfeet is one of the highest levels. I spent two hours trying to explain to my grandfather why the word *coyote* would be used as a criticism of a man rather than as a compliment. And to this day, if my grandfather were still alive, he would still be sitting there scratching his braids and trying to figure out what I was talking about, and he would be sure that I was lost because I understood.

My great advantage has been the fact that I was initiated into two worlds rather than one. Television has the opportunity of teaching in the most fundamental way, very much like those unusual teachers who gave me the opportunity of seeing the validity of the world that I came from and the world that I was moving into. I think it must be possible, in the kind of images that are presented on television, to suggest that there are alternatives, that there are larger ways of looking at the world and different ways of looking at the world that are not simply amusing and exotic but valid and true. Maybe we simply have to learn to use the word *truth* a little more and the word *superstition* a little less.

In writing about native Americans I have made a particular effort not to talk about their beliefs in this and that but instead to talk about those things as actual facts. I have tried not to use the words *myths* and *legends* in the same way that I would not speak to a Christian audience and talk about the Jesus myth. In a fundamental way, it would shatter something we wish to believe and do believe. These ways in which the media express a kind of unintentional superiority and correctness are the insidious ways that liberal people actually destroy our greatest multiplicity and begin to make us confuse being equal with being uniform or conformist.

We don't have to be the same in order to be equal, and it is very difficult for us to grasp that, because, unfortunately, gentlemen from Africa wear suits and gentlemen from Japan wear suits and gentlemen from Indian reservations wear suits when they speak to big corporations. What this suggests to us is that the men have somehow changed, whereas they are simply disguised. They are disguised in terms of the dominant world so that they can wheel and deal in that world, but they may very well go home and put on kimonos or whatever they wear.

Different images make different impressions. I tried to make this point in my book, *Many Smokes, Many Moons.* I asked an Indian artist to draw a picture of a famous event that took place in 1492. I found a sixteenth-century etching that showed a marvelous galleon in a bay with handsomely dressed gentlemen coming on to the shore out of a landing boat. There were also some very European brown people who had gifts (one of them had brought a peace pipe along for the occasion). There was a gentleman in a robe planting a large old structure in the ground. It was a very familiar scene to all of us.

The same scene, painted by an Indian, was quite staggering. It showed three Indians crouched on the shore, staring in amazement at the water, where a floating island of rock was gradually approaching. The island was covered with tall defoliated trees in which vines and various leaves seemed to be blowing in the wind. Beneath them were strange men wrapped in some peculiar kind of shell, who looked as if they had squirrels in their mouths, they were so bushy.

I showed these two pictures to a group of Indians and to a group of non-Indians, and the Anglos said, "Well, if you think about it, the Indians really didn't see what they thought they saw. The island is really a ship and those defoliated trees are really masts, and those people had beards; there weren't squirrels in their mouths. They simply didn't know what they were looking at, so they made an error." The Indians looked at them for a long time and then said, "After all, isn't the ship really a floating island, and what are masts finally, but tall defoliated trees?" We see reality in terms of the way in which we experience it.

What if we saw the world as Einstein said it existed? What if we were an entirely alien kind of being who did not see these outward shapes and forms that are really whirling molecules but saw the particles that science tells us make up our world? In that case, finally, who sees reality? If we are in charge of showing our reality to our children and the children of others, don't we have to show them more than the reality that we have taken for granted for only a few thousand years?

Minority Role Models

Asian Americans

CHARLES W. CHENG AND
MARSHA HIRANO-NAKANISHI

DEROGATORY STEREOTYPES of Asians have been etched in American literature and history books and clutter old Hollywood movies. Similar images of contemporary Asians and Asian-Americans now are transmitted into virtually every American home by television.

There are very few instances of Asian or Asian-American contributions to television's library of offerings. One must strain even to recall when an Asian-American was last seen on the television screen. It is almost as though Asian-Americans are not part of American life but are invisible.

When Asian-Americans are visible, almost without exception the depictions promote stereotypic attitudes. Take, for example, the "Hawaii Five-O" series. Wo Fat is a contemporary version of Fu Manchu: powerful, threatening, inscrutable, and the quintessence of yellow peril. Jack Lord, who plays the Anglo chief, is backed by a rear guard of Asian-American assistants to track evildoers and bring justice to Honolulu. The first Asian image obviously fosters an unacceptable stereotype. The second is more subtle. One needs to ask whether Asian-American protagonists ever make independent decisions, not beholden to the astute, all-knowing McGarrett. This program and others suggest that whites almost always make the critical

---

* The late Charles W. Cheng was an assistant professor in the Graduate School of Education, UCLA, and an advisor to "Rebop."

* Marsha Hirano-Nakanishi is project manager of Language Minority Youth Studies at the National Center for Bilingual Research.

and final decisions. Such portrayals of Asians and Asian-Americans may, then, convey to young and old, but particularly to young people, that Asian-Americans sit in one of two camps: leaders of an Oriental band of evil or unthinking subservients to Anglo justice and intelligence.

Another major source of extreme irritation to many Asian-Americans is television's virtual failure to differentiate between Asian-Americans and Asians. This point can best be illustrated by summarizing some meetings between a group of Los Angeles Asian-Americans and ABC in 1977 and 1978.

To its credit, ABC had introduced an Asian cartoon character, Samurai, to integrate its extraterrestrial Super Heroes "force." ABC invited a group of Asian-Americans to review this addition to the program and to discuss the overall treatment of Asian-Americans in children's programming. These efforts of ABC are to be applauded. Such an outreach is one way in which minority groups can have at least a minimal influence in children's television.

Samurai is an Asian character, developed from the folklore on the ninja in Japan; he is not an Asian-American. It is a step forward that Samurai is a peer on the side of justice with the other super heroes, but the Asian-American group emphasized to ABC that treating Asians and Asian-Americans as one can be harmful to children of all colors. It is not that the group opposed programs that deal, albeit supernaturally, with the experience of Asians from their ancestral past. To be sure, Asian-Americans are as interested in their roots as anyone. But broadcasters all too frequently forget that Asian-Americans are not Asians; their roots and cultural life are based on being of Asian descent in America—not in Japan, China, Thailand, the Philippines, or Korea.

It angers and embarrasses Asian-Americans and their children to be almost exclusively typified in the medium by Asians with accented voices and foreign garb. Moreover, this tendency to focus solely on Asian characteristics misrepresents them to non-Asian-Americans in ways that cannot help to improve race relations in this country. By remaining ignorant of the Asian-American experience in the United States, television can neither successfully project more diverse images nor portray the struggles of Asian-American people to the wider viewing audience.

The commercial broadcasting industry continues to convey limited and unsatisfactory images of Asian-Americans, most of them based on subtle or blatant forms of racism and ignorance. Commercial television generally has failed to present diverse, sensitive, and honest portrayals of Asian-Americans in all dimensions and forms. The major networks and producers should take heed of some PBS breakthroughs, including Frank Chin's "The Year of the Dragon" and KCET's "Visions" series, which presented "The Gold Watch."

Producers should be cognizant of and should fully represent the Asian-American versus Asian distinction in their programming. It is equally important that programs not simply stress the Asian-American success story. Asian-Americans often are held up as models to other minorities and the dominant society. As the Council on Interracial Books for Children has suggested, the characters in such success stories are respected not on their own terms but for their display of "outstanding abilities, skills, or talents in order to gain the approval and esteem of white Americans." Moreover, this approach ignores many of the real-life experiences of thousands of Asian-American working-class families who face the same struggles encountered by other minority groups and other Americans who are not part of the mainstream of society. Specifically, producers and networks should explore the talents of Asian-Americans who are eminently capable of telling about and showing Asian-American life to its fullness. For a start, the television industry may find untapped creativity and competence in such people as the Los Angeles–based East-West Players, Maxine Hong Kingston (author of *The Woman Warrior*), and the lauded crew of Visual Communications of Los Angeles.

Whether we like it or not, television influences the thinking of children. We know we cannot initiate a national karate attack on the tube. We therefore must wage an intense effort to improve significantly television's portrayal of minority-group experiences in this country, for the sake of our children and ourselves.

Minority Role Models

A Case Study, "The Righteous Apples"

TOPPER CAREW

SOCIETY SUFFERS from a lack of values, morals, and positive role models, and American youths—black, white, Chicano, Asian, and Native American—need to know that these still exist. They need to know that justice, equality, friendship, and cooperation are not just pipe dreams of a world that died long ago. They exist now, and "The Righteous Apples" was created to let young people know. Teenagers need to understand that it is acceptable to want to right wrongs and care about people.

"The Righteous Apples" are a multiracial group of high school students who have come together to make music. They attend the formerly all-white Sherwin High School in a formerly all-white, working-class Boston neighborhood. The series explores the inter-actions between the Apples themselves and their friends in this some-times racially tense, recently desegregated neighborhood school.

The group is composed of Charles "Big Neck" McMorris, leader, deal maker, and conga player; Gloretta Benson, singer and book-keeper; Sandy Burns, singer, choreographer, and mechanic for their van; and Samuel "D. C. Jr." Rosencrantz, piano player and equipment manager. The group also has a backup band that appears at their gigs, at periodic rehearsals, and at recording sessions.

* Topper Carew, Ph.D., is president and executive producer of Rainbow TV Works. In addition to "The Righteous Apples" he has produced "Say Brother" and "Rebop," PBS. Currently he is producing dramas and dramatic musicals for children, also for PBS.

Although they are the first multiracial group in the neighborhood, that is not the primary reason for their being together. To them, music is the primary and unifying element. Each member of the group has his or her own particular motivation for being one of the Righteous Apples. Sandy sees the success of the group as her ticket out of the ghetto. Gloretta loves music and always believes in giving herself totally to her commitments. She does not intend to make music a career, but she likes the attention that comes with being part of the group. D.C. Jr.'s only interest is in playing good, noncommercial black music, and the Righteous Apples allow him to fulfill his assumed "black" identity. Big Neck, as leader of the group, has an ego investment in the Righteous Apples: he founded the group, so he wants it to succeed. He leads the Apples, so he wants them to be the best.

It is important to know who the Apples are because they are presented as realistic role models to the viewing audience. Big Neck is the precocious, charismatic, and stylish leader of the Righteous Apples. He is street wise and scholarly. As the group's leader, Neck spends much of his time mediating differences: D.C. Jr., Glo, and Sandy always have differing points of view—about almost everything. While Neck tends to be pragmatic in his thinking, his intolerance for racial injustice can be incensed to the point of physical reaction; his temper is fierce. But most often Neck is in control and very much aware of his surroundings. He is the group's assertive manager, bold negotiator, articulate spokesman, and shrewd deal maker. His own support comes from his family: an older brother who has had a brush with the law, a younger brother and sister, a father who is a postal worker, and a mother who is a teacher's aide. He feels responsible for his younger brother and sister and wants to be a good role model for them. Neck's parents want him to go to college. He will, but he wants the band to go too.

Sandy, sixteen, Irish-Catholic, is the youngest member of the Righteous Apples and the youngest of two girls in her family. Her mother died a few years ago, and her father tries hard to make a home for himself and Sandy even though his job as a factory worker tends toward occasional layoffs. Sandy's sister, though only three years older, is married and has two children. She and Sandy disagree on all questions of race; she cannot understand why Sandy hangs around with blacks. While Sandy has never belonged to a multiracial group before, the opportunity that she senses and the enthusiasm that she feels blind her to all problems. Sandy is not an academic achiever. She is, however, very talented and has chosen to fight her way out of the mire of the lower class by employing her musical abilities. Interested only in the development of her musical career, Sandy has chosen not to go to college.

Gloretta, seventeen, is unusually well adjusted for an only child. She has a mature relationship with her parents and discusses everything with them. A good, conscientious student, Glo thrives on intellectual discussions and analyzing problems. She has always been an avid reader. Her tennis game is fair, but she gets little exercise during the winter so she is constantly dieting. Glo's parents are older than would be expected, and this contributes to her conservatism. Her father was on the board of the NAACP during the legal push to desegregate the schools and insisted that Glo be bused. She was twelve years old the first year of busing and was subjected to some abuse, which she bore stoically. By the end of that year, she understood the purpose for going through it. This experience has had a strong effect on her growth and maturity. Although she intends to go to college, Glo plans to participate in the group until then. She enjoys the friendship of the Righteous Apples and the secretly relished recognition, fun, social value, and fame that it brings, but she will not abandon her career goals for the possibility of being a star; she wants to be a doctor. Glo has a strong sense of fairness and justice. She is also highly opinionated and outspoken and sometimes finds it hard to defer to Big Neck, especially since she feels equal to, if not better than, any boy. She is becoming almost militant about the injustice of the role of women in society and does not let a sexist remark go by unchallenged.

D. C. Jr. is from a middle-class Jewish family. His family is very liberal and extolled the black cause as he was growing up. He identifies with, and values, things that are black—to the point of exaggeration. He only "loves" black girls but does not dislike white girls. He thinks whites are square and racist folks crazed. His parents are somewhat concerned that he does not identify as much with his Jewishness, but they are too liberal to object. When he does identify with his Jewishness, he does it in a hip way. D.C. Jr. is basically a "mama's boy" and a bit of a coward in a pinch, but he always tries to cover it with his "cool." D.C. loves music, knows every bit of black music history and trivia, and maintains the group's equipment. He craves attention and likes to have the last word—always. D.C. has always done well in school but does it by coasting. While he will probably go to college, his ambition lies in music, particularly since he can be a "black" Apple. His politics are liberal on everything but feminism, and he is very impatient with injustice; he wants black justice now.

D.C. Jr. is his own most ardent fan; he initiates and consumes flattery.

The Righteous Apples characters are real. They are not pasteboard figures or cartoon characters. They have ambitions, faults, goals, hopes, and histories. They share a similar dream: to believe in themselves and to reach whatever end they look for, whether it is college, a medical profession, a singing career, or just being with friends. They care not only about one another but about people in general. If their young dreams tend toward the naive, it is in an effort to suggest positive images of racial cooperation for teenage viewers to follow. And, judging from the volume of letters Rainbow TV Works receives from the Apples' teenage fans, they not only want this type of programming but they believe in it and want to perpetuate it.

The series premiered on May 15, 1980, carried by 197 PBS stations across the nation. In all statistical reports, "The Righteous Apples" was far more popular with teenagers than with older audiences. It was created to reach a broad audience, but the teenage audience was its prime target. The messages in the stories were made strong so that they would reach the hard-to-reach adolescent audience. The Apples dealt with prostitution, abortion, racism, self-respect, violence—subjects that younger audiences relate to because they often face these problems in their own lives. The stories were also presented in such a way that an answer did exist.

"The Righteous Apples" took the night in New York City (WNET) ratings as well as in Dallas (KERA). The series rated number two in San Francisco (KQED) and fluctuated between two and three in Chicago (WTTW). Its total weekly viewing audience, mostly teenagers, was estimated at well over 4 million.

The goals of the series are important; they reflect what Rainbow wants to achieve in every project that emanates from this production company:

1. *To encourage and reinforce in all children a positive regard for themselves that grows out of an understanding and pride in their own unique cultural heritage, experience, and environment.* "The Righteous Apples" was created to provide minority children with heroic and successful peer and role models who exemplify, convey, and put into practice the best features and attributes of a moral and just world. In "A Dream Fulfilled" (episode 107) Big Neck spearheads a movement at Sherwin High to recognize the contributions that Dr. Martin Luther King, Jr., made to this nation and to the black cause. The story concerns the education of a young black girl who learns how much Dr. King did for his people and that the struggle for justice, recogni-

tion, and self-respect is far from won. In "Love Has Two Left Feet" (episode 108), D.C. Jr. falls in love with a girl who has cerebral palsy and is not Jewish. He does not see racial, physical, or religious barriers, but his parents are upset that he has fallen in love with a gentile. Big Neck, whom the parents love and care about, helps them realize that they must look beyond themselves and be proud that their son is able to care about and love another person without worrying about what she is.

2. *To portray for children the positive aspects that the rich diversity of cultural pluralism brings into American society.* In the mixture of the personalities of the Apples, their parents, and their friends, viewers can find real people—not stereotypes or time-old caricatures—of great diversity. The story of "Secret Love" (episode 110), concerns Glo's new boyfriend, Martin, who is half-black but passes as white. His socially conscious mother has raised him to feel that he must hide the fact that he is half-black. Glo helps him understand that he cannot hide that fact anymore, that he does not need to hide it because it is something to be proud of. When he decides not to pose as white anymore, he feels a sense of relief because he is accepting himself for what he really is.

3. *To demonstrate and encourage intercultural communication, cooperation, and friendship.* This, in essence, is "The Righteous Apples." They are a band composed of two blacks and two whites—a multiracial group in a neighborhood and school that does not appreciate this kind of group at this time. They are together because they want to be, because they are friends, and because they enjoy what they represent. In all their stories, it is because they work together as a group that they are able to help other people. They are not crusaders for justice, but they believe in justice, for blacks and whites. They are not supermen or superwomen, but they do their best to help people. In "Josh's Run" (episode 101), the Apples help an elderly blues musician and a friend escape from a mismanaged, destructive nursing care home. They also help him realize that he still has much to offer. In "Point of View" (episode 102), they help a fellow student who is accused of stabbing the assistant principal to realize that the stabbing was an accident that happened because the student was trying to smooth over tensions in the school. In the same episode, the Apples make an aggressive black student realize that violence will not solve race problems and that the solution does not lie in ignoring it or pretending it doesn't exist.

"The Righteous Apples" offer to teenage viewers answers—not just problems—to the pressures they face daily, both with their peers and with society in general. The Righteous Apples show these teenagers that dancing, music, love, caring, silliness, and friendship all go together with justice, equality, and goodwill toward all people. Big Neck loves to dance and he loves to party, but he also cares about the people around him and is not afraid to become involved to right a wrong. D.C. Jr. is a bit of a coward but if Neck can do something, so can he. Glo wants everything orderly and nice, and when it is not she is not afraid to help change the situation. Sandy is young, somewhat self-centered, but is not afraid to stand by her friends in whatever they choose to do. These are the Righteous Apples, and Rainbow TV Works is proud to present them to America's viewing audiences.

Resources, Chapter Three

ABC. "Afterschool Special," "Family of Strangers," September 24, 1980. A one-hour drama about a shy and sensitive teenage girl who feels that her world is crumbling when her boisterous new stepfather and his three not-so-friendly daughters move in. Based on the book *Bugs in Your Ears* by Betty Bates. Produced by Highgate Pictures.

————. "Afterschool Special," "Home Run for Love," April 2, 1980. A sixty-minute drama about a twelve-year-old Brooklyn Dodgers fan who overcomes his shyness and gains a valuable understanding of life through his friendship with an elderly black man who takes him to his first baseball game. Based on the novel *Thank You, Jackie Robinson* by Barbara Cohen. Produced by Martin Tahse.

————. "Afterschool Special," "Make Believe Marriage," February 14, 1979. Ten high school seniors "get married," get jobs, have children, and deal with divorce, all in a twelve-week modern marriage course. Produced by Highgate Pictures.

————. "Afterschool Special," "Me and Dad's New Wife," February 18, 1976. A thirty-three minute drama about a twelve-year-old girl's emotional crises in trying to accept her parents' divorce and her father's remarriage. Produced by Daniel Wilson Productions.

————. "Afterschool Special," "New York City Too Far from Tampa Blues," 1979. A one-hour drama about a young Puerto Rican boy who moves to Tampa with his family, forms a rock and roll band with a boy from a local street gang, and learns pride when he earns more money as a musician than his father does as a truck driver. Based on the novel of the same title by T. Ernesto Bethancourt. Produced by Daniel Wilson.

————. "Afterschool Special," "Rookie of the Year," 1975. A one-hour drama about a young girl's struggle to gain acceptance on an all-boy baseball team. Produced by Daniel Wilson Productions.

————. "Afterschool Special," "The Secret Life of T. K. Deering," 1978. A one-hour drama about a young girl who secretly joins an all-boy club. Her young-at-heart grandfather discovers her secret and also joins the club. The two become very close and realize that being old has as many problems as being young. Produced by Daniel Wilson.

————. "Afterschool Special," "A Special Gift," October 24, 1979. A teenage boy must chose between playing on his school basketball team or ballet rehearsals for his first professional appearance. He must also face the taunts of his father and friends, who think dancing is for sissies. Produced by Martin Tahse Productions.

————. "Afterschool Special," "What Are Friends For?" April 29, 1981. A sixty-minute drama about a twelve-year-old girl who gains understanding of her parents' divorce through the disappointments she suffers in a close friendship. Based on the book *What Are Friends For?* by Mildred Ames. Produced by Martin Tahse Productions.

————. "Afterschool Special," "Which Mother Is Mine?" January 21, 1981. A teenage girl is torn between her natural mother and the foster parents who have given her a loving home for six years. Produced by Martin Tahse Productions.

Action for Children's Television. *Heroes, Hamburgs, and Hard Rock: Television and Young Adolescents: An ACT Conference.* Transcripts. Newtonville, Mass.: Action for Children's Television, 1978.

————. *Television Role Models and Young Adolescents: An ACT Research Workshop.* Transcripts. Newtonville, Mass.: Action for Children's Television, 1978.

"A Man's Place," 1979. A thirty-minute film for junior and senior high school students showing people of traditional orientations and men who are trying new roles at work and at home. Available on 16-mm film from Institute for Research and Development in Occupational Education, City University of New York, 33 West 42d Street, New York, N.Y. 10036.

American Association of Retired Persons. "Children's Attitudes towards the Elderly." Report on file at the association. 1909 K Street, N.W., Washington, D.C. 20049.

Arlen, Michael J. "The Air: Baretta's T-shirt; or, Youth Must Be Served." *New Yorker* (November 14, 1977): 167+.

Aronoff, Craig. "Old Age in Prime Time." *Journal of Communication* 24:4 (Autumn 1974): 86–87.

Artel, Linda, and Wengraf, Susan. *Positive Images: A Guide to 400 Non-Sexist Films for Young People.* San Francisco: Booklegger Press, 1976.

Belotti, E. G. *What Are Little Girls Made Of? The Roots of Feminine Stereotypes.* New York: Schocken Books, 1976.

Busby, Linda. "Sex Role Research on the Mass Media." *Journal of Communication* 24:4 (Autumn 1975): 107–131.

————. "Sex Roles Presented in Commercial Network Television Programs Directed toward Children: Rationale and Analysis." Ph.D. dissertation, University of Michigan.

Butler, Matilda, and Paisley, William. *The Flawed Mirror: Sourcebook on Women and the Mass Media.* Washington, D.C.: Communications Press, 1977.

Commission on the Status of Women. UNESCO. *Influence of the Mass Communication Media on Attitudes toward the Roles of Women and Men in Present-Day Society.* Report; E/CN/.6 601. New York: United Nations, 1976.

Dates, Jannette. "Race, Racial Attitudes and Adolescent Perceptions of Black Television Characters." *Journal of Broadcasting* 24:4 (Fall 1980): 549–560.

Donnagher, P. C., et al. "Race, Sex and Social Example: An Analysis of Character Portrayals on Inter-racial Television Entertainment." *Psychological Reports* 38 (1976): 3–14.

Family Life Theatre. Improvisational educational theater workshops for adolescents. Family Life Division, Metropolitan Hospital, 1901 First Avenue, Room 417, New York: N.Y. 10029.

Gerbner, George, and Gross, Larry. "Aging with Television: Images on Television Drama and Conceptions of Social Reality." *Journal of Communication* 30:1 (Winter 1980): 37–47.

Gerbner, George, and Signorelli, Nancy. *Women and Minorities in Television Drama 1969–1979.* Philadelphia, Pa.: University of Pennsylvania Press, 1979.

Glock, Charles Y., et al. *Adolescent Prejudice.* New York: Harper & Row, 1975.

Goldberg, Herb. *The New Male: From Self-Destruction to Self-Care.* New York: William Marrow, 1979.

Gorsoni-Stavn, Diane. *Sexism and Youth.* New York: Bowker, 1974.

Greenberg, Bradley S. *Life on Television: Content Analyses of U.S. TV Drama.* Norwood, N.J.: Ablex, 1980.

Harmonay, Maureen, ed. *Televised Role Models and Young Adolescents: An Act Research Workshop.* Transcripts. Newtonville, Mass.: Action for Children's Television, 1978.

Hendry, Leo B., and Patrick, Helen. "Adolescents and Television." *Journal of Youth and Adolescence* 6:4 (1977): 325–336.

Kernan, Michael. "Old Age: TV Tells It Wrong." *Washington Post*, September 18, 1979, p. C3.

Klinger, Judson. "TV's Teen Idol Comes down with Adult Movie 'Fever.'" *New York Times*, December 11, 1977, pp. D15, D32.

KQED. "Up & Coming." A fifteen-part series of half-hour dramas about an upwardly mobile black family that presents honest black role models for young people. Broadcast over the PBS network. Produced by Avon Kirkland.

Lemen, Judith. "A Content Analysis of Male and Female Dominance Patterns on Prime Time Television." Qualifying paper, Harvard University Graduate School of Education, 1975.

McDonald, Gerald W. "Parental Power and Adolescents' Parental Identification: A Reexamination." *Journal of Marriage and the Family* 42:2 (May 1980): 289–296.

MacDonald, J. Fred. "Black Perimeters—Paul Robeson, Nat King Cole, and the Role of Blacks in American TV." *Journal of Popular Film and Television* 7:3 (1979): 246–264.

Miller, W. C., and Beck, T. "How Do TV Parents Compare to Real Parents?" *Journalism Quarterly* 53:2 (1976): 324–328.

Morgan, M., and Harr-Mazer, H. "Television and Adolescents' Family Life Expectations." Manuscript, University of Pennsylvania, 1980.

Multimedia Program Productions. "Young People's Specials," "Andrew." December 1980. A half-hour drama depicting the conflict between a son and his father when the son decides to pursue a career that has been traditionally identified as women's work.

———. "Young People's Specials," "Suzy's War." October 1980. A half-hour drama about a black ghetto girl's fight to rid her neighborhood of violent crimes.

Murray, John P. *Television and Youth.* Boys Town, Neb.: Boys Town Center for the Study of Youth Development, 1980.

NBC. "Hot Hero Sandwich," 1979–1980. An eleven-part series of half-hour programs featuring interviews, comedy sketches, and filmed sequences focused on the fun and frustration of growing up.

———. "Special Treat," "The House at 12 Rose Street." March 4, 1980. A one-hour drama about a young boy's mixed reactions when a black family moves into his all-white neighborhood and his struggle to stand up against the prejudice of his friends. Based on the book of the same title by Mimi Brodsky. Produced by Daniel Wilson.

———. "Special Treat," "The Rocking Chair Rebellion." October 23, 1980. A one-hour drama about a fourteen-year-old girl who befriends the residents of a nursing home. Based on the novel of the title by Eth Clifford. Produced by Daniel Wilson.

PBS. "Freestyle," 1978–1979. A thirteen-part dramatic series promoting alternatives to traditional sex-role stereotypes. Designed for young adolescent viewers. Produced by Norton Wright.

Rosen, M. "Farrah Fawcett-Majors Makes Me Want to Scream! A Look at TV Sex: 'Charlie's Angels,' 'Police Woman,' and Now 'Soap.' " *Redbook* 149 (September 1977): 102.

Singer, Robert P., and Caplan, Robert M., eds. "Television and Social Behavior." *Journal of Social Issues* 32:4 (Fall 1976): 1–247.

Slater, Jack. "Is TV's Image of Blacks Improving?" *New York Times*, September 16, 1979, sec. 2, p. 33.

Starr, Paul. "Hollywood's New Ideal of Masculinity." *New York Times*, July 16, 1978, sec. 2, p. 1.

Tuchman, Gaye; Daniels, Arlene Kaplan; and Benet, James. *Hearth and Home: Images of Women in the Mass Media.* New York: Oxford University Press, 1978.

Wartella, E. *Children's Impressions of Television Families.* New York: John and Mary R. Markle Foundation, 1978.

Weigel, Russell H., and Jessor, Richard. "Television and Adolescent Conventionality: An Exploratory Study." *Public Opinion Quarterly* 37 (1973): 76–90.

Weiss, Robert S. "Growing Up a Little Faster: The Experience of Growing Up in a Single-Parent Household." *Journal of Social Issues* 35:4 (1979): 97–111.

WGBH-TV, Boston. "The New Voice," 1981. A fourteen-part dramatic series for teenagers about the students who work on the school newspaper of a racially-mixed high school.

Organizations

American Institute of Family Relations, 5287 Sunset Boulevard, Los Angeles, Calif. 90027.

Family Service Association of America, 44 E. 23d Street, New York, N.Y. 10010.

Young Adult Fiction

Adler, C. S. *The Silver Coach*. A twelve-year-old girl who has to spend a summer with her grandmother after her parents' divorce learns something new about family relationships. New York: Coward, McCann & Geoghegan, 1979.

Cleaver, Vera, and Cleaver, Bill. *Queen of Hearts*. Young adult novel about a twelve-year-old girl who reluctantly agrees to play housekeeper for her grandmother for the summer. The two have a stormy time together and develop a unique relationship. New York: Lippincott Junior Books, 1978.

Guy, Rosa. *The Friends*. Story of a young West Indian girl who moves to Harlem and is rejected by her classmates because she "talks funny." Only poor, ragged Edith accepts her, and the two girls learn about friendship and prejudice. New York: Holt, Rinehart & Winston, 1973.

Harris, Marilyn. *Hatter Fox*. About the gap between the safe, normal world of middle-class whites and that of a maverick teenage Indian girl. New York: Random House, 1973.

LeGuin, Ursula K. *Very Far Away from Anywhere Else*. An intellectually inclined teenage boy finds companionship with a music-loving girl. New York: Atheneum, 1976.

Lipsyte, Robert. *The Contender*. Story of teenagers searching for acceptance and dignity. A young black boy who has dropped out of school is rejected by his friends for working at a Jewish-owned grocery store and for refusing to help them rob the store. New York: Harper & Row, 1967.

Peck, Richard. *Don't Look and It Won't Hurt*. Story of an adolescent girl growing toward maturity as she confronts the problems of family life. New York: Holt, Rinehart & Winston, 1962.

Sebesteyn, Ouida. *Words by Heart*. Story of a young girl in the only black family in a western settlement who is rejected by well-to-do whites because of her intellectual capabilities and by poor sharecroppers because of her father's success as a farmer. Boston: Atlantic-Little, Brown, 1979.

Wartski, Maureen Crane. *A Boat to Nowhere*. Novel about the tragedy of the Vietnamese people and the triumph of their spirit. New York: New American Library, 1980.

Yep, Laurence. *Child of the Owl*. A twelve-year-old Chinese-American girl from a poor family moves in with her grandmother in San Francisco's Chinatown and learns the richness of her cultural heritage. New York: Harper & Row, 1977.

4 The World of Work

Over Tudor Gothic plastic trays
They speak of essays, count the days,
Till deadlines due begin to fall
And April 15th says it all.

Ivy, not spinach, they calmly munch,
Planning their futures over lunch.
"She has good scores, it's not her fault
If she's rejected—pass the salt."

Harvard, Wellesley, MIT
(Give your extra roll to me.)
Radcliffe, Rutgers, Smith, and Brown
(They shake their milks and drink them down.)

Brandeis, Vassar, Wheaton, Reed
(This broccoli has gone to seed.)
"What if after this he flunks?"
(Do you want your pineapple chunks?)

The question on their minds these days
(Who just swiped the mayonnaise?)
Is who'll survive the college crunch
(And what they're going to have for lunch.)

C. Palmer
Camden-Rockport High School

Career Choices

CAROL HULSIZER

ASK A BUNCH of teenage girls to track down a discount source for designer jeans, and they will tear the town apart to locate designer labels at bargain prices. Ask adolescent boys for the inside story on professional team player trades, and you will be deluged with arcane information on game statistics, dollar deals, and idiosyncratic behavior of managers and owners. Ask either group what jobs they will have when they are thirty, how to get into that occupation, what it is like to work in that field, how to move ahead, what is the most one can earn, and you will probably get a blank stare and the comment, "I haven't thought about it yet." Ask what kind of life-style they expect to have as adults and what level of income will be adequate to support it. You will hear about houses, children, cars, TVs, stereos, absurdly low estimates of what these all cost, and no mention of money to pay for medical care, insurance, education, or taxes. In short, teenagers have little understanding of the work connection and of what it takes to maintain a comfortable standard of living for a single person, much less a family.

It's cool to be up on fashion and sports. It's not cool to talk about work. Sooner or later the inside story will reveal itself anyway, and who can picture a future fifteen years down the road? The ingenuity that adolescents apply extravagantly in areas that their culture deems meaningful is untapped when it comes to preparing for jobs. Instead, they drift, just as many of their parents did.

* Carol Hulsizer works in career education and has developed curricula and counseling materials for adolescents and women entering the work force.

For many teenagers, especially girls, this may mean a decade or so of wasted time. There are changing social and work place realities that they should recognize now, while students can take advantage of free school training opportunities. A few facts should matter to young people.

1. Distinctions between breadwinners (males) and bread makers (females) are vanishing. Girls finishing high school in the 1980s will spend about thirty years in the work force. Now over half of all U.S. women are employed outside the home; by the year 2000, half of the entire labor force will be women. Most girls will end up in poorly paid, dead-end occupations because they lack the skills to compete for good jobs in fields dominated by men.

2. Most families cannot get by on just one income. According to the Department of Labor, men who are sole family wage earners bring home an average of $16,774 a year, or $322 a week (1980). This doesn't buy much in today's marketplace. Women as sole wage earners make less than half this amount. They average $7,852 a year, or $151 a week, a dismal fact of economic life that bodes ill for single and widowed women and the rapidly rising number who will become separated or divorced.

3. The top professions are crowded. Medical, law, and business schools are pouring out graduates, making the outlook in these fields less rosy, except in rural areas distant from major cities. Opportunities in architecture, publishing, and teaching are shrinking along with the contracting economy and declining birthrate.

4. Forecasts indicate a large number of openings, great job diversity, and high wages in trade and technical occupations. Expanding high-technology industries such as electronics need skilled workers, particularly on the East and West coasts and in Texas. But the mushrooming growth of electronic aids will threaten employment potential in factories, offices, and banks as more and more jobs are automated and fewer workers are needed.

Information such as this, based on timely labor market data, is not the sort that is conveyed by parents, peers, relatives, or neighbors from whom young people usually obtain career information. Their recommendations are most likely to reflect prevailing stereotypes and traditional choices for both boys and girls. Such advice often tends to steer them awry or serves to close off future options.

Schools do not pick up this slack. Guidance counselors in large institutions frequently have fewer than twenty minutes of contact a year with individual students; many are woefully out of touch with today's labor market and may themselves communicate old-fashioned attitudes about suitable career goals for either sex. Studies show, for example, that junior high school girls are as competent at math as boys the same age. But only lately have math and science courses been viewed as legitimate pathways to rewarding jobs for girls. It has become apparent that when girls drop these subjects after completing the minimum requirements, they are effectively barred from further training for a vast range of promising nontraditional occupational fields.

Television also supplies career information to teenagers, much of it superficial and some of it misleading. Commercials, especially those portraying working women, highlight a degree of affluence that is pure myth. How these feed adolescent fantasies about what it is like to hold a job and run a home has yet to be assessed. Many entertainment formats are equally hollow. Work sites are uniformly pleasant, job tasks indeterminate, wardrobes attractive, and bosses caricatured. Program content does little to make teenagers aware that jobs in the real world do not come through central casting. Topics that are not dealt with are: How did Trapper John decide to become a surgeon and where did he get the $40,000 or more to put himself through medical school? Why has Jennifer, a young woman of obvious competence, settled for a routine office job at WKRP, and how does she manage to dress so well and live in such a posh apartment on a secretary's salary? Can Fonzi really make a living as a motorcycle mechanic? In what other occupations could he use his prodigious mechanical skills? What combination of school courses and work experience helped him become such an expert? Any of these themes might make an interesting show.

And they help young people address some key career planning issues. Finding out about all the available possibilities (the government lists more than 400 occupations and over 20,000 different job titles), focusing on job fields that make sense for the years ahead, and figuring out sensible ways to explore or "try them on" is what the career-development process is all about. Television can do a lot to bring this process to life by highlighting critical factors that should be weighed in choosing one's life work.

Specifically, television can prompt young people to ask the right questions as they start thinking about careers and jobs. First of all, what is a career? Perhaps as some who specialize in youth transition problems, including a former secretary of labor, have noted, a career is something you can identify only when you look back on it. "Career" may be an elegant academic concept that misrepresents reality. Most people move from one kind of job to another in our exceedingly mobile society; with increasing freedom they try different types of work, develop different types of skills. Not only are experimentation and changing direction acceptable, they make possible second—and often better—starts. Young people should understand this and not feel that decisions made at age sixteen will lock them into permanent occupational slots.

"One skill, many options" is an even more practical lesson that television might teach. Too many teenagers float into elective vocational courses by picking classes that their friends choose or by how the course fits into unassigned hours of their schedules. Then they float into jobs, with no inkling of the implications of these choices.

A better approach is to convince teenagers that they should get all the mileage they can out of the time—and after high school, the money—they invest in training. They should be encouraged to acquire basic skills that will be transferable to a variety of occupations. Girls as well as boys should know that basic trade and technical skills will give them additional labor market leverage. Technical training can pave the way into fields where jobs are plentiful, will enable them to start on a higher rung of the job ladder in terms of earning power, and will help them move across occupational boundaries.

Other questions that TV can help young people formulate concern the nature of jobs. What makes a job good? A number of facets should be considered: Is the job in a field that is growing or at least stable? What are the educational requirements that will make me a competitive job candidate? Can I afford them or get financial assistance, if needed? Will the entry-level salary allow me to support myself? What can I earn later? Does the company offer on-the-job training that will help me advance? Does it provide tuition reimbursement for outside education? What other benefits are available, such as health insurance, savings plan, and credit unions? Is the job environment healthy and safe? And—an essential question—will I be doing work that I feel is worthwhile? Consideration in adolescence of elements that afford job satisfaction and self-respect might help this generation confer more status on work itself—and may ultimately lead to improvements in the quality of work place life.

Television can also point up new ways to use educational resources. Parents and counselors as much as teenagers might profit from this kind of information. Low-cost or free career training is now widely available through corporations and the armed forces. New programs are mushrooming throughout the country to link schools and industry; many provide opportunities to learn and earn simultaneously and to gain supervised experience, using actual industrial equipment. Internships, cooperative education projects, and volunteer placements introduce young people to insurance offices, health care facilities, real estate agencies, and a host of other community work settings. They also give employers a chance to evaluate and help shape tomorrow's work force.

Television could build on this valuable exposure by dramatizing the experiences of young people in a variety of authentic work sites. Why not, for example, develop a program series based on the experiences of a high school class engaged in testing out different types of work roles? A wealth of comic and serious story material could be mined from this central idea, especially if scripts incorporated the freshness, skepticism, and irreverence that teenagers generally bring to "sacred cow" situations.

Authenticity is the prime clue. It is the ingredient that lets viewers of all ages feel the intense pressures of the "M*A*S*H" scene. The high pitch of activity in the operating room, where personnel scurry to carry out procedures, the deadly boredom and loneliness of off-duty time, the dreary food—all tell the truth about life in a military medical outpost. Moreover, the literal atmosphere lends credence to aspects of character development. Radar starts as a naive boy, assumes a work load that would make a strong man buckle, and becomes a pivotal team member. Although the comedy is broad, the message gets through that it is okay to be inexperienced, it is good to accept job challenges and responsibilities, and there is more to growing up than just getting taller.

Laverne and Shirley, on the other hand, are rarely seen at their jobs. The impression persists that their work weeks are very short since most of their adventures happen in off hours and concentrate on fun and games. Several intriguing work-related issues might frame scenarios on this show more useful to young audiences; for example, what it is like to be on an assembly line; how male and female co-workers get along in a factory; what it means to be supervised; how employers and employees negotiate about job conditions. These could be packaged with amusement as well as depth.

Opportunities abound on the home screen to give work its real flavor, to show its stresses and satisfactions, and to make young people aware of the need to develop marketable skills. More attention to these concerns on the part of broadcasters will enable adolescents to make more informed career choices and may help arm them for the difficult passage into the labor market.

Michael (Ethan Tucker) must decide between going to art school or following the family tradition of lobster fishing in "The Fisherman's Son," a Multimedia Young People's Special.

Sam takes over the family bakery but doesn't really want to be a baker in "On the Level," a production of Agency for Instructional Television.

WOMAN: Let's talk woman-to-woman.

Nowadays, we're free to do so many things. Women have more alternatives.

Semicid is one of those alternatives.

It's a safe, simple way to prevent pregnancy...

a vaginal suppository. Semicid is effective. Yet has no hormonal side effects.

And Semicid is incredibly easy and convenient to use.

Don't just take my word for it. Ask your doctor about Semicid.

It's a safe, simple way to prevent pregnancy. Semicid.

This commercial for Semicid Contraceptive Suppositories (which are made by Whitehall Laboratories) has aired in a number of cities.

Billy's (Noelle North) relationship with Craig (John Crump McLaughlin) helps her learn the difference between love and friendship in "A Friend in Deed," a Capital Cities Family Special. Photo courtesy of Paulist Productions.

Tony (Anthony Candell) and Debby (Marta Kober) face the possibility that Debby may be pregnant in "Is That What You Want For Yourself?," a production of Health Video Services. Photo by Diane Smook.

A fatherless teenager (Rob Lowe) tries to raise his own illegitimate son in "Schoolboy Father," an ABC Afterschool Special. Photo courtesy of ABC, copyright © 1978, 1979, 1980, 1981 by American Broadcasting Companies, Inc.

TV Professions

MICHAEL MORGAN AND GEORGE GERBNER

ASKING CHILDREN, "What do you want to be when you grow up?" is something of an historical novelty. The very notion of occupational choice was largely nonexistent in traditional societies. For males, it was "like father, like son"; for females, home and children. But the technological, social, and economic transformation of the post–Industrial Revolution has made going into the family business the exception.

Asking adolescents the same question is an equally recent phenomenon. Formerly, they already were grown up and either apprenticing or well into doing whatever it was they would continue to do. Today adolescents do not have it so easy. The responses of their younger years (like "fireman") will not suffice, and our relatively mobile system does not insert young people into predetermined, specific occupational slots. Aspirational fantasies of childhood must slowly give way and be replaced by more realistic expectations of the roles they will take as adults—in a future that may seem quite distant but is coming closer.

* Michael J. Morgan, Ph.D., is a research specialist of the Cultural Indicators Project for the Annenberg School of Communications, University of Pennsylvania.

* George Gerbner, Ph.D., is professor of communications and dean of the Annenberg School of Communications, University of Pennsylvania.

Much of the research presented here was conducted by the Cultural Indicators Project at the Annenberg School of Communications. George Gerbner and Larry Gross were co-principal investigators, Nancy Signorielli the research coordinator, and Michael Morgan the research specialist.

To make things even tougher, we also tell young people that they can be anything they want to be. It is up to them. Given ambition, initiative, and dedication, the possibilities are endless. But we do not really tell them what the choices are, much less the mechanisms of preparing for and entering a job.

Somehow young people acquire bits and pieces of information about various jobs, sometimes through direct contact, sometimes through the guidance of parents or other adult advisers, and sometimes through mass media—particularly TV. Of the tens of thousands of different types of jobs in this country, young people are exposed to only a small handful through any given source.

Suzanne Jeffries-Fox interviewed adolescents about their sources of information for six jobs: police, lawyers, judges, doctors, paramedics, and psychiatrists.[1] She found that TV was by far the most frequently cited source of information about these jobs, and the students discounted the TV information only when it was directly contradicted by another source, such as personal contact. Reading was rarely credited as a source of job information.

A growing body of evidence suggests that television's portrayal of occupations has some influence on young people's career outlooks. In 1967, Melvin DeFleur and Lois DeFleur asked children about three kinds of occupations:[2] (1) those with which children are likely to have direct, personal contact (teacher, mailcarrier, school janitor); (2) those seen often on TV but rarely in real life (lawyer, reporter, butler); and (3) those seen rarely on TV or in real life (electrical engineer, printer, bank president). They found that the children knew the most about the personal-contact jobs but more about the TV-contact jobs than the general-culture-contact jobs. If we assume that the only difference between the TV-contact jobs and the culture-contact jobs is that the former appear on TV, then this study demonstrates that children acquire knowledge about occupational roles from TV. They also found that children are better able to rank jobs according to their prestige in the TV contact category than in the other two; this led them to conclude that TV is a more potent source of information about job status than either personal contact or the general culture.

One aspect of our long-term, ongoing research project—called Cultural Indicators—has been the study of the portrayal of occupations on television and the consequences of that portrayal of adolescents' career choices. Cultural Indicators has been monitoring network television drama ("message system analysis") and assessing its impact on viewers' conceptions of social reality ("cultivation analysis") since 1967. At the end of 1979, the data contained information about 1,500 programs, 4,100 major characters, and 14,200 minor characters. This information is used to describe and analyze the complex but coherent world of television and is then used as the basis for investigating the implications of regular exposure to television's most recurrent messages on people's attitudes, outlooks, and behaviors.

The research has shown that the amount of television viewing makes a distinct, independent contribution to viewers' attitudes and behaviors in terms of violence and victimization, sex roles, age roles, academic achievement, family life, law enforcement, political activity, minorities, and health. In numerous samples of children, adolescents, adults, and the elderly, it was found that heavier viewers of television are more likely than lighter viewers to report outlooks and expectations that are congruent with television's imagery, even when controlling for other factors and information sources, such as education, age, and newspaper reading.

The research is aimed at uncovering the patterns of content and effects of television. The analyses focus on the most stable, recurrent images and not on individual programs or characters. The research also looks at what happens to large numbers of people rather than what a few individuals might learn from television. It is quite likely that some young person may decide to become a doctor because he or she likes Marcus Welby, but the research approach is designed to examine the images of doctors cultivated in large audiences after seeing hundreds of TV doctors over long periods of time.

Underlying all of television's images about the world of work is one dominant, insistent message: the labor force presented on television is largely comprised of professionals. From the earliest content analyses in the 1950s to the present, researchers have continually reached this conclusion. Working-class occupations are vastly underrepresented in television drama.

About 57 percent of all prime-time and weekend daytime major and minor characters are employed. Among prime-time major characters, occupation is a highly common aspect of portrayal; only about 15 percent have no discernible occupation. The two largest groupings are classified as professionals (about 20 percent) and law enforcement agents (about 17 percent). Professionals include doctors, lawyers, astronauts, entertainers, teachers, athletes, clergy, nurses, and accountants. Managers, officials, and proprietors comprise another 10 percent of prime-time major characters.

The remaining categories, particularly the blue-collar jobs, are all relatively small. Clerical and sales workers constitute 3 percent of the prime-time major character population; 4 percent are laborers, repair workers, factory workers, and skilled and semiskilled crafts persons; another 3 percent are service workers, such as servants and waiters. Four percent are in the military, 3 percent are housewives, less than 1 percent are retired, and only 3 percent are explicitly unemployed. In contrast to these small numbers, 7 percent are criminals. The final 10 percent are mixed or other roles, such as witch, fortune teller, superhero, student, hunter, juror, genie, and aide to king.

Occupational roles on television vary according to the sex of the characters. Jobs are more likely to be part of the way males are portrayed and somewhat less important for females. Nine of ten male television characters can be placed in some occupational category, but no information is given for one of four women. Sometimes the distribution of jobs by sex matches the real world, but more often than not, television occupations are dominated by males (as is the entire world of television, by a ratio of three to one). Although about the same proportion of males and females are classified as professionals, over half of the female professionals are entertainers.

A study by Linda Glennon and Richard Butsch that examined all family programs on television from 1947 to 1977 found that while working-class occupations constitute about 70 percent of the real world labor force, only 6 percent of the television programs featured heads of household with blue-collar jobs.[3] One of the major themes of these few shows is upward mobility; dignity is achieved not by being working class but by becoming middle class.

A dozen studies over the last twenty-five years show that the world of television is dominated by active, high-status, glamorous professionals who are portrayed more positively than other major characters. More common, more mundane, and less prestigious workers make up a marginal proportion of their true numbers. The affluence of television professionals is exaggerated; generally they have either already succeeded or are on their way to promising, lucrative careers. In the Glennon and Butsch study, one of four family series featured a servant; servants were found in almost half of all single-parent series.

We are not implying that television must faithfully and accurately reproduce reality; drama involves selection, invention, and amplification. The important question is not whether there are deviations but rather what kinds of deviations exist and what the possible consequences are.

Roles are created according to their usefulness in the television world. Those roles for which television has more use—because they imply adventure, sex, status, or power—are created and cast in greater numbers than those with more restricted dramatic uses. The result is that the dominant social groups—whether defined by age, sex, or occupation—tend to be overrepresented, usually in a manner that emphasizes their affluence and spending power. Minorities on television—women, the old and the very young, the working classes —have less than their proportionate share of values and resources. Their underrepresentation means that they are portrayed with restricted scope of action, stereotyped roles, diminished life chances, and undervaluation.[4]

Cultural Indicators studied more than 200 adolescents over a three-year period. (In the first year of this project, they were in the sixth, seventh, and eighth grades.) Each year of this study, it was found that heavy viewing among adolescents correlated with lower aspirations, lower IQs, lower achievement scores, and more traditional values, such as sex-role stereotypes and the desire for early marriage, early childbirth, and large families.

It would be difficult to argue that television content could cultivate lower aspirations, given the virtual invisibility of the working classes on television. More likely, such a relationship might be due to heavy vewing per se; the very act of spending a large amount of time watching television might signal and reinforce a lack of ambition.

But in an examination of the effects of viewing in early adolescence on career goals in later adolescence among the same students, a very different pattern emerged: those who watched more TV when younger had significantly higher aspirations two years later than did lighter viewers. Even controlling for powerful factors like IQ, social class, and age, heavy viewing seems to raise career goals over time. This effect is more pronounced among girls. These findings suggest that television may lead to some real and difficult conflicts. Even girls who want to get married and have children at relatively young ages and even girls who want to have many children are influenced toward jobs with higher prestige. Given our present social situation, it may be difficult for women to mix family responsibilities with working at high-status careers. Few female teenagers will be able to handle the demands of early marriage and large families and at the same time become high-level professionals.

Television may be seen as an influence on adolescents' notions about occupations, much like other social, cultural, and psychological forces. It may be the major or only source of information about many jobs, particularly white-collar professional jobs. Television may make a powerful contribution to adolescents' general career orientations, if not to specific jobs, by cultivating underlying desires, norms, and expectations. Its repetitive, frequent messages about middle-class affluence and upward mobility, designed ultimately to stimulate the consumption of products and services sold on television, can be seen as reaffirming a great American myth.

References

1. Suzanne Jeffries-Fox, "Television's Contribution to Young People's Conceptions about Occupations" (Ph.D. diss., University of Pennsylvania, 1978).

2. Melvin L. DeFleur and Lois B. DeFleur, "The Relative Contribution of Television as a Learning Source for Children's Occupational Knowledge," *American Sociological Review* 32 (1967): 777–789.

3. Linda M. Glennon and Richard J. Butsch, "The Devaluation of Working Class Lifestyles in Television Family Series, 1947–1977" (Unpublished manuscript, 1978).

4. George Gerbner, Larry Gross, Nancy Signorielli, and Michael Morgan, "Aging with Television: Images on Television Drama and Conceptions of Social Reality," *Journal of Communication* 30:1 (Winter 1980): 37–47; and George Gerbner and Nancy Signorielli, "Women and Minorities in Television Drama, 1967–1978" (The Annenberg School of Communications, October 1979).

Resources, Chapter Four

Agency for Instructional Television (AIT). "Jobs: Seeking, Finding, Keeping." A series of sixteen twenty-minute programs. Available from AIT, Box A, Bloomington, Ind. 47402.

CBS. "Going Places," August 9, 1980. Documentary about teenage journalists discovering America.

Gitlin, T. "The Televised Professional." *Social Policy* 8 (November–December 1977): 94–99.

Leifer, Aimee Dorr, and Lesser, Gerald S. *The Development of Career Awareness in Young Children.* Cambridge, Mass.: Center for Research in Children's Television, Harvard Graduate School of Education, 1976.

Masserman, Jules Hymen. *Adolescence, Dreams, and Training.* New York: Grune & Stratton, 1966.

Multimedia Program Productions. "Young People's Specials," "The Fisherman's Son." A half-hour drama about a sixteen-year-old boy's conflict with his father over his career plans. He wants to go to art school; his father wants him to follow the family tradition of lobster fishing.

Seeger, John R., and Wheeler, Penny. "World of Work on TV: Representation in TV Drama." *Journal of Broadcasting* 17:2 (Spring 1973): 201–214.

Solnit, Albert J. "The Adolescent's Search for Competence." *Children Today* 8:6 (November–December, 1979): 13.

Taking on Tomorrow. Film and book. Film available for rental or purchase from National Audiovisual Center (GSA), Order Section, Washington, D.C. 20409; book available from Dissemination and Utilization for Vocational Education, Ohio State University, 1960 Kenney Road, Columbus, Ohio 43210.

Working on Working. Film and book. Film available for rental or purchase from National Audiovisual Center (GSA), Order Section, Washington, D.C. 20479; book available from Dissemination and Utilization for Vocational Education, Ohio State University, 1960 Kenney Road, Columbus, Ohio 43210.

WSB-TV, Atlanta. "Makin' It." A weekly talk-show series designed for high school students that focuses on different career possibilities.

Organizations

American Federation of Teachers, 11 Dupont Circle, N.W., Washington, D.C. 20036.

5 Sex and Sexuality

It must have been
The heat of that summer night.
We rested our wary minds
Only for a moment
Against each other's needs,
And found our arms
Reaching out.

Milbanke Holz
Camden-Rockport High School

Sex on Prime Time

JOYCE SPRAFKIN AND
L. THERESA SILVERMAN

THROUGHOUT EARLY television history, the broadcasting industry perpetuated and maintained a puritanical television world in which the use of words such as *pregnant* was taboo, and all married couples apparently slept in separate beds. By the late 1960s and early 1970s, when public criticism was firmly centered on the issue of televised violence, network officials and TV producers were already engaged in behind-the-scenes battles over the limits of sexual reference. The resulting gradual and progressive relaxation of strictly held taboos attracted little public attention until 1977 when "Soap," a prime-time situation comedy with explicit sexual themes, set the stage for a new era of sex on television.

The controversy continues today. Religious-based organizations and special-interest groups have called for the removal of sex from television, while advocacy groups, such as the National Organization for Women, call for a more diversified portrayal of sex roles and relationships and decry the emotional banality of sex on TV.

What is all the fuss about? Certainly TV has not suddenly become a pornographic medium. Much of the concern centers on the impact of TV sex on children and young adolescents. According to a recent survey, adults' standards of appropriate sexual content for television

* Joyce Sprafkin, Ph.D., is chief of the Laboratory of Communication at the Long Island Research Institute, State University of New York at Stony Brook.

* L. Theresa Silverman, Ph.D., is an assistant professor at New York University School of Journalism.

vary depending upon the age of the projected audience, turning to strong disapproval when directed to a teenage or child audience.[1] What, then, is TV teaching young adolescent viewers about sex and sexuality?

While the impact of television on young people's psychosexual development has not been systematically explored, there is ample documentation of the medium's effects on a variety of other behaviors and attitudes, suggesting that TV is a significant teacher of social roles, attitudes, values, and behaviors, including those related to sexuality. Television has been shown to have effects on aggressive, prosocial, and consumer behaviors and on attitudes toward political issues and social realities.[2] While adolescents watch less television than do children aged six to eleven, they do watch an average of 24.1 hours per week, mostly during prime time. Clearly there is ample opportunity for television to act as a teacher.

In an attempt to contribute an objective, scientific account of what kind of sexual content is shown on prime-time television and how it is presented, several communications researchers have analyzed the portrayal of physical intimacy and sexual behavior on programs aired between 8:00 and 11:00 p.m. (Eastern Standard Time). Across several studies conducted since 1974, certain consistent findings emerge.

First, sexual intercourse has not been shown on television. References to intercourse occur verbally through descriptions and innuendos or are contextually implied through indirect scenic and behavioral clues. While such verbal and contextual references have appeared in fair number, the overwhelming majority of interpersonal touching on television is nonsexual in nature. The most frequent type of physical contact is ritualistic, including such casual acts as handshakes, pats to get someone's attention, and touches to emphasize a point or to guide someone. Also quite common are supportive touches and affectionate gestures. Viewers are exposed to a number of kisses (about seven per hour in a 1978 sample) and hugs (about five per hour) between adult characters during the prime-time hours.[3]

Sexuality, however, cannot be gauged by the number of kisses or hugs per hour. Most of the sexual content on television is more subtle and pervasive and is manifested in behaviors and attitudes. The majority of the sexual portrayals on television are verbal presentations in the form of sexual innuendos. The frequency of such allusions has increased steadily over the past few years, with hourly rates of about one per hour in 1975 to eleven per hour in 1978.[4] Throughout the years, the bulk of the innuendos have occurred in a humorous context, appearing almost exclusively in situation comedies and variety shows. To the adolescent viewer, the overall impression must be that sex is funny; joking about sex is a common and acceptable way to make people laugh. While this flippant or light-hearted attitude toward sex is not necessarily an unhealthy component of a total system of sexual values, it unfortunately has received disproportionate emphasis in the TV world.

Although the predominance and steady increase of "sex with a titter" characterizes much of prime time, there has been a recent increase in sexual themes and sexual references presented in serious contexts. Unlike the sex typical of comedies, sexual presentations in movies and dramatic series usually take the form of direct verbal references to or contextual implications of intercourse. The weekly frequency of such references increased from two in 1975 to seventy-seven in 1978, most of which appeared in movies and dramas.[5]

Broadcasters have become bolder in their treatment of sex, presenting it more and more frequently in both humorous and serious contexts. Perhaps the most socially significant aspect of such portrayals is the relationship of the individuals involved. One study found that the number of references to premarital and extramarital sexual encounters far surpassed those to marital sex.[6] Not only, then, is there a documented increase in TV sex, but the sexual relationships shown occur outside of marriage. The message to be extracted from prime-time television is that adults are preoccupied with sex—talking about it, joking about it, "doing it"—and, moreover, that most heterosexual encounters occur outside of marriage. Traditional social and sexual values are clearly discrepant with this message.

Also inconsistent with traditional values is the increasing tendency in televised portrayals to mix sex and violence. Between 1977 and 1978, the percentage of programs depicting violent sex increased from 0 to 10 percent.[7]

Socially taboo sexual behavior is more often talked about than acted out on TV.[8] Frequencies of such references (either as a direct verbal reference or a humorous innuendo) vary depending on the specific topic. The prime-time viewer is rarely, if ever, exposed to televised allusions to incest, pederasty, exhibitionism, fetishism, masturbation, or voyeurism.

During a typical evening of prime-time viewing, however, the viewer could experience at least one reference to homosexuality, prostitution, rape, transvestism or transsexualism, and pornography or striptease. Most of these references are concentrated between 9:00 and 11:00 p.m. The type of program largely determines the kind of sexual reference that appears. Situation comedies tend to contain references to homosexuality and transvestism or transsexualism, crime and adventure programs to deal with aggressive sex, and dramas to present the majority of references to prostitution. The different contexts in which the taboo acts appear may communicate a message in itself: while rape and prostitution are treated as serious topics, homosexuality, transvestism, and transsexualism are presented as humorous perversions. Unfortunately, this may discourage the adolescent viewer from seeking information about these behavior patterns that would lead to a sensitive and socially conscious understanding of them.

Adolescents may be particularly impressionable when it comes to television's portrayals of socially discouraged sexual behaviors. In one study, teenagers were asked where they obtain information about various sexual topics.[9] While biological and health-related information was a realm for parents and friends, television and friends were the sources considered most important for information about the more atypical sexual behaviors such as homosexuality, transsexualism, and transvestism.

TV contains many references to sexual behavior that create impressions of how people relate to one another sexually. The potential impact on adolescents of TV's presentations of sexuality cannot be overlooked, particularly since adolescents rarely have adequate sources of information about sexuality. The effects of television have been shown to be more pronounced for areas in which alternative sources of information are relatively unavailable. Adolescents are interested in sexual topics not currently taught by sanctioned authorities. Not only is available information about biological and health-related aspects of sex inadequate but information about the emotional component of sex is practically nonexistent.

Sexual socialization generally takes place largely outside the family, probably because many parents report being uncomfortable about discussing sexual topics with their children.[10] The General Mills American Family Report for 1976–1977 listed homosexuality, death, and sex as the top three topics that parents find most difficult to talk about with their children.[11] This is indeed unfortunate since, when given a choice of possible alternate sources, teenagers consistently report that their first choice for more sexual information about a wide range of topics is their parents.[12]

A distinction exists between the kinds of sexual information available from formal societal sources and the kinds of sexual information that teenagers and young adults need and desire. While biological facts about sexuality can be found by the enterprising youth, many teenagers are so ignorant about sex that they fail to recognize a need for such information. Most, however, are bewildered by the new and powerful feelings and sensations they are experiencing. It is into this self-recognized knowledge gap about romance and love that the media—whether print, music, film, or TV—become important for adolescents. TV in particular is important in this respect because it is readily available (in the home) and easily accessible (requiring no particular skills).

Learning about sex and romance from television circumvents the embarrassment of asking friends or parents. But the messages about sex and romance that television promotes may not lead teenagers to mature sexual attitudes or responsible sexual behavior. There is some evidence that suggests that in comparison with their nonpregnant peers, adolescent girls who have become pregnant are both more frequent viewers of TV and place more credence on the sexual and romantic experiences of TV characters.[13]

I am not claiming that teenagers turn on the TV in order to learn about sex and romance; such information is merely a bonus to being entertained. However, conscious use of television to learn about social relations has been reported. During the recent revival of regular viewing of soap operas on college campuses, many dedicated soap-opera viewers reported that part of their viewing was motivated by what they learned about human social relations from such shows.[14] As prime-time television programs portray more serious treatments of sexual relationships, we might expect adolescents to turn more to such programs for the lessons they provide. Whether the effects of the messages they obtain are positive or negative depends largely on how responsible broadcasters are in their treatment of sexual topics and how willing parents become to use such presentations for initiating family discussions about sexuality.

References

1. J. N. Sprafkin, L. T. Silverman, and E. A. Rubinstein. "Reactions to Sex on Television: An Exploratory Study," *Public Opinion Quarterly* (1980): 303–315.

2. G. A. Comstock et al., *Television and Human Behavior* (New York: Columbia University Press, 1978).

3. J. N. Sprafkin and L. T. Silverman. "Update: Physically Intimate and Sexual Behavior on Prime-time Television: 1978–79," *Journal of Communication* 31:1 (1981): 34–40.

4. Ibid.; S. Franzblau, J. N. Sprafkin, and E. A. Rubinstein. "Sex on TV: A Content Analysis," *Journal of Communication* 27 (1977): 164–170.

5. Sprafkin and Silverman, "Update"; Franzblau, Sprafkin, and Rubinstein, "Sex on TV."

6. C. Fernandez-Collado and B. S. Greenberg. "Sexual Intimacy and Drug Use in TV Series," *Journal of Communication* 28:3 (1978): 30–37.

7. G. Gerbner. "Sex on Television and What Viewers Learn from It" (Paper presented at the annual conference of the National Association of Television Program Executives, San Francisco, California, February 19, 1980).

8. Franzblau, Sprafkin, and Rubinstein, "Sex on TV"; L. T. Silverman, J. N. Sprafkin, and E. A. Rubinstein. "Physical Contact and Sexual Behavior on Prime-time TV," *Journal of Communication* (1979): 33–43; Sprafkin and Silverman, "Update."

9. L. T. Silverman and J. N. Sprafkin. "Adolescents' Reactions to Televised Sexual Innuendos" (Report prepared for the American Broadcasting Companies, April 1980).

10. E. J. Roberts, D. Kline, and J. Gagnon, *Family Life and Sexual Learning* (Cambridge, Mass.: Population Education, Inc., 1978).

11. Yankelovich, Skelly, and White, Inc., *The General Mills American Family Report 1976–77: Raising Children in a Changing Society* (Minneapolis, Minn.: General Mills, 1977).

12. Silverman and Sprafkin, "Adolescent's Reactions."

13. W. Robins, "The Jiggly Effect Takes Off," *Newsday*, April 23, 1978, pp. 4–5.

14. F. M. Bordewich, "Why Are College Kids in a Lather over TV Soap Operas?" *New York Times*, October 20, 1974, sec. 2, p. 31.

Teenage Sexuality

SOL GORDON

PEOPLE IN THE TELEVISION industry do not have to be reminded how awesome is their power and influence. It is certainly to their credit that they have, in many areas, responded responsibly, particularly in news coverage and in revealing and sensitive documentaries and special programs.

In one area of concern, however, the TV industry has been either unresponsive or grossly irresponsible. Apart from an occasional Norman Lear episode or a "M*A*S*H" incident, prime-time commercial TV is macho and sexist and caters to the worst instincts of humankind, from rape to murder. Its portrayal of love is pathetic and does a lot of damage in reinforcing stereotypes and unrealistic expectations. (In terms of presenting responsible programs on sexuality, PBS does not have a better record than commercial broadcasting.)

But this kind of global criticism turns off television people, and I shall not continue. Instead I offer some positive messages and ideas that sex educators would like to see on TV. These messages can be incorporated into commercially viable situation comedies, afternoon soaps, "tits and ass" extravaganzas, detective stories, westerns, and even nostalgia specials:

1. Girls get pregnant because they have sexual intercourse.

* Sol Gordon, Ph.D., is director of the Institute for Family Research and Education. He is the author of numerous books about sexuality for adolescents and their parents, including *The Sexual Adolescent*, *The Teenage Survival Book*, and *Facts About Sex for Today's Youth*.

2. It's not romantic to have sex without birth control, it's stupid.

3. When someone says, "If you really love me, you'll have sex with me," it is always a line.

4. Sex is never a test of love.

5. "No" is a perfectly good oral contraceptive.

6. Men who boast about all the women they have had and how they need sex a lot basically hate women.

7. More than 85 percent of all boys who impregnate teenage girls will eventually abandon them.

8. Girls who feel they don't amount to anything unless some guy loves them won't amount to much afterward.

9. People who feel good about themselves are not available for exploitation and don't exploit others.

10. If he says, "Honey, if you really love me, you'll have sex with me," she could say, "I love you, but do you have a condom?" And if he were to answer, "I get no feelings from a condom," she could reply, "All the other boys I know get plenty of feelings with a condom. What's the matter with you?"

11. Of the ten most important things in a relationship, sex is number nine. Number one is love and caring. Two is a sense of humor. Three is communicating, and ten is sharing household tasks together.

The bottom line for the next decade must be prevention. Here are some of the basic concepts:

1. Knowledge is not harmful. Young people who are knowledgeable about their sexuality tend to delay their first sexual experience, and, when they have sex, they use birth control.

2. The promiscuous girl is not the one who is getting pregnant. She is on the pill. The girls who are getting pregnant are those who don't believe in having sex (they are making love). They are the ones who don't believe in premeditated sex.

3. Parents are the sex educators of their own children—whether they do it well or badly. They need help and support to do it well.

4. Sex education in the public schools has not been tried. Less than 10 percent of American schools have anything approaching a valid sex education program.

5. Sex education without values is valueless. We need to help people make a distinction between moral and moralistic education. A moral education encourages self-esteem and nonexploitive behavior. A moralistic education seeks to influence children to accept a particular religious and personal point of view. Moral education represents the highest aspirations of a society.

6. Sex education on TV is essential. That does not mean that if in the next decade TV did a significantly good job of it, the problem would be eliminated. We could, however, reasonably expect a 10 to 20 percent reduction in unwanted teenage pregnancy and venereal disease. In the long run, if we encourage young people to develop healthier attitudes about themselves, they could become the sex educators of their own children (if they become parents). This would effectively break the cycle that forces each generation of young people to discover from their equally misinformed friends what sexuality is all about.

7. Problems associated with sex will not be substantially eradicated unless we effectively reduce poverty, racial discrimination, sexism, and the pernicious double standard that exists in our society.

8. Finally, we need to support the basic principles of the women's movement, a movement that comes with the potential for the liberation of us all. But we must get across to the American public that the women's movement means equal opportunities for decision making, career choice, leisure, and equal pay for equal work. The notion that the movement means women don't want to have babies or wash dishes and are so aggressive that men are becoming impotent is the figment of the imagination of extremists who oppose the women's movement for political reasons.

The sexual revolution has not started yet. We need one that binds intimacy with sex, for many people today use sex as an avoidance of intimacy rather than as an expression of it.

We must prepare today's children for tomorrow's family by educating them for self-respect and the respect for the rights of others. If we want responsive, responsible children, we must provide mature models, not critics, and a sound basis for decision making, not antics and stereotypes.

Teenage Pregnancy

JANE MURRAY

ONE OF THE MOST compelling social issues to surface in the public consciousness during the 1970s was the dramatic increase in sexual activity among young unmarried teenagers and the distressingly high rates of teenage pregnancy that resulted. Teenagers today are apparently as preoccupied with sex as their elders, and much less constrained than in the past from acting on their sexual impulses. According to a 1980 study by Melvin Zelnick and John F. Kantner of Johns Hopkins University, 50 percent of all fifteen- to nineteen-year-olds in metropolitan areas of the United States were sexually active in 1979, compared to 30 percent in 1971, with all of the increase since 1976 attributable to sexual activity by white females. And despite the fact that proportionally more sexually active teens than ever are using contraception, the percentage of those who become pregnant out of wedlock has risen steadily—from 28 percent in 1971 to 33 percent in 1979. But even more dramatically, the 1979 figure means that 16 percent of all women aged fifteen to nineteen have been pregnant out of wedlock.

These statistics are deeply disturbing. They translate into tragedies of traumatic abortions, or of unwanted babies and misspent young lives; they pose some hard questions for society in general and for those who work directly or indirectly with youth in particular. The questions are many, but at the top of the list is this: Are we, as

* Jane Murray is director of communications and development for The Alan Guttmacher Institute.

members of the adult society, being truthful with our children about sex, or are we passing on to them our own ambivalence about sex and sexuality in the form of impossibly mixed messages that create problems for them that they are ill equipped to solve? Do we on the one hand promote and celebrate sex through every available medium —television, movies, magazines, books—and on the other hand withhold from our children the information they need to make responsible, confident decisions about their sexuality and their interactions with each other? Do we practice a ludicrously inconsistent kind of prudishness when it comes to talking to them directly about their bodies and the endless fascination and power of sex?

Consider some facts of adolescence. The age of menarche, or the onset of menstruation for girls, has been getting steadily younger over the last decade until it is now at an average of 12.5 years. At the same time, the median age at which young people marry has been rising—to twenty-one for women and twenty-three for men. This means that the average young woman in 1980 will be fecund and at least potentially sexually active for nine years or more before she marries, if she marries, during which time she may complete an extensive education and launch a career. Is it reasonable to expect her or her male counterpart to delay intimate relations for so long when he, at least, is in his sexual prime? Is it even desirable to stunt their physical responses and foreclose such a potentially rewarding means to emotional growth?

Sexual activity among the young seems a forgone conclusion today, given their degree of freedom from supervision, the amount of sexual stimulation they are exposed to in our culture, and the fact that we expect them to delay marriage until they are established. It is our responsibility to minimize the obstacles they encounter in avoiding the negative consequences of adolescent sexual activity—chiefly unwanted pregnancy. We must find a way to be more honest with them about a preoccupation that we all share and that, if handled directly and sensitively, has the possibility of bringing our generations closer together rather than forever driving us apart.

Teenage Pregnancy: The Numbers

As with any other statistics, one can look at those relating to adolescent fertility in a variety of ways. For example, teenage childbearing has been declining steadily during the last decade; at the same time, however, the incidence of teenage pregnancy has been increasing steadily. The real problem is the more than 1 million pregnancies that occur each year to the country's 10 million women under twenty. Here are the facts:

1. Over 1.1 million American teenagers now become pregnant each year (the latest available figures are for 1978).

2. Three-fourths do not intend to get pregnant.

3. Four in ten have abortions (419,000 in 1978).

4. Two-thirds of the pregnant teens (721,000) are unmarried. Only one in seven means to get pregnant, but one in twelve gives birth.

5. About half of births to teens are to married teens (56 percent in 1978), but six in ten of these babies were conceived before marriage. The result is that in 1978, about 182,000 young women under twenty probably got married just because they were pregnant.

6. More than three-fourths of all births to teens are conceived out of wedlock (78 percent, or 442,000, in 1978).

Our greatest concern is for young teens who become pregnant—those aged seventeen or under—since they are unlikely to intend to get pregnant, and they and their babies are subject to the greatest risk of health problems, educational and economic deprivation, and family disruption if they carry a pregnancy to term.

7. Nearly half a million young women aged fifteen to seventeen become pregnant each year (428,000 in 1978); of these, nearly half (203,000) become mothers. Six in ten of these young mothers are not married when they deliver.

8. These young women are less likely to have abortions than eighteen- and nineteen-year-olds (52 percent compared to 57 percent of the older girls).

9. In addition, 30,000 girls under fifteen conceived during 1978 (an average of 600 per state), resulting in 11,000 births and 15,000 abortions (the rest were miscarriages). Virtually all of these pregnancies were unintended.

There has been a tendency until recently to dismiss teenage pregnancy as a problem confined largely to black and poor teenagers. However, white middle-class teenagers are now sexually active almost as early and at nearly the same rate as their black peers, and pregnancy among young white girls is rising proportionally. Suddenly teenage pregnancy is a problem among all segments of the population.

Undoubtedly so many young women are getting pregnant because early sexual activity has become the rule, not the exception. Kantner and Zelnick's 1979 survey found that the average age of first intercourse for girls is now 16.2 years, and that by age 18, six of ten metropolitan women and seven of ten men have had premarital intercourse. And although more of them than ever before are trying to prevent pregnancy by using contraception (49 percent at first intercourse in 1979 compared to 38 percent in 1976), not enough of them are using effective methods or using them soon enough. Kantner and

Zelnick found that the use of the most effective contraceptives—
the pill and the IUD—by teenagers at first intercourse dropped 41
percent between 1976 and 1979, and use of the least effective methods
—withdrawal and rhythm—rose by 86 percent. In 1976, the three
most popular methods of birth control among teens were the condom,
the pill, and withdrawal, in that order; in 1979, they were withdrawal, the condom, and the pill.

This reversal in the use of effective contraception by teenagers is
disturbing, considering its consequences in unwanted pregnancies,
abortions, and births. One reason for it may be that young women—
those who are least vulnerable to any adverse effects of oral contraceptives but most vulnerable to the damaging effects of early pregnancy—are apparently more influenced than older, more experienced
women by misleading publicity about the dangers of pill use. This
is cruelly ironic, since, in fact, there is little evidence that pill use
is risky to young women who are properly screened by doctors or
clinic personnel; on the contrary, theirs is precisely the age group
for which this method is safest.

Among the most important reasons for the high teenage pregnancy
rate is the high incidence of early, unprotected sex. A study conducted by Laurie Zabin, John Kantner, and Melvin Zelnick in 1979
revealed that of those teens who become pregnant outside of marriage,
22 percent do so within the first month of sexual activity and 50
percent within the first six months. Many become pregnant the first
time they have intercourse, due in large part to the fact that half
of all teenagers do not use any kind of birth control when they first
have sex. The average delay between first intercourse and first contraceptive use may be more than a year—ample time to become pregnant. The rationalization given by most young women for not using
any kind of birth control is that they did not intend to have sex,
a degree of denial that has resulted in countless unintended pregnancies and hundreds of thousands of unwanted babies.

Assuming, under the circumstances presented by our culture, that
there is very little we can do in the short run to keep teenagers from
having sex and that we do not wish to punish them, or worse, their
children, by withholding the services they need, how can we help
them be better prepared for the sexual initiatives they will take?

It is becoming increasingly apparent that, beyond making contraceptive services as easily and freely available to teenagers as possible and
providing abortion services when preventive measures fail, the answer
to this urgent question lies in finding new ways to define and provide
sex education—a term that has become so vague that it is nearly

meaningless, although it has the power to provoke passionate argument and violent opposition in some quarters. Partly because of the aura of controversy surrounding the issue, policy makers and school administrators tend to assume that parents do not want the schools, or any other public agency, to participate in the sex education of their children. Certainly the impression given by the most vocal opponents of school sex education is that parents generally wish to take sole responsibility for the instruction of their children in the complex matter of sexuality and human reproduction and, moreover, feel quite capable of doing so. But do they and are they?

"American Families in 1980," a public opinion poll of 1,600 adults throughout the United States conducted for the White House Conference on Families by the Gallup Organization, revealed widespread support for sex education in the public schools. Of those surveyed, 87 percent endorse public school instruction in marriage and family life, 79 percent approve of school sex education with parental consent, and 34 percent support sex education without parental consent. These findings are consistent with those from a survey by the National Opinion Research Center in 1974 that found that 78 percent of adults favored sex education in the schools, and a recent Cleveland study by the Project for Human Sexual Development that found 80 percent of adults in support of sex education in the schools. However, only Kentucky, Maryland, New Jersey, and the District of Columbia require local school districts to include sex education in the curriculum. State policies are even less reflective of public opinion on teaching about contraception. Although a 1977 Gallup Poll shows that at least 70 percent of Americans believe contraceptive information should be included in school sex education curricula, just six states and the District of Columbia support the provision of birth control information. It appears that a very small minority of Americans is influencing policy decisions in the provision of sex education in the schools.

Even if parents feel they are competent to undertake sex education, there is strong evidence that many of them are not much better informed than their children. A study conducted by Warner Qube in Columbus, Ohio in 1979 of well-educated, middle-class adults revealed that only 65 percent of those over twenty knew the time of the month when the risk of pregnancy is greatest, compared to 40 percent of teenagers. Furthermore, it has been shown repeatedly that educated young parents (themselves the products of the liberated 1960s) have difficulty talking to their children about sex.

Ignorance begets ignorance, and ignorance is one of the primary causes of teenage pregnancy. Joy Dryfoos, senior fellow of the Alan

Guttmacher Institute, believes that the cycle will not be broken until "parents, schools, churches, and the society in general are willing to acknowledge that human sexuality is a subject that needs more open discussion, at least as open as it receives in the pornographic magazines, suggestive songs, and lurid movies that are currently the instructors of youth." Dryfoos suggests that television might play a role in demystifying the subject for parents and children and helping teens avoid unwanted pregnancy:

> In only a few instances has television been used either to recruit patients for family planning clinics or inform them about reproduction or contraception. At the same time, the subject of teenage pregnancy has received dramatic coverage in a number of TV movies and soap operas. Advertising of contraceptive methods is not allowed, not because of the law but because of the negative policies of TV networks. America's youngsters are considered a prime market for "hucksters"; it is interesting to postulate what would happen to the adolescent pregnancy rate if condoms were marketed with the same enthusiasm as rock-and-roll tapes.
>
> If children grew up with the same exposure to contraceptive advertising that they have to toothpaste ads, they would be far more likely to use contraception when they initiate sexual activity, the moment at which the practice of pregnancy prevention must begin.

It may be unrealistic to suppose that such a revolution in the world of television advertising will occur overnight, or even at all. There is, however, a good possibility of achieving a strong impact through television programming. Until now, television has dealt with teenage sexuality in terms of its melodramatic consequences for girls: pregnancy, out-of-wedlock births, even, in a few cases, abortion. What seems not to have been shown are models of healthy interaction between parents and children on the subject of sexuality—open discussion of the consequences of teenage sexuality that might have a preventive, educational effect. Perhaps if parents and children could watch dramatizations of other parents and children having such interchanges, they would learn from them and find the subject less threatening. Certainly sexuality and sexual expression are more openly acknowledged in all our lives than they have ever been. This fact is at least tacitly accepted by virtually everyone in the society in nearly every area, except the most important: between parent and child.

We must find ways to communicate with our children about sex before they have already made mistakes that could have been avoided. They need the security that knowledge and a sense of solidarity with their parents can give them, the security that might enable them to say "no," to postpone their first sexual encounters until they are really ready for them. Boys and girls need preparation for engaging respon-sibly in sexual relationships so that they can avoid hurting themselves and others, including their own unborn children. They need balanced, straightforward information on contraception: the relative risks and benefits of various methods, weighed against the risk of unmarried pregnancy at, say, sixteen. They need role models that will show them how they might behave in situations that require decision mak-ing on the subject of sexual activity. They need to have sex made a real fact of life for them, instead of a source of embarrassment, titil-lation, anxiety, and confusion.

If creative, concerned television programming can help meet this need, parents and children will benefit, and the medium and society in general will have taken a giant step toward maturity.

Teenage Pregnancy

A Case Study, "Is That What You Want for Yourself?"

DIANE SMOOK AND
PEGGY STEVENS

HAVING GROWN UP in an electronic environment, today's children are highly saturated with information by the time they begin school. By adolescence, they are frequently resistant to the acquisition of new information, whether presented in print form or by audiovisual means. The Triggertapes Project began as an attempt to penetrate this resistance in teenagers. The challenge was to get a message across to these young people without spoon-feeding them information; to make them think about something that had relevance to their own lives and encourage them to seek whatever information they decided was necessary. We felt that broadcast television was not successfully reaching the teenage audience. Although we had innovative ideas and were experienced in other areas of production, we lacked the track record necessary to produce for children's television. We had to find another route leading to this end.

In 1978 we formed Health Video Services, a not-for-profit educational production company. After much discussion with educators, psychologists, and teen counselors, we began by tackling the area of teenage sexuality and pregnancy, an area in which there was a lack of good educational film and videotape materials. All but a handful of those on the market were preachy and stilted and were considered useless by the teachers and counselors who work with young people.

* Diane Smook and Peggy Stevens are film and videotape producers and co-directors of Health Video Services.

Any film longer than fifteen minutes did not allow sufficient time for discussion before the end of a class period.

After a great deal of research, we defined our own approach to this problem of communications. In Triggertapes, we would attempt to strike a responsive chord in young audiences through thought-provoking dramatic situations. We would produce a series of short, open-ended videotapes for classroom use. If the adolescent viewers could identify with the characters in a predicament and if they were not presented with a solution to the problem after becoming emotionally involved in the story, then they might be seduced into thought, discussion, and a search for information. They would have to supply their own endings or possible conclusions; the process might help them in making their own decisions.

This decision-making process is a critical feature in the maturation process of young adolescents, particularly in the area of sexuality and sexual activity. Teenagers want to make their own decisions but often lack the information and experience to do so. They receive so many contradictory messages about sexuality from parents, teachers, television, and popular music that they need to define their own feelings. Fourteen- and fifteen-year-olds are at a physical developmental level that allows them to participate in sexual activity but at a psychological level that makes it difficult to deal with the consequences realistically. We wanted our materials to help them realize what information they need in order to make their own decisions.

To achieve this goal, we needed to reach teenagers at their own level. Imposition of adult ideas and approaches would not allow the materials to trigger the emotional reaction needed to begin the learning and thinking process. To ensure that the tapes and films would strike a responsive chord, we devised an innovative developmental process that made the adolescents themselves a major source for the scripts. In the spring of 1979, we held drama workshops with urban teenagers who expressed their thoughts, feelings, questions, and reactions to various adolescent problem situations through role playing and improvisations. Each session began with simple warm-ups and drama games and then focused on typical situations in the areas of human sexuality, pregnancy prevention, and family relationships. The sessions were conducted in an open and nonthreatening manner. As rapport was established and the teenagers became more comfortable and involved, their responses and improvisations moved from superficial to more meaningful levels. During each session, time was given to discussion of the improvisations and alternative solutions to the situations presented.

Five scripts that incorporated the dramatic situations, conflicts, and questions that emerged from these sessions were then written. The first of these scripts, "Is That What You Want for Yourself?" is the story of Debby, a fifteen-year-old who thinks she may be pregnant. Her boyfriend, Tony, is sympathetic, but neither of them knows what to do. Debby's parents are not aware of the potential problem, but her father throws Tony out of the house when he finds him in Debby's room with the door closed, and her mother hits the roof when she discovers birth control pills hidden in a drawer. There are many loose ends left for the teenage audience in this tightly constructed script: What did Debby really want from this sexual relationship? Why didn't she use any one method of contraception properly? What are Tony's feelings toward her? What do you think of his friends' advice? Or of Debby's plan to move in with Tony and "make it on their own"? How will Debby's parents deal with the news of her pregnancy if she is pregnant? How do you feel about Debby's parents' relationship? If you were a parent, how would you have handled the situation? How would you react if you thought that you or your partner were pregnant?

To ensure that the program elicited the emotional involvement and reaction of adolescent viewers, we prepared a rough videotape of the script and did formative testing with groups of teenagers in a variety of settings in New York City, suburban Long Island, and New Jersey. We asked if any lines seemed corny, if the characters were believable. We found that while the father seemed strong and unpleasant to a number of adults, teenagers found him totally realistic. Tony and Debby were presented as nice teenagers who really cared for each other but were confused. Was their relationship believable and real? For the most part, the response was gratifying. The young people in the test audiences became involved with the characters and always protested when the tape abruptly ended without a resolution of the problem. At every testing session it was necessary to conduct a lengthy discussion of the story and its possible outcomes before exploring the ways in which the script and characters could be improved. In the end, there was only one major change. The story was originally written for a working-class black family. This presented a problem. Although the white students felt that the story cut across ethnic and racial backgrounds, many black students became defensive. Did the mother work only because she was black? Why were they so poor? Would a white family be shown as less than middle class, living in less than a suburban home? We decided to switch to a white lower-middle-class urban family.

The final script was filmed on location in Brooklyn. Learning Corporation of America now distributes the thirteen-minute film in both 16-mm and videocassette formats. A curriculum guide is available, and the reviews and feedback from educators have been enthusiastic. "Is That What You Want for Yourself?" reflects life. The parents are not role models. The two young people must find their own way, determine their own values, make their own decisions, and so must the teenage viewers. Even the toughest teenagers become involved in the story and are stimulated to think and to question. To this extent, we are gratified in the achievement of our goals.

The financial realities of running a small not-for-profit company with very little funding, however, were ever present and have checked our optimistic enthusiasm for producing the second script in the series, despite the success of the first. What follows is a detailed account of the financial obstacles we faced as nonprofit producers.

September 1978: Health Video Services is incorporated as a not-for-profit educational production company. Letters of inquiry are sent to thirty relevant foundations after consultation with the Foundation Center. Twenty-four are not interested. Five never respond. The secretary of Lavanburg Corner House is interested but noncommittal. We set out to learn how to write a proposal for foundation funding and are advised to follow government proposal guidelines so that we can use the same proposal for both foundations and government agencies.

November 1978: Well-researched eighty-five page proposal mailed to numerous foundations and many government agencies.

December 1978: Rejections dribble in after the holidays. Foundations with adolescent programs want to use the materials once they are produced. None will support a media project. The Ford Foundation sends a letter that their program officer describes as an "enthusiastic rejection."

January 1979: Trip to Washington, D.C. Meetings with aides of New York City congresspersons and senators. All are accessible, kindly, interested; none turn up sources for government funding that have not already been tried. Do receive letters of support to forward to the new Office of Adolescent Pregnancy. Proposal sent to New York State with great hopes. Get letters of support from all whom we saw in Washington, D.C. (Find out a year later that many jokes were made in Albany about this. One is supposed to get state officials' support rather than national leaders'. Overkill.) One bright spot: a grant from the Gold Foundation; it is small but pays for legal fees and phone.

February 1979: New York State turns down proposal. Although they had specifically requested curriculum development programs, they decide to fund only direct service projects with their limited social services budget. Three months of drama workshops at the Door are begun. Perhaps this will illustrate that project is alive. Officer at United Fund informs us that foundation program officers never read long proposals. Proposal version 2 is born and sent to additional foundations, both corporate and private. New York City Chapter of the March of Dimes grants funds to cover cost of scriptwriter and first five scripts.

June 1979: Scripts in hand, proposal version 3 is written. With mounting photocopying fees, foundations are reapproached, letters of inquiry and copies of scripts sent out. Many meetings. No funding.

October 1979: Metropolitan Life Foundation sponsors a reading of the first script to try to help raise production money. Luncheon is well attended by corporate and private foundation representatives.

Version 4 of a yet shorter proposal is prepared, which limits request to funding for the five extant scripts. First things first. This proposal sent to all who attended luncheon and many who did not. Preliminary responses good. Decisions await board meetings in January and March.

November 1979: The Federal Office of Adolescent Pregnancy has been inundated with proposals and has had its funds cut. Ten copies of government version of Triggertapes proposal mailed in to compete for remaining funds. Congressional support is secured.

New York State Department of Social Services issues request for proposal (RFP) that sounds promising. Definitely want creation of new media curriculum this time. We apply. Still optimistic.

January 1980: With $10,000 from Metropolitan Life Foundation and a small grant from the Gold Foundation, production of first script begins. Funds received will cover half of the production budget, with no staff salaries and reliance on friends in the industry for favors. Field testing of cassettes of Met Life reading begins. Minor dialogue changes made at suggestions of teenagers in test groups. Major change is move from black to white family.

February 1980: Take revised script to Learning Corporation of America. They like it but tell us the educational market is still basically 16-mm. Triggertapes becomes Triggertapes Films. Learning Corporation is noncommittal regarding distribution and wants to see a rough cut before making a decision. Realization begins to dawn that none of the corporations that attended the Met Life luncheon is going to contribute money. Ensuing corporate depression is offset by a surprise small grant by the Lavanburg Corner House, which we had approached a year earlier. Once again, New York State turns down the proposal. All media projects have been cut from their funding budget.

March 1980: Attend ACT Conference in Washington. Everyone is supportive and interested. No one offers money. Preproduction begins in New York. Director and cameraman hired. Two weeks are spent lost in Brooklyn to find locations. Location service is not in budget. Exteriors will be shot in Greenpoint, fifteen minutes out of the city, and interiors in the apartment of a friend of a neighbor of producer's Aunt Millie. Call-backs go well. The day after call-backs, the New York City transit strike begins.

April 1980: Numerous vehicles are rented to transport cast and crew as the strike continues. The first shooting day is the exterior at Greenpoint. Fifteen minutes of travel takes two hours as heavy rain complicates the strike. It is a horrible day, but the rushes are beautiful. Three hours after the final wrap, the strike ends.

Emergency phone calls are made to more foundations. Small discretionary grants made by the Astor Foundation, New York Community Trust, and the New York City Chapter of the March of Dimes cover overruns.

The rough cut looks more like a fine cut. We hold our corporate breaths as it is screened by Learning Corporation. They agree to distribute and to advance us enough money to cover finishing costs. Still no salaries, but at least the film will be seen.

July 1981: Posh Magno screening room is selected as the site of the joint Learning Corporation/Health Video Services premier of "Is That What You Want for Yourself?" Turnout is excellent and feedback is positive. The film will be on the New York City list of films recommended for purchase. Still no salaries. No royalties until advance is repaid. The search for funds to produce second script continues.

September 1981: New York's Metromedia station wants to use "Is That What You Want for Yourself?" for a school vacation special. The film will be combined with a follow-up discussion by a teenage studio audience. The program is canceled when Screen Actors Guild talent broadcast buy-out fees are beyond what the station can afford for a one-time daytime program.

New plan: efforts made to develop a series of dramas for commercial television about a variety of problems facing teenagers ranging from divorce and shoplifting to anorexia nervosa and sibling rivalry. All will use the Triggertapes original developmental sequence of drama workshop-script-field testing-production. Thus begins a new round of proposals, meetings, attempts to find funding—this time in the commercial arena.

Teenage Sex and TV

What They Want to Know

BETH WINSHIP

SOME ADULTS BELIEVE that today's adolescents already know everything about sex. Despite the sophisticated appearance and sexual ex-
perimenting of young teenagers, however, their letters to my column
reveal staggering ignorance and misinformation: "He told me I couldn't
get pregnant the very first time"; "How can I be pregnant? We only
had sex between my periods"; "I thought you couldn't get caught if
you did it standing up!"

Adolescents get very little education about sex, either at home or at
school, yet they feel enormous pressure from all sides to "get with it."
In 1979, one of every four girls had started sexual activity by the age
of fifteen, and by age nineteen, more than two-thirds of them were
having intercourse. One in every six babies born in this country has
a teenage mother.

To help adolescents avoid the negative consequences of sexual experimentation, we have to help them make wise decisions about having intercourse in the first place. Teenagers are not scared away from
sex out of fear of pregnancy or venereal disease. When adults tell
them to act responsibly, they interpret this as code words for, "Don't
do it." Teenagers think about sex in terms of what they feel at the
moment, what their partner is saying or wanting or doing, not what
may happen in nine months. We must prepare them for the situations
they will actually meet—in the back seat of a car, at the drive-in, or

* Beth Winship is the author of the *Boston Globe's* syndicated teenagers' advice
column, "Ask Beth."

in the empty house—and not talk only about the dangers of pregnancy and parenthood.

First of all, adolescents need to understand that some of the reasons they feel pressured into sexual activity are inappropriate, such as having sex to gain status, to rebel against parents, to win love, or to become popular. They need to be forewarned about common lines, such as, "You would if you loved me," or the one I hear so often, "He said he'll leave me if I don't say yes."

Young adolescents need to be warned about the pressures that traditional sex stereotypes put on them, like the myth that to score makes you a "real man," or the myth that a girl should do almost anything to please a male. They should be taught to recognize the false premise in the media message that to be sexy is to be successful.

Most students get some facts about reproduction in school, but sex to them is not a matter of reproduction, it's a matter of curiosity and excitement, who they are with, and how to act grown-up. They need information about infatuation, what sexual desire feels like, and the difference between love and lust.

They need the facts too. Contraceptives are widely available, but most teenagers don't know what to use or how to get them, privately and without embarrassment. They need to know that venereal disease doesn't happen only to other kids; "nice" kids get it too. They need to know that if they get pregnant, wise counseling is available to help them make the right decisions about abortion or keeping the baby. Ninety-four percent of teenaged girls who carry their babies to term are now keeping them, little understanding how crippling this is to the life of the young girl and to her child as well.

Television has enormous influence on children. Indeed, a lot of pressure for sex comes from TV's heavy emphasis on sexual material in much of the programming and in commercials as well. A cover on a recent issue of *People* magazine shows three teenaged girls with the headline, "Torrid Teens on the Soaps: With Sugar and Spice and Lots of Vice They're Luring the Younger Generation." Most television programs are not so blatantly out to corrupt adolescents, but the sex that does appear is almost uniformly seductive, furtive, out of wedlock, exploitive, or downright violent. It does not answer any of the questions that kids so plaintively write to me.

Good programs that address the issues of teenage sexuality honestly and sensitively can do so much to enlighten young people. Recently I watched three programs that show adolescents coping with pregnancy and in everyday life at home and at school. "The New Voice" is a new PBS series for adolescents that focuses on the students who work on a high school newspaper. In a two-part special on pregnancy, one of the student reporters discovers that her friend Gina is pregnant. She researches an article on teenage pregnancy, which shows that Gina's fear and shame and frustration are normal feelings for a young pregnant girl. Visiting a home for unwed mothers, the young reporter interviews teenage girls discussing how hard they found it to face the anger and disappointment of their parents and how difficult it was to decide among abortion, adoption, or keeping their baby. They had not realized how big an effect having a baby would have. They yearned to graduate, just like everyone else.

Unable to tell her parents or her boyfriend, Gina plans to drop out of school. Her boyfriend, Bernard, suspects there is a problem. His friends ask, "How do you know it's your kid?" and tell him not to get tied down. Only one boy understands Bernard's feeling of personal responsibility. Gina and Bernard finally confront the issue, first in anger, then constructively. Neither knows what to do. They discuss future plans for college, and, at the show's end, they resolve to tell their parents.

The strength of "The New Voice" is its honest portrayal of a pregnant high school girl. Peer reaction is vividly shown. It is clear how accidental pregnancy changes Gina's life. One of the strongest messages is the good relationship between Gina and Bernard and Bernard's belief that a boy is as responsible for accidental conception. A few boys will agree, but most still say, "She got herself into it; let her take care of it!"

Gina and Bernard are good actors but seem old to be high school students. It is essential that an adolescent audience identify with the actors if they are to take the message to heart. Also, Gina and Bernard are black, and it would be a shame to risk the impression that teenage pregnancy is a black problem. It is everybody's problem.

An opportunity was missed to give a clearer message about contraception, in connection with Gina's failure to protect herself. The ending is also weak. Will telling her parents really solve all of Gina's and Bernard's problems?

"Is That What You Want for Yoursef?" is a short, open-ended program for classroom use that chronicles the day a mother discovers contraceptive pills in her fifteen-year-old daughter's room. Debby, afraid that she might be pregnant, discusses the potential problem with her boyfriend. Debby tries to persuade him to get a job and find a place for them to live, but he says he wants to finish school. When they suspect that Debby might be pregnant, her parents are outraged. The father tells Debby's boyfriend, "Get outta' my house!" The mother, having just learned that her older daughter has been deserted by the father of her baby, asks Debby, "Is that what you want for yourself?" The frame freezes and the program ends with many tough questions left for classroom viewers to tackle.

This program presents accidental pregnancy as a calamity. It also gives a valuable message about a common misconception about birth control: Debby tells her boyfriend, "I only take the pill when we're going to do it." It highlights teenagers' ignorance about the actual issues involved in having a child or setting up housekeeping. It might have been still better if it had included some remedial information.

This is an Archie Bunker type of household but without the warmth. The mother copes only by yelling; the father is already full of beer when he arrives home and gets more vituperative. Little affection is apparent, which might serve to make viewers even more afraid to confront their parents.

"Schoolboy Father" is an ABC Afterschool Special about a boy who finds out his summer romance with Daisy has produced a baby. Daisy has put the child up for adoption, but Charles, raised by a divorced mother, is determined to raise his son himself. He talks his mother and the social worker into letting him have his baby on a trial basis. He soon finds baby care far too demanding. Charles becomes inattentive in class, late for work, careless, and preoccupied with worry. Having to miss a party is the last straw, and he sorrowfully returns the infant. Frivolous? Not really. Loneliness and isolation are two real threats to a school-age parent of either sex.

Daisy's anger about her pregnancy and Charles's ignorance about it are accurate glimpses of teenage responses. So is Daisy's reason for not using birth control: "I really liked you. I never thought I'd get pregnant." "Never thinking" is the underlying message in programs like these and is so necessary.

The weakness here is that the situation is not lifelike. Few sixteen-year-old boys have the motivation or the courage to try to raise a baby. Nor is the romantic image of paternity that is portrayed realistic. Although the baby cries and soils his diapers, by and large he is usually well behaved. Fortunately, the scenes of Charles at work and at school are believable and show how distracting parenting is for him.

One significant factor in this show is that a social worker is present. Daisy's reaction to giving up her baby is bitter, so bitter that it risks making adoption seem an impossible alternative. However, a more positive attitude is provided by the social worker. I wish she had not been presented, at first, as such a disagreeable woman, but in the end she proves sympathetic and supportive.

The presence of the social worker raises a fundamental issue that needs to be emphasized in all programs about adolescent sexuality: there is abundant help available to pregnant teenagers. No adolescent should have to make such heavy life choices alone. These shows could easily include a girl consulting with her counselor, going over the alternative solutions. It should also be possible to name local resources, or at least national referral agencies, such as Planned Parenthood.

These three programs have much to offer adolescents concerning the problems involved in accidental pregnancy at their age. Such TV programs will find an interested and absorbed audience. Teenagers I have talked to do watch them. Further shows could address the basic issues of deciding whether to have sex, how to get along socially if one decides against intercourse at this time, peer reactions, and so on.

The fate of a girl, not a boy, who keeps her baby must be explored. The current adolescent dream of having a sweet little baby like the ones in baby food advertisements must be explored. Other issues that could be aired are parent-teenage communication about sexuality, sex education programming in schools, community reactions, what happens to the children of teenage parents, teen marriage, and the effect of drugs and alcohol on sexual desire and behavior. Television can reflect the way life really is. It can be a potent way to show adolescents the realities in their lives as maturing, sexual people.

Contraceptive Advertising

HARRIET PILPEL AND EVE PAUL

THE IDEA PROMOTED by Anthony Comstock in the later nineteenth century that contraceptives are "obscene" or "immoral" is obsolete. Today contraception is widely accepted as a legal, necessary, and indeed a government-sponsored and supported form of health care. It is therefore astonishing that the National Association of Broadcasters Code still contains what can only be described as an archaic prohibition of commercial messages about contraception.

One argument in support of the code prohibition is that television reaches children and adolescents. This argument, however, reflects an ostrich-like attitude about teenage sexuality. It has been wrongly assumed that youngsters who do not know how to protect themselves from pregnancy will not engage in sexual activity. Statistics prove the folly of this view.

U.S. teenage childbearing rates are among the world's highest. Of the 21 million young people in the United States between the ages of fifteen and nineteen, more than half—7 million young men and 4 million young women—have had sexual intercourse. Each year, over a million women in this age group become pregnant. Of the 540,000

---

* Harriet F. Pilpel is a senior partner of the Greenbaum, Wolff, and Ernst law firm, general counsel of Planned Parenthood Federation of America, Inc., and one of the general counsels of the American Civil Liberties Union.

Eve W. Paul is vice president for legal affairs of Planned Parenthood Federation of America, Inc.

pregnancies each year of unmarried fifteen- to nineteen-year-olds, 90 percent are unintentional.

How are young people to learn about effective means of contraception? Pervasive Victorian attitudes in our society make it impossible for a high proportion of teenagers to discuss this subject freely and comfortably with their parents. Many parents would like to delegate this responsibility to professional educators.

Television and radio have an important role to play in reaching adolescents. To a limited extent, both television and radio already contribute to the education of teenagers about sexual responsibility through programs such as "James at 16," "Facts about Girls" and "Facts about Boys," public service announcements of agencies where contraceptive services are available, and messages about where venereal disease diagnosis and treatment can be obtained. Recently there have been isolated instances of contraceptive advertising on radio and television. However, the industry ban on commercial messages remains a significant restraint on the dissemination of vital health information.

We are not primarily addressing here the advertising of prescription drugs and devices, since these are ordinarily not advertised to the general public, although we see no reason why an advertising campaign could not be developed around prescription contraceptive drugs and devices—for example, based on the theme, "When you go to your doctor for contraceptive advice, ask about our product." Nor are we specifically concerned here with the issue of parental consent to medical services for minors, since that question generally does not arise until a health professional actually dispenses a prescribed contraceptive to a patient. (Many state laws permit minors to consent to their own contraceptive care, and we believe that an absolute requirement of parental consent for contraceptive care of all minors would be held unconstitutional, as have absolute requirements of parental consent for abortion.) Our concern here is the dissemination of information about nonprescription contraceptives—condoms, foams, and jellies— the so-called barrier methods. These methods do not require a doctor's prescription because their use entails no health hazards.

The controversy over the NAB Code restriction on the advertising of nonprescription contraceptives in many ways is similar to the controversy that arose over a New York State statute that prohibited the dispensing of nonprescription contraceptives to persons under sixteen. A case challenging this statute as unconstitutional came before the United States Supreme Court in 1977: *Carey* v. *Population Services International*. In that case, the state of New York conceded that physicians in the state could legally prescribe contraceptives for their minor patients, but the state argued that it had a legitimate interest in preventing the sale to minors under sixteen of over-the-counter contraceptives.

Seven justices agreed that the statute was an unconstitutional interference with minors' privacy rights to decide to use contraceptives. The reasoning of the various justices reaching this result differed, however, and they wrote four separate opinions setting forth their views. The plurality opinion was delivered by Justice William Brennan, joined by Justices Blackmun, Marshall, and Stewart. Justice Brennan began by reaffirming the principle, clearly established in 1976 in a case involving abortion, that minors, like adults, have a constitutionally protected right to decide, free of state interference, whether or when to bear or beget a child. He went on to say that state restrictions inhibiting privacy rights of minors are valid only if they serve "any significant state interest . . . that is not present in the case of an adult."

Since the Supreme Court had already ruled that a state may not impose a blanket prohibition, or even a blanket requirement, of parental consent, on the choice of a minor to terminate her pregnancy, Justice Brennan held that a blanket prohibition against the distribution of over-the-counter contraceptives to minors under sixteen was not permissible. A state's interests in protecting the health of the pregnant minor and in protecting potential life, he said, are clearly more involved in the decision to have an abortion than in the decision to use a nonhazardous contraceptive.

New York State argued that significant state interests were served by restricting young minors' access to nonprescription contraceptives because their free availability would lead to increased sexual activity among the young, in violation of New York's policy to discourage such behavior. The state conceded, however, that "there is no evidence that teenage extramarital activity increased in proportion to the availability of contraceptives."

While Justice Brennan did not argue with the assumption that the state may regulate the sexual behavior of minors, he said it would be unreasonable if the state "prescribed pregnancy and the birth of an unwanted child (or the physical and psychological dangers of an abortion) as punishment for fornication." In a concurring opinion, Justice John Paul Stevens concluded that "an attempt to persuade by inflicting harm on the listener is an unacceptable means of conveying a message that is otherwise legitimate. . . . It is as though a state decided to dramatize its disapproval of motorcycles by forbidding the use of safety helmets."

The decisions of the Court in constitutional cases like the *Carey* case apply only to government and government agencies, and the National Association of Broadcasters is not a government agency in the usual sense of those words. It has been argued, however, that because broadcasters are governmentally licensed to monopolize a segment of the publicly owned airwaves, constitutional guarantees do apply to them. That question has not been finally resolved. The code ban on contraceptive advertising might well be challenged on the same constitutional grounds as the challenge to the New York statute in the *Carey* case. The issue to be decided would be similar: shall young people have access to information about over-the-counter contraceptives (as well as to the contraceptives themselves), or must those millions who are already sexually active be compelled to seek medical advice (which many of them are unwilling or unable to do) or continue to risk pregnancy with the choice of abortion or an unwanted, out-of-wedlock birth?

Closely related is the issue of sexually transmitted diseases. All states and the District of Columbia now have laws enabling physicians and health agencies to diagnose and treat minors for venereal disease without parental consent. Nevertheless, sexually transmitted diseases have reached epidemic proportions among teenagers in the United States. Condoms are the one contraceptive method that is also highly effective in preventing the transmission of venereal disease. Yet the code prohibition of advertising of condoms in effect prevents this vital information from reaching millions of teenagers.

There is an enormous public health need for greatly increased dissemination of information to young people about contraception and sexually transmitted diseases. Young people also need to know where to obtain prescription methods of contraception. These needs can be adequately filled only by a combination of public service announcements and commercial advertising.

At a time when television programming includes a great deal of sexual content, the industry is clearly failing to meet its responsibility to function "in the public interest, convenience and necessity" when it bans contraceptive and venereal disease advertising needed by millions of young people. This ban may well be unconstitutional; it also may be legally vulnerable on antitrust law grounds as an unreasonabe combination in restraint of trade. The ban represents a failure to satisfy the public health needs of the teenage population. Unless it is lifted, the ban is likely to cause litigation that will inevitably lead to recognition even by the NAB that contraceptives and venereal disease advice and supplies for minors are safe, legal, necessary, and here to stay.

Resources, Chapter Five

Baizerman, Michael; Thompson, Jacquelyn; and Stafford-White, Kimata. "An Old, Young Friend: Adolescent Prostitution." *Children Today* 8:5 (September–October 1979): 20.

Bell, Ruth, et al. *Changing Bodies, Changing Lives: A Book for Teens on Sex and Relationships*. New York: Random House, 1981.

CBS. "The Body Human," "Facts for Boys." November 6, 1980. A half-hour information special with host Ken Howard who talks to teenage boys about their evolving sexuality.

————. "The Body Human," "The Facts for Girls." October 7, 1980. A half-hour special for young people that focuses on a girl's journey from childhood to adolescence.

————. "CBS Reports," "Boys and Girls Together." February 6, 1980. A one-hour news special examining the increase in teenage sexual activity, sex education, and the influence of adult attitudes on teenagers.

————. "30 Minutes," "Teen-age Parents and Teen Tycoons." January 13, 1978. Produced by Joel Heller.

Cannon-Bonventure, Kristina, and Kahn, Janet. "Interviews with Adolescent Parents: Looking at Their Needs." *Children Today* 8:5 (September–October 1979): 17.

Capital Cities Communications. "Capital Cities Family Specials," "When Jenny When." January–February 1979. A twenty-five minute dramatic presentation of the dilemma two teenagers confront in dealing with sex and the importance that their peers attach to it. Produced by Paulist Productions.

Card, Josefina J., and Wise, Lauress L. "Teenage Mothers and Teenage Fathers: The Impact of Early Childbearing on the Parents' Personal and Professional Lives." *Family Planning Perspectives* 10:4 (1978): 190–205.

Children as Parents: A Progress Report on a Study of Childbearing and Childrearing among 12- to 15-Year-Olds. New York: Child Welfare League of America, 1981.

Chilman, Catherine S. *Adolescent Sexuality in a Changing American Society: Social and Psychological Perspectives*. DHEW Pub. (NIH) 79-1426. Bethesda, Md.: National Institute of Health and Human Development, Center for Population Research, 1979.

Fox, Greer Litton. "The Family's Influence on Adolescent Sexual Behavior." *Children Today* 8:3 (May–June 1979): 21.

Gordon, Sol. *You Would If You Loved Me*. Fayetteville, N.Y.: Ed-U-Press, 1979.

Gordon, Sol; Scales, Peter; and Everly, Kathleen. *The Sexual Adolescent: Communicating with Teenagers about Sex*. Belmont, Calif.: Duxbury Press, 1979.

KQED. "Up & Coming," "A Little Romance." January 7, 14, 1981. A two-part segment about two teenage girls who discover they are pregnant, wrestle with their parents and with their own feelings, and try to make the right decisions. Produced by Avon Kirkland. Broadcast over PBS.

Lindsay, Jeanne Warren. *Teens Parenting: The Challenge of Babies and Toddlers.* Buena Park, Calif.: Morning Glory Press, 1981.

Moore, Kristin; Hofferth, Sandra L.; and Wertheimer, Richard. "Teenage Motherhood: Its Social and Economic Costs." *Children Today* 8:5 (September–October 1979): 12.

Multimedia Program Productions. "Young People's Specials," "I'm Soooo Ugly." February 1981. A half-hour drama about a girl who, convinced that she is homely, learns an important lesson about true beauty after an especially disappointing Valentine's Day.

Paul, Eve; Pilpel, Harriet; and Wechster, N. F. "Pregnancy, Teenagers and the Law, 1976." *Family Planning Perspectives* 8:1 (1976): 16–21.

Paulist Productions. "A Friend in Deed." A twenty-eight-minute drama about a homely teenage girl who volunteers to wheel an injured basketball player to and from class and soon falls in love with him. She discovers the true meaning of friendship when he introduces her to his girlfriend.

Phelps, Edith B. "Adolescent Sexuality." *Common Focus* 1:5 (July 1979).

Prerost, Frank J. "Developmental Aspects of Adolescent Sexuality as Reflected in Reactions to Sexually Explicit Humor." *Psychology Reports* 46:2 (April 1980): 543–548.

Roberts, Elizabeth J. *Television and Sexual Learning in Childhood.* Rockville, Md.: National Institute of Mental Health, 1980.

Roberts, Elizabeth J.; Kline, David K.; and Gagnon, John H. *Family Life and Sexual Learning.* Cambridge, Mass.: Population Education, 1978.

Scales, Peter, and Gordon, Sol. "Preparing Today's Youth for Tomorrow's Family." *Impact* 1:2 (1979): 3–7.

Silverman, L. Theresa; Sprafkin, Joyce N.; and Rubinstein, Eli A. *Sex on Television: A Content Analysis of the 1977–78 Prime Time Programs.* Stony Brook, N.Y.: Brookdale International Institute of Applied Studies in the Mental Health Sciences, 1978.

Teenage Pregnancy: The Problem That Hasn't Gone Away. New York: Alan Guttmacher Institute, 1981.

Tierney, Joan D. "Facing Up to Fantasy: Using 'Sooner or Later' to Open Communication between Parents and Children." *Teachers Guides to Television* 11:2 (Spring 1979): 10–11.

WTTW/Chicago Public Television. "Guess Who's Pregnant?—An Update." June 11, 1980. A one-hour documentary about the increasing incidence of teenage pregnancy, the status of sex education, and services available to pregnant teens.

Organizations

American Association of Sex Educators, Counselors, and Therapists, 5010 Wisconsin Avenue, N.W., Washington, D.C. 20016.

Center for Population Options, 2031 Florida Avenue, N.W., Washington, D.C. 20009.

Council for Sex Information and Education, Box 23088, Washington, D.C. 20024.

Institute for Family Research and Education, Syracuse University, 760 Ostrom Avenue, Syracuse, N.Y. 13210.

National Sex Forum (Sex Education), 1523 Franklin Street, San Francisco, Calif. 94109.

Office of Adolescent Pregnancy Programs, DHEW, 4144 North 71st Street, Milwaukee, Wis. 53216.

Planned Parenthood Federation of America, 810 7th Avenue, New York, N.Y. 10019.

Project on Human Sexual Development, 27 Longfellow Hall, 13 Appian Way, Cambridge, Mass. 12137.

Sex Information and Education Council of the United States (SIECUS), 34 Fifth Avenue, New York, N.Y. 10021.

Young Adult Fiction

Blume, Judy. *Are You There, God? It's Me, Margaret.* Twelve-year-old Margaret and her friends are preoccupied with their physical maturity. New York: Bradbury Press, 1970.

———. *Then Again, Maybe I Won't.* A story of a young boy entering into puberty. New York: Bradbury Press, 1973.

Donovan, John. *I'll Get There, It'll Be Worth the Trip.* A teenage boy who fears he has homosexual tendencies when he and his friend engage in some affectionate play. New York: Harper & Row, 1969.

Holland, Isabelle. *The Man Without a Face.* Story of a fatherless fourteen-year-old boy who first learns about love from a man who becomes his teacher and his friend. New York: Lippincott, 1972.

LeRoy, Gen. *Cold Feet.* Coming-of-age novel about a young girl who is terrified of sexual maturity, is unwilling to embrace traditional femininity, and is on the edge of a full-blown identity crisis. New York: Harper & Row, 1979.

Mazer, Norma Fox. *Up in Seth's Room.* Story of a fifteen-year-old girls' first love and the mounting sexual pressures from her friends. New York: Delacorte, 1979.

Pascal, Francine. *My First Love & Other Disasters.* Kaleidoscopic complexities of a fifteen-year-old girls' first love. New York: Viking, 1979.

Smith, Doris Buchannan. *Dreams and Drummers.* The story of a fourteen-year-old girl who tries to cope with her first romance. New York: Crowell Junior Books, 1978.

Zindel, Paul. *My Darling, My Hamburger.* Novel dealing with abortion, premarital sex, and interpersonal relationships. New York: Harper & Row, 1979.

6 Youth in Crisis

There is a crack in the Earth
And I have fallen in.
Down in the darkness, where I have never been.
People are looking, staring at me;
I lie here and wonder what do they see?
Shall I be here forever
I can not climb back
Rotting and dying in this horrible crack
Am I alive or am I dead.
Oh God, who will save me from
This crack in my head?

Sixteen-year-old female suicide,
Illinois institution

Adolescents and Alcohol

A Case Study, "The Late Great Me"

DANIEL WILSON

"THE LATE GREAT ME: Story of a Teenage Alcoholic" follows a fifteen-year-old girl's road into alcoholism and her long and difficult journey back. It is not so rare a story as one might think. There are an estimated 3.3 million teenagers in our society who are problem drinkers.

Young people are under tremendous pressures from parents, peers, and even from themselves to be "hip," to be the best athlete, to have the highest grades, to be attractive, to have a boyfriend or girlfriend, or just to be something other than what they think they are. Struggling with these demands, teenagers can easily fall prey to alcohol, which seems to make things easier but in the end leaves them with an even bigger problem.

"The Late Great Me" is the story of a teenager, who, desperate for attention and popularity, is easily talked into trying a little wine by a boy who seems interested in her. She becomes increasingly dependent on the false sense of confidence that alcohol provides and, as a result, sacrifices many of the things and people she cares most about.

"The Late Great Me" was the first ninety-minute "ABC Afterschool Special." It started in the fall of 1978 when Daniel Wilson Productions was asked by the ABC television network to develop a program dealing with teenage alcoholism. Our objective was to produce a film that would inform the adult audience as well as the youth audience of the seriousness and dangers of the problem on a level they both could relate to.

* Daniel Wilson is executive producer of Daniel Wilson Productions.

First we looked for an existing piece of material—a book, an un-published manuscript, or a newspaper or magazine article—that would lend itself to being translated into a screenplay for television. Many books and articles were researched and read by our story editor, Phyllis Minoff, and ultimately rejected. One book, however, stood out. *The Late Great Me* by Sandra Scoppettone was chosen as the basis for the screenplay because of its sensitivity in handling the issue of teenage alcoholism and its strong character development.

ABC finally agreed that *The Late Great Me* had such an informa-tive and compelling story to tell that the normal sixty-minute time period should be expanded to ninety minutes. From the network's point of view, this decision was not taken lightly because expanding time periods requires them to go to each affiliate throughout the United States—over 200—and seek their permission to do so. Networks do not like to do this unless there is an overwhelming and compelling reason to do so. It creates problems for them because local stations never want to relinquish time to networks that they program them-selves. Expanding to ninety minutes was a difficult decision for ABC to make and was done due to the significance attached to the theme of teenage alcoholism.

Having convinced the network to undertake the project, we set out to start the development process: optioning the property and hiring a television writer to adapt that property into a meaningful drama. After buying the rights to the book, we discussed who would be the best choice to write and adapt the material. We decided on Jan Hart-man, who worked with us in the past. We met with him and discussed an approach, and he agreed to undertake the project. He was excited by its potential and also by the fact that it was going to be the first ninety-minute Afterschool Special produced in the seven-year history of the series. We agreed on March 30 as the deadline for the first draft of the script; this gave him a rather comfortable three months.

Hartman worked out his story outline and discussed it with Minoff. Some alterations were made, and then we met with the ABC program staff to get their approval so Hartman could begin writing. During this time he met with various research organizations and sources who deal with the treatment of teenage alcoholics. Among these were John Severinghaus of the Smither's Rehabilitation Center at Roosevelt Hos-pital in New York City and Scott Hicks, director of the Teenage Alco-holic Rehabilitation Program in Troy, New York. It was important that the necessary factual information about teenage alcoholism be woven into the dramatic fabric of the screenplay. The film needed to be realistic. We relied on the experts particularly in the scenes of Alcoholics Anonymous meetings; they advised us on how the meetings are run, what people say, and how an alcoholic teenager might react at a meeting.

Before we knew it, March 30 was upon us and Hartman delivered his first draft on time. This point in the process is always the most trauma-filled for me. I never know whether or not the idea will be translated to script form in a way that allows the project to go forward toward a successful conclusion. In this case, because it was the first ninety-minute special done in the series, there was even more pressure on the project.

The first draft of the screenplay had some problems but essentially worked. We met with the network representatives and worked out revisions so Hartman could proceed to a second draft. Normally that would take four to six weeks. For a variety of reasons, however, the second draft was not delivered until the end of June.

ABC had planned this project as the season's premiere of the Afterschool Special series; it was to be aired in September. We were already running a little late for this. I figured we needed a minimum of ninety days from the time the network bought the film to delivery of the finished film. The network likes to have a film delivered at least two to three weeks in advance of its air date so that it can be advertised, screened for critics, and generally promoted.

At this point some friction surfaced between the network and me. "They" were a little concerned that it was taking so long to develop the property and consequently could no longer schedule it effectively as the premiere show. Also, some of their stations resisted clearing ninety minutes as opposed to the customary sixty. It has been said in jest that "owning an individual television station license in the United States is comparable to having a license to steal." While this may be a slight exaggeration, I believe that in many cases the profit motive does overmotivate local television stations. Consequently, they do not like to give up thirty minutes where they are getting full revenue unless they have to. And because networks don't like to make waves with their stations, I felt that not enough effort was being put forth by the ABC stations clearance department to convince the recalcitrant stations that it was in their best interest to clear for this specific program.

The friction developed into a major confrontation. The network said that because we couldn't deliver the show on time for the Afterschool Special premiere, they couldn't get the stations to clear ninety minutes. Consequently they suggested that we cut the script to sixty minutes. I refused. My response was not capricious. The writer, the story editor, and I had spent months preparing a script that dramatically displayed the disintegration that takes place in a teenage girl due to her dependence on alcohol. It was a carefully crafted story that needed every moment to convey the attitudes, character development, physical and mental disintegration, and subsequent recovery.

We wanted to take in everything the book dealt with, and ninety minutes was the only way to do it. It was vital to develop Geri's character completely in order for the drama to be realistic, to hit home. The development of alcoholism is subtle, and we wanted to show this slow progression over several months. A major problem with alcoholics is how difficult it is for them to accept the fact that they have a problem and how long it takes them to do something about it. This is particularly true for young people, and we wanted to show this struggle in Geri. I felt it was impossible to cut one-third of the story and be faithful to the integrity and intent of the project. I did not want to do the production if it could not be done well.

At this point, the network had not ordered the film. Their financial expense was simply the development costs. If they had chosen not to go ahead, the writer would, of course, have been paid for his screenplay. However, there would have been no fees paid to Daniel Wilson Productions for the six months of work that had been put into the project.

There were many meetings. Finally it was agreed that we would go ahead with the ninety-minute program as originally planned. Also the script would undergo another draft to take into account network changes. At this time, ABC still had not ordered the film; this was not to come until the end of July. In the meantime, we had to prepare for production by lining up a director and the technical staff that would implement the filming when and if the network gave us the go-ahead. In mid-July I assigned Linda Marmelstein, a staff producer, to the project. She read the screenplay, and we decided to send it to a director who had done a considerable amount of work for us in the past, but he declined. I was told later that he had thought it was the worst script he had ever read. We then sent it to another director who was mildly interested, but who for personal reasons and commitments, could not do it on the schedule necessary. We then sent it to a third director, Anthony Lover, and to this day I'm eternally grateful that we were turned down by the other two. Tony Lover became one of the primary creative forces in making "The Late Great Me" the success that it was.

We still could not commit him to the project, however, because we did not have the go-ahead from ABC. Finally, on August 15, we were told we could start production. Jan Hartman was working on his final polishing of the script, which was to be delivered on August 28; a casting director, Phyllis Kasha, was hired, and we began auditioning actors for the principal roles. We intended to begin shooting on September 10. We were given an air date of November 14, which meant we would be delivering very close to the wire. After what seemed to be countless hours of screening actors for each of the roles, we decided on Maia Danziger as the young girl and Charlie Lang as her boyfriend.

While the casting process was going on, we were involved in the normal preproduction process: hiring technicians, camera and sound directors, art directors, costume designers, caterers—all those many integral occupations that eventually coalesce into a functioning production unit—and finding locations that gave us the visual feeling and texture of the story.

The principal photography began as scheduled on September 10, 1979. It did not end on schedule, however. We ran three days over, and most of those days were very long ones, extending into fifteen or sixteen hours. We were over budget. A series of circumstances all culminated in the fact that the material simply needed more time. The budgets overruns were significant. Because of the tension that existed between me and the network, we had no expectation that ABC would help financially. From our best projection it looked like we were going to be $100,000 to $125,000 over budget. I had to make an evaluation while we were still shooting whether to cut back to minimize our losses. After considerable thought, I decided not to; I believed that the people who were entrusted with the making of the film could not do the job they had set out to do if they lacked the financial support. I also felt that the material was of such significance that it was important for us to make a film that would be lasting and meaningful.

We finished shooting on October 1 and immediately went into postproduction. We wanted to deliver the finished film to the network at least seven days in advance of the November 14 air date. That period is somewhat of a blur in my mind. All I can remember is a lot of long days and nights, seven days a week, until we finally delivered the program to ABC on November 10. Even with that schedule we had to cut short the laboratory process by transferring to tape rather than delivering on film.

We were all pleased with the end result and felt that we had treated the material with a seriousness of purpose and had created a most compelling drama that the audience would stay with. We scheduled a screening and a small reception in New York. The results of this screening were truly rewarding. The hundred people gathered were enthusiastic, and each of us involved felt good.

The true test of a television program is not how it looks in a screening room, however, but how effective it is in reaching and holding its audience when seen on TV. I don't think any of us was quite prepared for the tremendous response received by the program when it was aired on November 14, 1979. It achieved one of the highest ratings ever recorded in daytime television. The program was extremely well reviewed by critics, and most important, it seemed to have a significant impact on its audience. The first indication of that impact was the number of phone calls and letters that poured into ABC immediately after the showing. The second indication of impact was the intense interest it aroused among educational institutions around the country. Schools, museums, libraries, alcohol and drug programs, church groups, and youth groups have all requested copies of the film. "The Late Great Me" is not in distribution, however, because we have not yet found a distributor who will do the film in its entirety; they all want to cut it to sixty minutes. We refuse. We have also been trying to get the film on prime time but have had no luck. It's a shame that we cannot get this important film (in my mind, the best we have ever done) where it belongs, where more people—parents and youth —can see it.

Was it worth it? Sure it was; it was a program that had a definite effect on its audience. Would we do it again? Probably, but I would hope with less of an adversary relationship with the network.

Drug Abuse

A Case Study, "Stoned"

FRANK DOELGER

THE CHALLENGE in making "Stoned" was to produce a show that honestly deals with the dangers inherent in the use of drugs—in this case, marijuana. If our targeted audience had been parents, teachers, or anyone else predisposed to believe the very worst about the effects of marijuana, our task would have been considerably easier. The members of that audience, most of whom would probably have had little direct experience with drugs, would look at whatever facts we wished to present on the dangers of drug use as a reconfirmation of what they already knew. And, to a certain extent, that audience would be willing to accept our authority as producers and the authority of our consultants as informed and concerned spokespersons on the subject.

But the audience was the teenagers of America—an audience with a very different attitude and a very different set of experiences. The smugness of adolescence—that feeling we all had as teenagers that only the sixteen- and seventeen-year-olds of the world really know what's going on—would automatically predispose the audience to disbelieve what the adult world had to say. Since most teenagers have grown up in a world in which drugs are increasingly commonplace and have either used drugs themselves or have a lot of friends who have, their experience is very direct. They know firsthand about the use of marijuana and would be critical of any show that purported to

* Frank Doelger is director, Children's Programs, Highgate Pictures, a division of Learning Corporation of America.

172

be about an experience that is so much a part of their lives. So if "Stoned" were to succeed, we knew it was essential to tailor the show to the particular prejudices and experience of this audience.

This consideration influenced our decisions about what information to present in the show and how to present it. Much to the credit of the programming executives at ABC and the network's Department of Broadcast Standards and Practices, a decision was made to limit the amount of factual information on marijuana actually presented and to present those facts with as much restraint as possible. Rather than swamp the audience with all the information that is beginning to be available on the effects of marijuana, we chose just a few of the most recent findings (the suggested links between marijuana and chromosome damage, sterility in males, and possible increase in the occurrence of birth defects). These facts were presented in a section of the show in which a young teacher—who admits to having been a heavy user of marijuana—talks to his class in a familiar, casual manner. He doesn't try to scare the students, nor does he come on like a commanding authority figure. He simply presents what he has heard or read and tries to reach the class as best he can.

There were a lot of young people, of course, whom he couldn't reach. Some of the students in the show reacted with cynicism and even a certain amount of hostility toward the teacher. But what the teacher tried to do—and what the program as a whole was designed to accomplish—was to give his students something to think about. And whether that information was believed, we hoped it would at least raise some questions in our young viewers' minds as to the possible physical consequences of the use of marijuana.

So that the show did not appear too preachy, the psychological and behavioral dangers that many consider inherent in the use of marijuana were downplayed. Of all the things we could have said, of all the points we could have made, we looked for the one that we hoped would hit home most directly:

Mr. David (addressing his class): Pot made things seem better when they really weren't. Once I was feeling very low. My folks decided to split up. It hit me very hard. I smoked, and temporarily my problems would disappear. But I was just running away from the problem. When the pot wore off, my parents were still getting divorced.

The key was to acknowledge what every young viewer knew and what too many concerned critics of marijuana fail to admit in their treatment of the subject. Dope can make things a lot better—and can also be a lot of fun. There are several scenes in the show in which the teenagers get stoned and have a good time. Problems disappear, everything seems enormously amusing, no one has a worry in the world—for as long as the high lasts. Because of the honesty about that aspect of marijuana, the flip side of the show's argument—that escaping from a problem is not going to solve it—seemed more credible.

We tried to bring the same degree of honesty and restraint to the larger story as well. "Stoned" is a show about how one teenager's life changes once he becomes part of a group of heavy users of marijuana. The boy goes from being a loner to being a member of a tightly knit group of friends, from thinking he is a goon to thinking he is a much more popular and with-it kid, from freezing when girls approach him to being totally at ease with everyone.

The other side to the story is that he loses everything that is really interesting about himself in his obsession with always being stoned. But it was necessary to address all of the myths about what drugs, or being part of a drug-dependent crowd, promise before the darker side of the story could be shown. We wanted to avoid the mistake so many people make in dealing with the issue of drugs: suggesting that the most unbelievable evils befall an individual the moment he or she smokes the first joint.

Painting an honest picture was only half the battle. The real trick was how to get teenagers to watch. Fortunately, the rationale behind the ABC Afterschool Specials supplied the answer: make the show as entertaining as possible. It sounds like an obvious approach, but, unfortunately, it is one many programmers for children seem to forget. The seriousness of the problems of adolescence does not mean that it is inappropriate to entertain while teaching.

The ABC Afterschool Specials, NBC Special Treats, and CBS Afternoon Playhouse specials have tackled sensitive subjects and have managed to attract sizable audiences who seem to respond well to this combination of teaching and entertainment. "Stoned" not only said something very special about the possible dangers of drug use but also told a moving story about a teenage boy who loses sight of what is important in his life in his eagerness to find a group of friends. It was our hope that the personal story of the protagonist would give the audience as much to think about as all the information presented on the specific dangers of drugs.

Pressured by his friends, a boy gets involved in criminal actions and gets caught in "Going Along," a Multimedia Young People's Special.

Lisa is one of the thousands of young people who have found life too hard to bear and have killed themselves. Hers is one of the stories told in "Young Suicide . . . Too Sad to Live." Photo courtesy of WBZ, Boston.

Bill (James Bozian) dances with his senior prom date and then grieves at her funeral when she is killed in a drunk driving accident in "The Last Prom," a Multimedia Young People's Special.

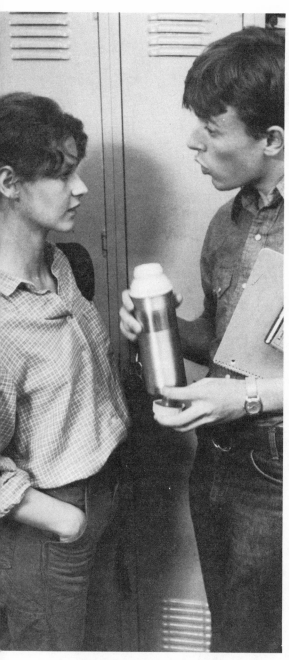

Afraid of losing the one boy who has been interested in her, Geri (Maia Danziger) is persuaded to start drinking, in "The Late Great Me," an ABC Afterschool Special. Photo courtesy of Daniel Wilson Productions, Inc.

Self-conscious in social situations, Geri seeks solace in alcohol in "The Late Great Me," an ABC Afterschool Special. Photo courtesy of Daniel Wilson Productions, Inc.

Geri's family is angry and confused about her drinking problem, in "The Late Great Me," an ABC Afterschool Special. Photo courtesy of Daniel Wilson Productions, Inc.

A lonely teenager (Scott Baio, left) feels better about himself when he is stoned until he almost loses his adored older brother in "Stoned," an ABC Afterschool Special. Photo courtesy of Learning Corporation of America/Highgate Pictures.

A student gang leader (Jackie Earle Haley) tries to intimidate his school's basketball coach (Le Tari) in "Chicken," a Capital Cities Family Special. Photo courtesy of Paulist Productions.

A troubled high school senior (Brad Reardon) contemplates suicide in "A Family of Winners," a Capital Cities Family Special. Photo courtesy of Paulist Productions.

Young people who are habital users of marijuana talk frankly about it in NBC's "Reading, Writing, and Reefer." Photo courtesy of the National Broadcasting Company, Inc.

Suicide & Depression

"Too Sad to Live"

PAMELA CANTOR

FREDDIE PRINZE, the twenty-two-year-old television personality, shocked friends and fans in 1977 when he shot himself in the head. Prinze was not alone; he was just better known than the other estimated 4,000 young people between the ages of fifteen and twenty-four who killed themselves that year.[1]

Suicide is not the privilege of rich and famous celebrities, nor is it confined to television scripts. It is a problem of serious proportions claiming an increasing number of lives each year. Suicide is the second cause of death among young people.[2] The increase in the rates of suicide during recent years is even more alarming. Among males ages twenty to twenty-nine, the rates doubled in the ten-year period between 1960 and 1970. Among females in the same age range, the rates quadrupled, and the rates for teenagers of both sexes, ages fourteen to nineteen went up 200 times.[3] The rates for the ten-year period of 1970 to 1980 were even higher. Current research indicates that attempted suicide among adolescents in the United States could run as high as 400,000 to 500,000 in 1981.[4] That means that approximately fifty-seven American children and adolescents attempt suicide every hour. It is not readily apparent why the suicide rate is increasing at such an alarming rate. One contributing factor might be the greater

* Pamela Cantor, Ph.D., is a developmental and clinical psychologist in private practice, a director of the American Association of Suicidology, and the Governor's appointee to the Statewide Advisory Board of the Office for Children, State of Massachusetts.

acceptance of cultural violence both within and outside the family. The inability to control aggression generates a steady rise in violent crimes in the United States.[5] Murders are occurring with increased frequency. In Boston, a murder occurs approximately once every four days.[6] Battered child cases are also on the increase, with about 2 million to 4 million cases reported in 1980.[7] We can only guess how many more remain unreported. Violence within the family leads children to be violent toward others and toward themselves. Aggression turned toward others increases the murder rate, and aggression turned inward accelerates the suicide rate.

A second factor may be the tendency of parents to spend less and less time with their children and to relegate child care to other agencies. Cross-cultural studies show that parents in the United States spend less time with their children than do parents of almost any other nation in the world.[8] A home where both parents are emotionally as well as physically available to the children is the exception rather than the rule. A study conducted in Boston showed that among intact families, the average time that fathers spend with their children is about thirty-seven seconds per day.[9] It is my experience that among adolescents who have attempted suicide, fathers are more often the absent or inaccessible parent.[10]

The dissolution of the family may be a third factor. One of two marriages ends in divorce, and one of three or four of these divorces involves children. When a divorce occurs, one parent, most frequently the male parent, becomes absent from the home. A child experiences a physically absent or emotionally inaccessible parent as rejection, and rejection inevitably breeds resentment and hostility. It is often difficult for the young person to differentiate between the intellectual concept, "Dad and Mom do not get along, and Dad and Mom do not choose to live together, but they both still love me," and the emotional concept, "Dad or Mom do not love me enough to stay with me." Children and adolescents often view divorce as a voluntary abandonment.[11] The child or adolescent may express feelings of abandonment outwardly through violence or inwardly through self-injury.

The most critical time for a divorce to occur with regard to the development of suicidal tendencies, particularly for a young female, is during adolescence.[12] During adolescence a young woman is most in need of a father with whom to test her femininity, from whom she can learn to delay gratification and tolerate frustration, and with whom she can formulate an identity.[13] Divorce and the subsequent absence of a father appears to affect adolescent women more than adolescent men, and women comprise 90 percent of all youthful suicide attempts.[14]

Another factor contributing to high suicide rates may be cultural frustration. Growing up and growing old hold little value. A prerequisite to growing up in our society is going to school. The time period committed to attending school is increasing, while the rewards and employment opportunities attached to the completion of schooling are decreasing. In our culture we have seen a delay in the commitment to marriage and, at the same time, an increase in the incidence of divorce. We have seen pointless and devastating wars along with the increased plausibility of total annihilation. Growing old holds minimal value. The elderly are often sent to old-age homes and too often are regarded by younger people as useless citizens because they are no longer economically productive.

Erik Erikson has said that the United States has done a fine job of augmenting the development of the human being with two notable exceptions: the periods of adolescence and old age. He said that if dignity were accorded to our elders, there would be a dignity and purpose to life perceived by our young.[15] Today young people too frequently witness depression among their parents and grandparents and a life without meaning among their peers. These trends in our society have produced an enormous number of angry, depressed, and suicidal young people. If we ignore these facts we can expect that crimes of violence, both murder and self-murder, will continue to increase, that family life will continue to deteriorate, and that the incidence of adolescents who feel dead while living will continue to rise.

What many of these young people feel can be summarized by the word *loss*—the loss of the love of their families, the loss of control over their own lives, the loss of identity, the loss of self-worth, the loss of meaning in life. Many young people ask themselves the question, "Why should I continue to live when I already feel dead?" Those who attempt or commit suicide often truly do not wish to die. They wish to change life in order to make it worth living.

The factors that contribute to the increasing suicide rate are both individual and societal in nature, and the solutions must also assume a dual focus. What can be done to counteract the tendency toward the acceptance of violence in our culture? Can we alter the private affairs of a family? How do we decrease the divorce rate? If a divorce does occur, how do we ensure that both parents will provide continued support and caring for their offspring? How do we modify cultural frustration, increase respect and utility for the elderly, eliminate war? How do we give life meaning? And perhaps, of equal importance, how do we teach children constructive methods of coping with stress early in life so that they do not resort to suicidal behaviors as a solution for problems? Children must be taught not to avoid crises but to meet crises intelligently, to live with the dilemma, and to seek help from others when necessary.

Violence has become an American way of life. It is endemic in our society, partially because of a child-rearing philosophy that encourages the use of physical force in disciplining children. The abuse of children and adolescents, tolerated by society as a whole by permitting children to grow up under conditions of severe deprivation, is a serious social problem. If the issues are societal, then the conventional treatment derived from the view of violence as an individual pathology might aid some children and their families, but it would not prevent or even significantly reduce the overall incidence of violence inflicted against oneself or others. Thus we must change the prevailing child-rearing philosophy that sanctions physical force in disciplining children, and we must eliminate financial and emotional poverty, which allows so many children to be at risk for self-abuse and neglect. Regardless of whether the violent adolescent is seen as a victim of his or her culture or of intrafamilial problems, changes in both areas would help decrease the number of terrified children and adolescents who are the source of our most heartbreaking statistics.

American society has often been described as child centered. Yet we spend little time with our children, and it appears that the national trend may be to spend less and less time. Women are entering the work force and men are not choosing to stay home to replace them. The family needs two incomes, women wish to have a life outside the home, and men still define themselves through their work. The new trend is to support child care agencies and encourage support systems outside the family.

One possible solution to this economic and social problem might be a return to an extended kinship system. At its best, the nuclear family offers a child two adult sources of support. At its worst, the system offers the child one source (or no sources) of support. The extended kinship family may offer the child aunts, uncles, grandparents, and peers as sources of affection, attention, and solace in times of need. In the extended family, the role models are numerous and the child's options are increased. It may be possible that Western culture has sacrificed a great deal in the stability of the life of the growing child for the sake of independence and mobility; which are so highly prized in the American tradition.

The divorce rate may not be subject to societal recommendations, but clearly the legal conditions of divorce could be altered to accommodate an understanding of the critical importance of a father to an adolescent girl.

A healthy old age requires a society that accords respect and support for the elderly and an individual whose life has given meaning to human striving. This is what Erikson meant when he said, "Healthy children will not fear life if their elders have integrity enough not to fear death."[16] Jobs that have personal and social meaning could be provided for the elder members of society, such as caring for children in institutions, caring for foster children, or being adoptive grandparents. Institutions for children could be built next to homes for the elderly so that each might use the resources of the other. The hope is that as people grow older, their lives might grow in meaning.

These implications have dealt with societal antecedents of suicidal behavior. Suggestions for primary prevention must focus on the practical rather than the theoretical. The most emphatic guideline in approaching the problem is that anyone trying to help a young person who is suicidal needs to pay attention and listen. The individual in psychological pain is trying to communicate his or her needs to someone. If the requests are not heard, or are ignored as they may have been in the past, the person may resort to a suicide attempt. Paying attention implies both concern and respect for the individual rather than a dismissal of the suicidal act as a gesture for attention. Attention may be just what the individual wants, but if it is necessary to go to these lengths to achieve it, then it is the desperation and the inability to cope with stress that must be noticed rather than the manipulative aspects of the act.

It is generally not wise to reassure an individual that "everything will be all right" without understanding the dynamics of the problem. Realistic acknowledgment of feelings is more helpful than offering glib reassurance.

It is worth noting that although many young people do not succeed in killing themselves when they intend to, many do succeed in killing themselves when they did not have that intention. It is therefore important to attend to every suicidal gesture, no matter how inconsequential it may seem.

It is best to avoid any diminution of self-esteem when someone is depressed. It is wise to be available and to give personal attention.

If you know someone is suicidal it is advisable to make a prompt appointment for that person with a professional. It may be even necessary to transport the young person, who may have summoned all his available energy to tell you of his or her pain.

Most emphatically, a person who seems suicidal should be asked directly, "Are you thinking about suicide?" The person needs to know that their confidant is able to talk about suicide directly and will not avoid the issue or condemn him or her for a sincere expression of feelings. The adolescent needs to know that it is not abnormal to think about suicide, that many young persons do so on a fairly frequent basis, and that your desire is to help the person to verbalize feelings in order to avoid the need to act on them.[17] The greatest life-saving device that anyone can offer, professionally or personally, is to talk about the suicidal feelings directly and be openly receptive to communication. Much more damage can be done by not talking about suicide than by talking about it. You will never give someone the idea of suicide by mentioning the word, but you may be able to keep him or her from suicide by listening.

Detection

Thinking about suicide is not a disease but rather a symptom of depression. Although there are few precise indications of exactly when a depressed adolescent will turn to suicide, there are indications of when an adolescent is experiencing severe difficulty. One is any sudden change in behavior. An adolescent who had taken pride in school work might suddenly begin to neglect academics. A young woman who had enjoyed a gregarious personality might withdraw from friends and begin to spend the majority of her time alone. A young woman who has had a boyfriend might sever the relationship and become socially isolated. A fight with a boyfriend or girlfriend is frequently the final precipitating factor in a suicide attempt. A young man may begin giving away his prized possessions in much the same manner as an adult might prepare a last will and testament. There may be sleeping difficulties or excessive fatigue, with subsequent sleeping used as an escape. There may be an increase in drinking or in the use of drugs or a sudden lack of interest in appearance or in sex. A number of signs are considered hallmarks of adult depression: lethargy, loss of interest in one's surroundings, pessimism, or a narrowed field of comprehension. But there also may be actions that adults might consider the antithesis of a depressive reaction. The adolescent may be constantly "up," frantically on the go, unable to remain at home for more than moments at a time. This is not a flight into health but rather an indication of the adolescent's extreme unhappiness and inability to tolerate being alone.

One other paradox is worth nothing: suicide and suicide attempts are most likely to occur at precisely the time when it appears that the depression is lifting. There are two theories that try to account for this. The first states that only when a young person is no longer depressed will he or she have the psychological strength to carry out a plan of suicide. The second states that the decision to force the ultimate control over life is the very factor that causes the renewed optimism. In either case it is difficult to remember this, particularly when the adolescent appears to take a new interest in life.

To regard every adolescent who is agitated or depressed as suicidal is to overreact. It is preferable, however, to institute some preventive measures rather than to find someone on the verge of suicide because no one has been sufficiently perceptive to hear the calls of distress. If an adolescent calls for help and no one listens, the individual may take another step and go a little further toward ending his or her life until, hopefully, someone does listen—in time.

"Young Suicide: Too Sad to Live"*

In the fall of 1978, WBZ-TV Boston was approached by the Massachusetts Committee for Children and Youth, an organization of mental health professionals, with the startling facts on the incidence of adolescent suicide. The station agreed to make a major commitment to programming that would inform viewers on this vital topic.

"Impact" is a monthly station effort in which all of WBZ's local programs devote part of one week to an issue of broad concern to the community. The centerpiece of this effort is a prime-time public affairs special. "Young Suicide: Too Sad to Live" was one Impact special.

The producer of "Young Suicide," Francine Achbar, contacted me to ask for information on the topic of adolescent suicide, assistance in script writing and editing, and to appear on the program as commentator. Our goal was to produce intimate documentary portraits of several different types of young people who tried to kill themselves. We wanted to create a program that would concentrate on the firsthand feelings and experiences of suicidal young people, in addition to providing competent advice to youngsters and parents on how to identify and cope with adolescent depression.

Finding subjects to profile turned out to be the most difficult task

* I would like to thank Francine Achbar, producer of "Impact" public affairs specials for WBZ-TV for her valuable contributions to this section.

of the production. As most television producers know, finding authoritative individuals to talk about a problem poses little difficulty; finding people who have actually experienced the problem and who are willing to talk openly about the issue is much harder. The issue of suicide is particularly sensitive. No one wants to talk. Everyone involved— youngsters, parents, friends, and counselors—may feel guilt, shame, or remorse. Psychiatric hospitals, clinics, and college mental health departments were understandably unwilling to divulge names of patients, but they were also unwilling to contact former patients to ask if they would be interested in participating in the program.

WBZ placed advertisements in one of Boston's weekly newspapers asking for young people who had attempted suicide to participate in a film project with no money involved. This produced several angry, disturbed young candidates who wanted to "get back" at their parents by appearing on TV. The producer interviewed these people and, after consultation, decided not to use them. They were unwilling to have their parents on the program, and there were questions regarding their present emotional maturity and the TV station's liability for accusations that could result from their appearances.

Ultimately, young people were found through the Massachusetts Committee for Children and Youth, Project Omega, a grief-assistance arm of the Samaritans (the suicide prevention group), and individual professionals. Because of these organizations' credibility and professional contacts, they were able to vouch for the integrity of the program and persuade parents and mental health workers to help find youngsters.

After two months, stories on four Boston-area young people were developed: Lisa, twenty-four, a talented artist; Pam, sixteen, a high school student; Michael, twenty, a landscape worker; and Carole, twenty-three, a graduate student. Lisa and Michael were now dead. Pam and Carole had not been successful with their suicide attempts; they were alive.

The next problem was how to produce complete portraits of these youngsters, particularly the two who were now dead. In the cases of Lisa and Michael, the pieces were constructed through on-camera interviews with parents, friends, and therapists who had worked with them. Lisa had left many letters to her best friend and a diary describing her depressions over many years. Her friend and her mother agreed to read from these writings on camera.

Through the interviews, letters, and scripted narrative, we endeavored to film reconstructions of what the young people were seeing and feeling as their depressions deepened to bring them to the intense pain that led to their suicide attempts. The on-air presentation included a discussion of the symptoms and behaviors each of the young people exhibited that are common in depressed youngsters and how they and their families can deal with them.

WBZ aired a follow-up program after the documentary that included a panel of Boston-area teenagers reacting to the portraits presented in the documentary and discussing depression with several experts from area mental health institutions.

The response to "Young Suicide" was positive and substantial. In addition to the several hundred phone calls generated by the program, the station has received many requests for tapes from mental health institutions and teaching hospitals to be used for training and discussion with staff and patients. The program won the United Press International Broadcast award for Best Public Service program of 1979, as well as the Associated Press Broadcast award for best enterprise reporting in a documentary.

"Young Suicide," which took fifteen weeks to produce, was staffed by a producer, associate producer, intern, cinematographer-editor, and sound person.

I would suggest that programs for adolescents be aimed at adolescents themselves and involve more than a statement of the facts. Since television is the most extensive experience all American children and adolescents share, it is an ideal medium through which to address the issues of adolescent suicide.

News broadcasts could offer information succinctly, with vignettes or with the reporter providing warning signs and resources available in a short time and with a minimal amount of money.

Talk shows offer a format that lends itself to the development and discussion of ideas at greater length. Producers of talk shows usually include young people who have attempted suicide. It would also be of value to interview adolescents who would discuss their suicidal thoughts and talk about why they have not attempted suicide.

A third avenue is the full-length documentary, such as "Young Suicide," or the full-length feature film. Both ventures require a greater commitment of resources but are clearly worthwhile. The dramatization of actual case presentations, having actors taking the part of suicidal young persons, is ideal, if the cost is not prohibitive. In this manner adolescents could be given information that might enable them to admit to their own feelings. Viewing an actual therapy session, or a dramatized one, might help to dispel young viewers' fears of seeking professional help.

I strongly recommend that other producers commit time to this major health problem and work in conjunction with a professional organization or a professional consultant who can be called upon for advice on how to handle potentially explosive psychological situations. One such situation occurred on "The Paul Benzaquin Show," a live talk show in Boston. A young woman called during the on-the-air telephone segment to say that she was about to commit suicide. She had made the beds, cleaned the house, left lunches for the children, and was now preparing to kill herself. That television show, the producer's and the host's willingness to turn their air time to efforts to locate the caller, saved the woman's life. Television can have a big impact.

References

1. Michele Kamisher, "Why Suicide," *Boston Globe*, April 2, 1978, p. 28.

2. Pamela C. Cantor, "Personality and Status Characteristics of the Female Youthful Suicide Attempter" (Ph.D. diss., Columbia University, 1972), p. 97.

3. Peter Bizen, "When a Youth Takes His Life," *Boston Globe*, January 6, 1973, p. 9.

4. Pamela C. Cantor, "The Effects of Youthful Suicide on the Family," *Psychiatric Opinion* 12:6 (July 1975): 6.

5. *Toward a National Policy for Children and Families* (Washington, D.C.: National Academy of Sciences, 1976), chaps. 2, 6.

6. Uniform Crime Reporting Unit, *Crime in Massachusetts, 1979* (Boston: Massachusetts Department of Public Safety, 1980).

7. E. F. Steele and C. B. Pollack, "A Psychiatric Study of Parents Who Abuse Infants and Small Children," in R. E. Helfer and C. H. Kempe, eds., *The Battered Child* (Chicago: University of Chicago Press, 1968).

8. *Toward a National Policy*, chaps. 2, 6; E. C. Devereux, U. Bronfenbrenner, and R. R. Rogers, "Child Rearing in England and the United States: A Cross-National Comparison," *Journal of Marriage and the Family* 31 (1969): 257–270.

9. F. Rebelsky and C. Hanks, "Fathers' Verbal Interaction with Infants in the First Three Months of Life," *Child Development* 31 (1969): 63–68.

10. Pamela C. Cantor, "The Adolescent Attempter: Sex, Sibling Position and Family Constellation," *Life-Threatening Behavior* 2:4 (Winter 1972): 252–261.

11. Pamela C. Cantor, "Suicide and Attempted Suicide Among Students: Problem, Prediction and Prevention," in Pamela Cantor, ed. *Understanding A Child's World: Readings in Infancy Through Adolescence* (New York: McGraw-Hill, 1977), pp. 433–443.

12. Pamela C. Cantor, "Birth Order and Parental Absence as Predisposing Factors in Suicide Attempts Among Youthful Females" (Address presented to the American Association of Suicidology, Los Angeles, April 1, 1976).

13. A. Gorceix, "Le Suicide, L'Adolescence et le poison," *Semaine des Hospitaux de Paris* 39 (1963): 2371–2374; R. Gould, "Suicide Problems in Children and Adolescents," *American Journal of Psychotherapy* 19 (1965): 228–246; J. M. Toolan, "Suicide and Suicide Attempts in Children and Adolescents," *American Journal of Psychiatry* 118 (1962): 709–714; N. Zimbacca, "Suicide in Adolescents," *Concours Medical* 87 (1965): 4991–4997.

14. B. H. Balser and J. F. Masterson, "Suicide in Adolescents," *American Journal of Psychiatry* 116 (1959): 400–404.

15. Erik H. Erikson, *Childhood and Society* (New York: W. W. Norton, 1950), p. 269.

16. Ibid.

17. Pamela C. Cantor, "Frequency of Suicidal Thought and Self-Destructive Behavior Among Females," *Suicide and Life-Threatening Behavior* 6:2 (1976): 92–100.

Juvenile Crime

GEORGE COMSTOCK

THE QUESTION of the contribution of television to juvenile crime and violence has a noisy history. Since the 1950s, congressional committees have investigated programming practices on the assumption that media portrayals of crime and violence might encourage similar behavior on the part of young viewers. Increasingly, social and behavioral scientists have come to believe that the empirical evidence from experiments and surveys of adolescent behavior suggests some truth to this view, while broadcasters insistently argue that the evidence is inconclusive. Most people associated with the making of television and film drama would prefer to ignore the question, either on the grounds that the answer might prompt some restraint on freedom of expression, a concern in which they are joined by many civil libertarians, or on the grounds that it might necessitate a change in the way they do business. Yet the question has been posed for decades and will never be silenced while more than 40 percent of those arrested for serious crimes are juveniles.

Despite the loudness of the argument, a quiet resolution is possible. First, it is necessary to distinguish between rights and responsible behavior. Second, it should be recognized that there are two questions: whether television and film portrayals of crime and violence should be held suspect, and through what particular features they might have undesirable influence.

* George Comstock, Ph.D., is S.I. Newhouse Professor of public communications at Syracuse University. He is the senior author of *Television and Human Behavior* and the author of *Television in America*.

The courts generally have held form and content inseparable in regard to First Amendment protection, and film and television drama is protected speech. Although its unrestrained reach into the home may sometimes subject broadcasting to court-imposed limits that other forms of communication escape (as in cases relating to obscenity, for example), on the whole television enjoys the same freedom as any other medium. Whatever one may conclude about the relationship between violent entertainment and juvenile violence, freedom of expression remains. This does not preclude the possibility that the Federal Communications Commission could weigh the quantity of violent programming against a station's public service record at license-renewal time. This would allow the FCC to discourage violent programs without intruding directly into the way a particular drama unfolds.

Legal right established, there remains the question of responsibility. When restraint on communication has been at issue, one concept frequently introduced by the courts has been that of redeeming social value. Most violent television and film dramas would have no difficulty meeting such a test, and in many cases the violence arguably is central to content on which the social value rests. The responsible position, however, is to confine violence in television and film to those instances in which it is absolutely dictated by moral and aesthetic purpose and not merely justifiable because it is part of a whole that cannot be deemed wholly worthless.

It has not been proven that television and film violence increase juvenile crime and violence, and given the complexity of human behavior, it is not likely to be. The proper query is whether the available evidence tends to discredit or give credence to such a possibility, and the answer is that the evidence makes such a connection seem probable.

When science is asked a question difficult or impossible to address directly, its solution is to address lesser approximations that are within its means. The answer to the initial question, although necessarily probabilistic, will be the answer that is consistent with the findings science can reach. For example, we might design an experiment comparing the behavior of young people who have just witnessed a violent television or film portrayal with the behavior of those who have not. This has been done dozens of times, and the results have been consistent: those who saw the violent portrayal subsequently expressed a greater degree of punitiveness or aggressiveness against another person than those who did not. We might also design an experiment in which we observe whether children imitate the acts they have just seen on television or film. This too has been done dozens of times, and the results also have been consistent: those who saw an example of violent behavior behaved more frequently in a manner just like what they had seen than those who did not see the violent portrayal. None of these experiments demonstrates an influence on crime, but they do demonstrate that exposure to television and film portrayals can affect behavior, and the behavior effected is of the type that could readily figure in criminal actions.

While these experiments have shown that violent portrayal can influence behavior within the context of an experiment, they have not told us much about everyday behavior. After all, an experiment is an artificial experience, abnormal in time frame and setting. In an experiment a person might display behavior that he or she would suppress in real life, where such actions could lead to punishment, retaliations, and social disapproval. The next question, then, is whether aggressiveness and the viewing of violent programming tend to go together in real life. Scientists would reply by collecting data on the television-viewing habits of teenagers through self-report and data on their aggressive behavior from their peers. This has been done a number of times, and in a majority of the instances there has been a significant positive correlation between the two. Teenagers who viewed greater amounts of violent television programming were in fact more aggressive in everyday behavior than those who did not.

One might suspect that this correlation is caused by the fact that teenagers who are more aggressive prefer entertainment that is more violent. This did not prove to explain the observed correlation, however. Other possible explanations were that both the television viewing and the aggressive behavior were associated with some other factor, such as doing poorly in school, feeling deeply frustrated, or coming from a household low in socioeconomic status. No such factor could be found. Although these alternative explanations may hold true for thousands of young people, they did not on average explain why teenagers who regularly viewed more violent television actually behaved more aggressively. In the earlier instances in which this association between television viewing and behavior was observed, the aggressiveness did not cross the threshold of criminal behavior.

In a recent investigation encompassing 1,500 teenage males in London, the aggressive behavior associated with television viewing extended to criminal behavior.

Correlation alone, of course, does not lead to an inference of causation any more than it should dictate a verdict of guilty. However, the evidence clearly dictates concern about the possible contribution of violent television and film portrayals to juvenile crime and violence.

The experiments demonstrate the possibility of causation; the surveys of everyday behavior corroborate that aggressiveness and exposure to violent television are associated in real life and that this aggressiveness extends to criminal behavior. These surveys do not turn up an alternative explanation. Thus the evidence suggests that the viewing of violent drama contributes to juvenile violence.

These examinations of mass media and aggression have helped identify some of the issues that deserve special attention by writers, directors, and producers. Television and film violence appear to be able to affect behavior by three broad means. First, observing others behave can change the inclination of the viewer to behave in a similar way. Aggressiveness may not be affected as frequently or as widely as social mannerisms, and criminal and violent behavior may be only rarely affected, but the principle is the same: observation is a means of learning ways to behave.

Second, for a young viewer, a vicarious experience through a television or film portrayal may change the meaning of an act, an object, a set of circumstances, or another person, just as a real-life experience could. A television portrayal may suggest that a brutal or vicious act can lead to money, fame, admiration, or a position of leadership. It may suggest that a household tool or appliance can be employed as a weapon. Or it may suggest that physical confrontation is the normal way of resolving conflict. In real life, an act of vengeance may be suppressed out of the fear that it will be scorned by friends and, if brutal enough, by the public at large. A television portrayal may change a young viewer's mind about the likelihood of retribution. A portrayal may also make an act previously unthinkable in certain circumstances seem more plausible by presenting it in those circumstances—such as in a classroom or a neighborhood grocery.

Third, because a television or film portrayal can leave a young viewer feeling excited or tense, it may precipitate behavior that would not otherwise occur.

Responsible film and television producers should exercise care in the treatment of certain elements of storytelling. I offer some suggestions:

1. Criminal and violent acts should not be rewarded by social approval, sexual conquest, or material gain, and if possible they should be punished. Punishment in the end is not necessarily sufficient; sometimes it is important to avoid a chain of earlier successes that lead the viewer to rewrite the ending internally.

2. Bitter and ruthless conflict between persons and groups should not be portrayed as the ordinary state of affairs.

3. Mass murders and the elimination of large groups of people should not be portrayed in a way that suggests human life is of low value.

4. Families, gangs, and clubs should not be depicted as shifting from tightly knit, loyal groups to divided and violently opposing forces without care to avoid the message that bonds promise little human security.

5. Extreme and excessive violence courts the risk of exaggerating the level of response appropriate to the offending act as well as the risk of leaving the viewer unduly stimulated.

6. Do not be afraid to depict violence as having painful and sometimes horrifying consequences for the victim and for those around him or her. Sanitized violence suggests that consequences are negligible and encourages the portrayed behavior.

7. As often as possible, show that violence and crime draws the scorn of others.

8. Characters that commit violence and crime should not be consistently attractive. Neither should they resemble typical young viewers, for this encourages viewers to identify with the character and model their behavior after the violent behavior shown.

9. Violence should not always appear justified by prior events because the belief that violence is appropriate in a certain situation implies that it holds social approval.

10. Be careful when portraying violence in realistic circumstances that a young viewer may encounter when he or she leaves the television set or theater, for the effect may be to make violent action relevant in surroundings that formerly elicited noncombative behavior.

11. In a fictional drama, convey that the violent events are part of a story and not an accurate account of real events. Fact is more likely to be taken as a model for behavior than fiction.

The Wild Bunch was a film foolishly shredded by network scissors, for the violent episodes that are strung like pearls on a string between its opening and closing frames occur far outside the realm of viewer experience. *Star Wars* and *The Empire Strikes Back*, like all other science fiction, enjoy the same liberty. *The Warriors*, on the other hand, was likely to have incited violence between members of rival gangs who saw it. This movie featured brutal violence, stylized and without emotional consequence; real life New York City as a setting; weapons common to gang fights; a stimulating, arousing experience; and an example of gangs at war. *Fuzz* had much the same characteristics. A person who would allow the torching of sleeping tramps to be shown in *Fuzz* while cutting gunfire from *The Wild Bunch* is attuned neither to psychology nor film. *Death Wish* and *Dirty Harry* both espouse vigilante behavior, but the latter had the saving grace of placing its hero in circumstances immensely distant from those of its audience. *Death Wish* had a justifiably aggrieved, highly attractive man disposing of one young criminal after another, each not too different from the people one would see each day in any big city. The author of the novel upon which the film was based, Brian Garfield, displayed both insight and honor in urging, futilely, that it not be broadcast on network television. *Easy Rider*, in contrast, is a stunning preachment against violence, for the audience is subjected to the appalling loss, in a manner in no way attractive or admirable, of the very people through whom they have vicariously achieved so much pleasure.

Taxi Driver, except for the double ending that made the psychotic killer a New York hero, would seem to be a perfect example of a brutally violent movie that is not likely to encourage violent behavior. The violence in this film is distasteful, the consequences ghastly, and the perpetrator beyond admiration or perception as resembling the viewer. That the movie may have influenced the thinking of the accused assailant of President Reagan on March 30, 1981, however, emphasizes the fact that violent entertainment can be powerful, and whatever the intentions of the film, it may entail grave risks.

Psychology offers producers cautionary advice of a more general nature. First, neither Nielsen ratings nor audience reactions are enhanced by interpersonal physical conflict when action is already at an attention-holding level; violence per se is not a key to popularity. Second, when a point is to be made, it should have a weight in the telling of the tale appropriate to its importance, or it will be lost and the opposite of what is intended may be communicated. Every story of racial conflict, for example, carries the risk that what will be conveyed is not the possibility of harmonious resolution, tolerance, and the like but examples of discord that may be emulated. Third, when conveying a message, a visual portrayal as well as a verbal statement should be employed, for the two together enhance the likelihood that a young viewer will get the point. Here the basic principle of television and filmmaking is in accord with psychology: show what you have to say.

Resources, Chapter Six

"ABC Afterschool Specials," "The Late Great Me." November 14, 1979. A ninety-minute drama about a teenage girl's dependence on alcohol to gain acceptance and self-confidence, and her long and difficult fight against the trap of alcoholism. Produced by Daniel Wilson.

ABC. "Afterschool Special," "She Drinks a Little." September 23, 1981. A sixty-minute drama about a teenage girl who is trying to cope with her mother's alcoholism. Produced by Martin Tahse.

———. "Friday Night Movie," "A Last Cry for Help." January 19, 1979. A two-hour drama about a seemingly model teenage girl who, unable to cope with everyday problems, is driven to a suicide attempt.

Belson, William A. *Television Violence and the Adolescent Boy.* Lexington, Mass.: Lexington Books, 1978.

CBS. "Afternoon Playhouse," "The House That Half-Jack Built." January 3, 1980. A one-hour drama about a lonely thirteen-year-old boy who experiments with drugs to gain acceptance. Produced by Half Jack, Inc., in association with Scholastic Productions.

———. "The Boy Who Drank Too Much." February 6, 1980. A two-hour drama about the tortured existence of a talented high school hockey player who is caught up in the throes of alcoholism. Produced by MTM Enterprises.

———. "30 Minutes," "Drug-Busting." November 10, 1979. A two-part report on drugs, schools, and law enforcement. Produced by Christopher Glenn.

Comstock, George. *Television in America.* Beverly Hills, Calif.: Sage Publications, 1980.

Comstock, George, and Rubinstein, Eli A., eds. *Television and Social Behavior,* vol. 3: *Television and Adolescent Agressiveness.* Rockville, Md.: National Institute of Mental Health, DHEW, 1972.

Comstock, George, et al. *Television and Human Behavior.* New York: Columbia University Press, 1978.

Edgar, Patricia. *Children and Screen Violence.* St. Lucia, Australia: University of Queensland Press, 1977.

Hamburg, B., and Hamburg, D. "Becoming Mature." *World Health* (December 1976): 12.

Johnson, Nicholas. "The Booze Tube." *Access,* June 14, 1976, p. 5.

McEwen, William J., and Hanneman, Gerhard J. "The Depiction of Drug Use in Television Programming." *Journal of Drug Education* 4:3 (Fall 1974): 281–294.

Miller, Walter B. *Violence by Youth Gangs and Youth Groups as a Crime Problem in Major American Cities.* Washington, D.C.: U.S. Government Printing Office, 1977.

Multimedia Program Productions. "Young People's Specials," "Goin' Along." April 1980. A half-hour drama about a teenage boy who is pressured by his peers into using pot, then into pranks and petty thefts, and finally to join in a robbery.

————. "Young People's Specials," "The Last Prom." May 1980. A half-hour drama about four teenagers who are involved in a fatal car wreck while drinking the night of their prom. Study Guide available. Produced by Metromedia Productions, Inc., 140 West Ninth Street, Cincinnati, Ohio 45202.

National Institute of Drug Abuse. *For Parents Only: What You Need to Know About Marijuana.* Washington, D.C.: U.S. Government Printing Office, DHEW, 1980.

NBC. "Death Penalty." January 22, 1980. A two-hour dramatic special about the relationship between a concerned psychologist and a hardened inner-city teenager convicted of murder and awaiting sentencing. Produced by Brockway Productions.

————. "Quincy," "No Way to Treat a Flower." September 20, 1979. Quincy discovers that a marijuana-related chemical, colchicine, is responsible for the death of a teenager.

————. "NBC Special Treat," "NBC Reports: Reading, Writing and Reefer." April 17, 1979. A one-hour special presentation documenting the startling increase in the use of marijuana by the nation's youth and its effect on their lives. Produced by NBC News.

Office of Education and the National Institute on Alcohol Abuse and Alcoholism. "Jackson Junior High." A series of four fifteen-minute films and related curriculum materials for grades five through eight on the responsible use of alcohol. Available from National Audiovisual Center, General Services Administration, Order Section, Washington, D.C. 20409.

Paulist Productions. "A Family of Winners." A twenty-eight minute drama about a high school boy of high-achieving parents who seems to have everything going for him until one by one his accomplishments fall apart and he contemplates suicide.

Rarick, David L.; Townsend, James E.; and Boyd, Douglas A. "Adolescent Perception of Police: Actual and as Depicted in TV Drama." *Journalism Quarterly* 50 N3 (1973): 438–446.

Roloff, Michael E., and Greenberg, Bradley S. "Resolving Conflict: Methods Used by TV Characters and Teenage Viewers." *Journal of Broadcasting* 23:3 (Summer 1979): 285–300.

Rothenberg, Michael B. "Effect of Television Violence on Children and Youth." *Journal of American Medical Association*, December 8, 1975, pp. 1043–1046.

WBZ-TV, Boston. "Young Suicide . . . Too Sad to Live." April 27, 1979. A one-hour documentary presentation of portraits of four young people who tried to kill themselves; two succeeded.

Organizations

American Association of Suicidology, 2459 South Ash Street, Denver, Colo. 80222.

Coalition for Children and Youth, 815 15th Street, N.W., Bowan Building, Washington, D.C. 20037.

Metro-Help/National Runaway Switchboard, 2210 North Halsted, Chicago, Ill. 60614.

National Council on Alcoholism, 733 Third Avenue, New York, N.Y. 10017.

National Family Council Against Drug Abuse, 315 W. 57th Street, New York, N.Y. 10019.

Young Adult Fiction

Arrick, Fran. *Tunnel Vision.* Story about a bright, popular fifteen-year-old boy who commits suicide, leaving behind his family and friends who struggle to understand his death. Scarsdale, N.Y.: Bradbury Press, 1980.

Childress, Alice. *A Hero Ain't Nothin But a Sandwich.* Story of a thirteen-year-old heroine addict in Harlem who cannot accept the fact that someone cares about him. New York: Coward, McCann & Geohegan, 1973.

Eyerly, Jeannette. *See Dave Run.* The story of a fifteen-year-old runaway told episodically by more than twenty people who know or encounter him. A portrait of a frustrated teenager that explores his feelings, his fortunes, and his misfortunes. Philadelphia: Lippincott Junior Books, 1978.

Harrah, Michael. *First Offender.* A thirteen-year-old boy ends up in a juvenile detention center after a street fight got out of hand. New York: Philomel Books, 1980.

Hinton, S. E. *The Outsiders.* Story of the loyalty and understanding among the members of a tough, lower-class gang. New York: Viking, 1967.

Neufeld, John. *Lisa Bright and Dark.* Story of a young girl whose parents refuse to recognize her growing madness. Only her teenage friends are there to help her. New York: New American Library, 1970.

Strasser, Todd. *Angel Dust Blues.* Story about a high school senior who is arrested for selling angel dust to a police officer. New York: Dell, Laurel-Leaf, 1979.

7 Radio

For "Moose"

A song just played on my radio.
Yes, I know, an innocent mistake.
Some unknowing DJ just didn't realize.
But I heard it in my ears and can see it in my eyes,
That haunting memory
Ripping my insides; lighting a fire
   I extinguished many years before.
I guess you never believed
Everything I told you then.
The night was cruel and gave no comfort
To our tears.
It's over now, I know, but
That song just played on my radio.

Karyn Chater
Camden-Rockport High School

Rock, Radio, and Responsibility

MICHAEL HIRSCH

LET'S BE PRACTICAL: a general manager at a major market radio station has only two basic concerns: making money and keeping the station's license. All else, including—or especially—serving the public interest, convenience, and necessity as defined by citizen watchdogs who never had to meet a payroll, pales by comparison.

It's not that the managers are bad folks or callous or venal; it's how they perceive their job, responsibility, and future. And it is very clear to them that all three will be determined by the ownership, not the public. And the ownership is generally interested in only ratings and profit. As one general manager said during an interview, "Ratings? Am I concerned about ratings? Let me tell you. Ratings are the last thing I think about . . . before I go to bed each night." So if this is the game we station managers are playing, what can be said about the responsibility of rock radio stations to participate in the socialization of their adolescent listeners?

If you've got a format that's working and the adolescents are tuning in in sufficient numbers to keep the concert promoters and the pimple cream pushers and the soda pop manufacturers happy, no one expects you to mess it all up with a format change in order to become responsible. I will not even suggest that stations stop telling postpubescent teens that "Tonight's the Night," that "Good Girls Don't, But I Do,"

* Michael Hirsh is president of Michael Hirsh Productions, executive producer for WTTW-Chicago Public Television; and producer of "Express," WLS-Radio, Chicago.

At the Metro-Help National Runaway Switchboard, there is always someone available to talk to young people in trouble. The Metro-Help staff works with the producer of "Express," WLS, Chicago, to reach teens with problems.

PUBLIC SERVICE RADIO SPOTS
ON RESPONSIBLE PARENTHOOD
Transcripts

LINDA RONSTADT:

I had a roommate, this girl had a kid and she stayed with me, and I really got a first-hand experience at caring for a kid. I know exactly how much responsibility is involved. It's more than anybody dreams of that doesn't have a kid and I know that sometime I'll have time for it. I don't think anything should stop people, like "Oh, this is a terrible world" to have children or any of that stuff, but what should stop them is whether they really think they're ready to handle it.

COMMODORES

Announcer: We asked William King of the Commodores about being a teenage parent.

King: It's the young mother that's really gonna find it hard. A 15 or 16 year old girl with a baby who has no help cannot go to those parties, cannot go to the movies, cannot go out with her friends, cannot go to the playground with the basketball game. She has to stay home and take care of that baby.

Announcer: For birth control information call THE ANSWER LINE at 942-6006. That number again is 942-6006.

CHIC

Announcer: We asked Nile Rogers of Chic about who *is* responsible for birth control.

Rogers: That's another thing that really bothers me is the lack of responsibility on both parts. In other words, it has to be a mutual thing. If she's not prepared and you're not prepared, oh well, then you just, you know, kiss and shake hands or something. You know, like, accidents, man, are a drag.

Announcer: For information about birth control call THE ANSWER LINE at 942-6006. That number again is 942-6006.

MUHAMMAD ALI

Announcer: Muhammad Ali, do you think being a teenage father would have affected your career?

Ali: I think it would have affected my life. I wasn't making no money at the time. I would have had to get out and work to support the child and take care of it. At the age of seventeen or eighteen I don't think I could have put my mind fully to boxing like I did.
Announcer: Nobody wins with an unwanted pregnancy.

Text of public service radio spots on responsible parenthood, by the Center for Population Options.

or that "My Sharonna should feel it growin' down my thigh, Sharonna."

What I am suggesting is that station owners look at what they're
doing now with the air time allotted to those things they promised
the FCC when they asked it to grant or renew their licenses: news,
public affairs programming, and public service announcements
(PSAs).

The public service director is the person responsible most often for
the mix of PSAs on air, and quite often is responsible for public affairs
programming. This person is likely also to be involved with ascertain-
ment. Once the director's slot is filled, the manager could care less
about it. The public service director is not looked to for a profit, or
ratings, or awards, but as someone to keep the community groups
off the manager's back, someone who can go to the rubber chicken
luncheons to reaffirm the station's concern about the community, and
someone who can spend hours on the telephone with obstreperous
citizens pushing a cause.

Given these circumstances, it's no wonder that we hear PSAs on a
hard rock station that sound like this: "That's The Knack, saying
Good Girls Don't . . . in a moment, the Doobies. Say, the Lake View
Presbyterian Church Women's Club is holding a potluck social this
coming Saturday night. For more information call 555-2345." Now the
station manager knows that there are not three listeners in his or her
vast audience who can or will relate to the Knack, the Doobie Brothers, and a potluck supper at a church on Saturday night. But he or she
doesn't think twice about it.

Think of it in this way. If the general manager tuned in and heard
the disc jockey say that right after Elton John we were going to hear
the Eagles, followed by Tony Bennett, it's likely the program director
and the music director would be on the line in seconds. All of this is
leading to my theory of socially responsible radio programming aimed
at teens: program PSAs for the target audience just as you would
program music to them. It's not hard to do. First, the public service
director is going to be thrilled to learn that you care enough about
what he or she is doing. Second, he or she will see to it that you get
some positive feedback (in writing for your public file) from the
groups he or she is starting to work with, and that will give you a
subtle sense of satisfaction. And third, you might even be doing some
good for your audience, which if we are to believe the statistics, needs
all the help it can get just to cope with growing up in the society
we've created.

A switch to audience-specific PSAs will require educating those groups and agencies in your area to understand what to submit for use on the station. This means that the public service director will have to learn enough about those groups so they can be channelled in the right direction. For example, the public service director can tell Alcoholics Anonymous that copy aimed at those who find liquor destroying their marriages and career may be important, but copy suggesting how a teenager can find a support group to help in coping with an alcoholic parent will get on the air. Copy from Planned Parenthood warning of an epidemic of venereal disease might be useful, but a PSA informing teens that under the law they have a right to treatment without parental knowledge or consent would be better. And instead of telling teenagers who see rampant unemployment that staying in school is the surest way to get a good job, the director can find out what agencies are offering counseling for dropouts and perhaps create some short, format-fitting PSAs that might be especially relevant.

There can be a profitable symbiotic relationship between youth-serving agencies and youth-reaching radio stations. Social service agency people need to co-opt the public service director. They can make this person feel important by asking him or her to serve on a media advisory committee and trying to make the director feel as if he or she has a vested interest in the agency's success.

The public service director is the gatekeeper to air time that could cost thousands of dollars if one had to pay for it. The station manager doesn't care whether the PSA on the schedule pushes the church social or the local teen hotline, and unfortunately neither does the FCC. Agencies that can make the director take a personal interest in them will find that the director will take every opportunity to help their cause.

When the director has ascertained community needs, agencies could help find leaders, both adult and teen, who speak to the needs of the audience served by the station. Agencies might also let the director's boss know, in writing, that she or he is an outstanding station asset.

Youth-serving agencies with more than one station in town programming to the teen market that don't already have a Radio Public Service Award to present annually at a major board meeting or dinner are missing a bet. The incentive of picking up an award has caused more stories to be done and programs to be produced than any other, save profit. The plaque should be presented to the general manager, but a duplicate inscribed to the public service director or station staff member who worked with the agency is also appropriate.

Agencies should not be afraid to honor more than one station at the same time. The people to whom the station manager is accountable don't care that they didn't get the only award; what matters is that they "won." If you doubt the validity of this theory, look at the number of local television Emmy awards presented in a city like Chicago. They give them away by the bushel basketful, and that doesn't stop the stations from taking out full-page ads to trumpet their victories.

Rock stations should examine their audience for public affairs programming as well. Are you producing a weekly panel show that looks "Inside Politics" or highlights "Issues in the News" and scheduling it in fringe time on the Sunday overnight because no one is listening? If you handled your bread-and-butter programming that way, you'd soon be on your way out of town. So why produce throwaway public affairs shows? The answer is obvious: you promised the FCC a certain percentage of such programming. The FCC doesn't care what it is as long as it can legitimately be called public affairs. The news director probably has enough to do fighting to keep a viable news operation at a rock station without battling for on-target public affairs programs in a decent time slot. So what's the point of this discussion? Forgive me a case history.

The station in question is ABC-owned WLS in Chicago, a 50,000-watt clear channel reputed to reach forty-three states on a good night. And Sunday is a very good night. Since July 1979, WLS has been reaching its primary evening audience, teens, with a twenty-five-minute public affairs show, "Express." The program is supplied to the station free of charge, it carries music from the WLS playlist, and does very well in the ratings.

Since it has been on the air, "Express" has dealt in detail with the entire panoply of subjects that fall under the heading of "coping information for teens." Some of these are problems, like VD, pregnancy, and sexual or physical abuse. But others are just concerns that young people have about growing up, concerns that have not been explained away by parents, peers, or teachers but that are very real to the young person going through adolescence. Teens are starved for an indication that what they're going through is not freakish or abnormal. They need to be told that the changeover from child to adult is routinely difficult, and they're not alone.

One "Express" show dealt with this by having the host read winning entries in an essay contest. The winners received an album for submitting a single-page letter beginning, "The hardest thing about being a teenager is . . ." Many of the entries talked about problems with parents, problems of freedom to be grown-up, to stay out late, to date. A week after that show aired, a letter received by the station confirmed that what it was doing was reaching the target audience. The signed letter goes this way:

> I listened to your program last night. You read some of the winners of the essay contest. The girls who didn't like their parents' questions every-time they went out reminded me of someone . . . me! I always hated it when Mom asked where I was going, who I was going to be with, what we were going to do, etc. I always felt that she was violating my privacy in some way. But now I think I understand why parents do that. Because the hardest thing about being a teenager, for me, happened this summer.
>
> My nineteen-year-old sister was home from college for the summer. Since she had been on her own for over a year, Mom didn't really ask her what she was going to be doing. One night she went down to the bars with a friend, but her friend didn't feel well and went home. My sister never made it home that night. When we got up the next day and she wasn't there we thought that she had gotten drunk and stayed at someone's house. By dinnertime when she still wasn't home we started to worry. Her friend had no idea what had happened to her. We started calling everyone that she knew to see if they had heard from her. No one had. Four days later they found her body. Some of her clothes had been ripped off but no one will tell me whether she had been raped or not. If she had called and said that she was going to such and such a place with so and so, we would have known who she was with and we would have caught the guy long before we did. Every time I hear one of my friends complain because their parents want to know where they are going to be, I think of my sister and pray that none of them ever have to go through the pain and agony that she must have gone through.
>
> Now I understand why parents want to know what's going on. They worry about us. Every time I'm late, Mom wonders if the same thing happened to me. At night I hear her crying herself to sleep, and I cry too. I'm seventeen and I've been through the same thing that the girls who wrote those letters are going through. But they haven't gone through the searching for their sister, finding her body, the visitation and funeral, and the search for the person who killed her. Please explain to them that all the questions are for their own good. It may save their lives someday.

A highly formated rock radio station has no time during regular programming hours to read a letter like that and have it mean some-thing. But the WLS management worked with my production company to develop a program series that has broken new ground on the radio in meeting the needs of a teen audience.

That's not to say that things always went smoothly. In the begin-ning there were some interesting conversations with management and the ABC network censors in New York. The censors were surprisingly supportive of the show, but despite the support, they were also concerned about the station's sense of responsibility to its audience. Nevertheless, we persevered, and in its first year on the air "Express" received several hundred pieces of positive mail, generated more than a thousand legitimate calls to the sponsoring hotline agency, and provoked no more than a half-dozen complaints.

Now in its second year, the program is paid for by Metro-Help, Inc., a Chicago-based, twenty-four-hour, seven-days-a-week hotline service for youth, which also operates the National Runaway Switchboard (NRS). The toll-free NRS number now enables us to serve young people outside the Chicago area who pick up WLS's powerful signal. It also is enabling us to begin distributing the show to other stations around the country, provided the stations are willing to pick up the cost of tape duplication and mailing.

"Express" is successful because the format works (approximately ten minutes of music mixed in with fifteen minutes of coping information played over a nonstop music bed), played on the right station (targeted at ages twelve to nineteen, and ratings indicate success in reaching females twelve to twenty-four), in a time slot that has an audience available to it (11 p.m. Sundays, not 3 a.m., where many other public affairs show play).

No subjects are off limits to "Express." There is a caveat, however, for providing sex and birth control on the air. Early on we struck a deal with WLS: if we are explaining birth control, we will also provide what became known as "virgin information." Surprisingly the mail indicated that coping with peer pressure to be sexually active when one didn't want to be was high on the list of subjects adolescents wanted to hear about. And it was not limited to twelve- and thirteen-year-olds expressing that concern. A number of letters from eighteen- and nineteen-year-olds asked if they were normal because they didn't want to have sex. This type of information is difficult to deal with because, unlike explanations of contraception, pat answers don't exist. Politically, however, it was essential to deal with these questions, and programmatically it was right to deal with them.

Finally, let's take a brief look at news programming that targets the teen audience. I am not suggesting that we talk down to adolescents or treat them as people who don't care or don't have to care about major events taking place in the world. Rather, news directors should sensitize writers, reporters, and newscasters to the teen angle in a story. For example, if teenagers (like many adults) listen with half an ear, it is important to emphasize that when the surgeon general expresses concern about women who smoke taking the pill, this does not mean that young women on the pill should quit taking it—until they find a suitable replacement. The danger of teenage pregnancy is significantly more harmful than the results of being a teenage pill user who smokes, and that fact should be emphasized to the teenage audience. Similarly, when the Supreme Court ruled that the government was not required to fund welfare abortions, many young people thought the Court had ruled abortions illegal. A line explaining that might have been helpful.

A routine contact with the local teen hotline service might have turned up the fact that callers were confused about issues like these, resulting in explanatory news stories aimed right at the audience. For example, Chicago's Metro-Help received a significant number of calls from young people who were completely confused about the problem of toxic shock syndrome and its relationship to tampon use. A radio station wired into such an agency would be led to a terrific story aimed right at its audience.

Contact between youth-serving agencies and the news department is a good idea if the news department is interested in keeping up with what's happening. Not too long ago, a Chicago television station was doing a hysterical mini-documentary series on high school drug use. At the same time, Metro-Help was logging a distinct drop in questions about drugs from adolescents and a concomitant rise in calls related to alcohol. I have no doubts as to which organization—the TV station or the hotline—was more in tune with reality.

Nothing I have suggested here will cost the station money. On the contrary, it might result in a larger audience in day-parts that were not doing well because of lackluster but obligatory programming. And at the risk of sounding Pollyannish, doing this kind of programming has been one way I've been able to show my own two kids that I care, and it has strengthened our ability to communicate.

That's hardly a witty, humorous way to conclude, but it's appropriate. If you need convincing, sit down for a chat about life with some young people—yours or anyone else's.

Resources, Chapter Seven

NBC-Radio. *The Source.* NBC Radio's Young Adult Network, Press Dept., 30 Rockefeller Plaza, New York, N.Y. 10020.

Sobel, Robert. "Maturing, Fragmented Audience Changes the Tune." *Television/Radio Age*, August 11, 1980, pp. 35–38, 68.

Weintraub, Neal T. "Some Meanings Radio Has for Teenagers." *Journal of Broadcasting* 15:2 (Spring 1971): 147–152.

8 Advertising & the Teen Market

Money has its foot on my neck
It controls me.

I turn flips
Jump through hoops
And tell him what I think.

Every now and then
I even get applause

For being . . . all that reflect
his thinking . . .
his culture . . .
his interest . . .

Maybe I should get his foot
Off my neck

But then . . .
I would have to stand.

Warrington Hudlin, II
East St. Louis, Illinois

Advertising to Adolescents

GEORGE MOSCHIS

THE ADOLESCENT MARKET is of particular importance to market-ers of consumer goods for several reasons: the number of teens, their purchasing power, their influence on family spending patterns, and their formation of attitudes and interests that influence their consump-tion behavior in later life.

A recent survey indicates that teenagers (thirteen- to nineteen-year-olds) number approximately 28 million. These consumers spent ap-proximately $30 billion on a variety of products in 1979. The largest portion of these expenditures was on clothes ($5.7 billion) and enter-tainment ($4.7 billion).[1] Teenagers also buy a staggering percentage of personal care products and sports and leisure equipment. Generally, expenditures by teenagers vary according to their age and sex. An earlier study by the Youth Research Institute found that older teen-agers (sixteen- to nineteen-year-olds) had more than three times as much discretionary income as younger teenagers.[2] Expenditures on items of personal appearance such as clothing and cosmetics are greater among teenage girls than boys primarily due to values stressed in the American culture.

Besides their purchasing power, teenage consumers have great in-fluence on adult and family purchases. Such influential spending (pur-chases in which youth play an influential role) was estimated several years ago at $145 billion.[3] A more recent study found that teenage

* George P. Moschis, Ph.D., is an associate professor of marketing at Georgia State University. He is the co-author of *Export Marketing Management*.

girls alone prepare an average of thirteen meals per week and spend over $13 billion a year on food, more than one out of every three family food dollars.[4]

Adolescence is a period during which consumption-related attitudes and interests are formed, patterns of consumer behavior that are likely to persist well into adulthood. A recent brand-loyalty study prepared by Yankelovich, Skelly & White for *Seventeen* magazine found that a significant percentage of women were using the same brands they first chose as teenagers.[5] Soft drink manufacturers are especially aware that brand preference develops during adolescence, and they advertise heavily to this market. An advertising executive for Pepsi-Cola recently said, "When you catch them young they stay with you."

Advertising to Teenagers

Advertising to adolescents tends to be limited primarily to products adolescents buy or influence family members to buy. Major categories include soft drinks, sporting goods, clothing (especially jeans), personal care products, models and games, and other entertainment items such as records and movies. These products are advertised in different media but especially radio, television, and magazines.

In many situations radio is considered to be the most effective medium for reaching the teen market, primarily because of its ability to reach a large portion of the teenage population. Because teenagers frequently listen to the radio for music and entertainment, many advertisers incorporate music and entertainment in their advertising message to keep teenagers listening throughout the commercial.

Teenagers are not considered to be heavy television viewers; they make up approximately 11 percent of the television audience, according to a 1981 A. C. Nielsen study.[6] Television commercials of products used by teenagers tend to emphasize the nonfunctional aspects of the product such as social significance of the product, group conformity, and acceptance. Common themes include humor, fun, excitement, and togetherness. These types of advertisements are believed to be appropriate for teenagers because teenage peer groups are significant sources of influence. Adolescence is a period of psychological transition of the child from his family into peer groups, substituting dependence on peers for his earlier dependence on parents. In this process, peer values and norms become very salient to the teenager who is looking for ways of identifying with peer groups.

Magazines are also effective in reaching teenagers. They represent one of the most diverse categories in the publishing business. Such youth-oriented publications are often tailored to certain audiences with respect to age group as well to the interests of youths. For example, *Boys' Life* is edited exclusively for boys ages nine to sixteen, while *Hit Parade* is geared to rock-oriented youth of various ages. Advertisements placed in youth publications tend to be consistent with the profile of the target audiences they serve.[7]

Adolescents' responses to advertising in different media appear to vary considerably. According to a study of youngsters (grades four through twelve), newspaper advertising is perceived as most credible and television advertising as least credible. (Credibility of magazine advertising increases and credibility of television advertising decreases with age.) Television advertising is the more interesting and best liked type of advertising and is likely to attract more attention than other types. Newspaper advertising, on the other hand, is the least interesting and least liked, but young people consider it to be the most helpful.[8] In another study of adolescents' preferences for sources of consumer information, television, newspaper, and magazine advertisements were rated equally, although these ratings tended to vary by type of product.[9] Teenagers' preferences for advertising in various media appear to be influenced by socioeconomic characteristics. Television advertisements are preferred more by blacks than whites, while newspaper ads are more likely to be preferred by upper-class than lower-class teenagers.[10]

Radio and magazines are often considered to be the most important media in reaching the teenage market, but most of the research on advertising's effects on adolescents has focused on television. Advertising effects generally refer to changes in the youth's thoughts and actions that occur because of his or her viewing of commercials in the various media. One major influence is the effect of advertising on the development of the youth's self-concept. Self-concepts examined in traditional studies of advertising effects tend to fall into three categories: consumer roles, occupational roles, and sex roles.

Studies examining consumer-role perceptions usually focus on either desirable or undesirable consequences of advertising on youths. Among the desirable consequences of television advertising is the development of positive consumer skills regarding purchase and consumption of products, such as budgeting skills; undesirable consequences include materialistic attitudes and nonrational motivations for consumption. Nearly all of the studies examining the effects of television advertising on consumer-role perceptions have found correlations between the amount of television viewing (consequently the number of advertisements teenagers are exposed to) and undesirable consumer orientations, such as materialism and social motivations for

consumption.[11] The effects of television advertising on positive consumer skills, on the other hand, have been mixed. For example, one
study found television viewing to be positively associated with good
consumer-role perceptions, while another found negative relationships
between economic motives and amount of television viewing.[12]

Advertising may also affect an individual's conception of occupational roles. Commercials provide occupational cues for athletes and
movie stars. Most occupational stereotyping in advertisements, however, concerns occupations portrayed by women. Content analysis of
advertisements shows that women in commercials have traditionally
been stereotyped as housewives and mothers, with such stereotyping
remaining relatively constant over the years.[13] Research suggests that
youths are likely to develop occupational stereotypes by viewing television commercials.[14] In addition to occupational stereotyping, viewing
of television commercials where portrayal of traditional sex roles regarding consumption activity is frequent may lead to the development
of stereotyped sex-role conception regarding consumer decision making. The results of a recent study show a positive relationship between
the amount of television a teenager watches and his or her likelihood
of holding traditional, nonegalitarian family decision roles.[15]

Studies of advertising effects on teenagers' self-concepts have been
limited to surveys. The results have been inferred from associations
found between amount of exposure to a particular medium and aspects
of the adolescent's self-concept. As a result, advertising effects can be
confounded by programming effects and by other factors that may
affect the development of the teenager's self-concept.

The effects of advertising on teenagers' self-concept development
are likely to depend on various characteristics of the teenage consumer.
A large number of studies show that advertising and other commercial
and noncommercial sources of consumer information are likely to have
a greater impact to the extent that the youth is black (or of other
minority background), of lower socioeconomic background, younger,
and lives in rural rather than urban areas.[16] This may be due to the
fact that teenagers possessing such characteristics are likely to be more
isolated from various paths of experience and that their lack of information may make them more susceptible to exploitation by commercials.[17]

References

1. "The New Teens," Today Show (NBC), May 14, 1980.

2. Youth Research Institute, *The Dynamics of the Youth Explosion* (Los
Angeles: Chamber of Commerce, 1967).

3. "Getting Across to the Young," *Business Week*, October 18, 1969, pp. 89.

4. "Teenage Girls Spend Billions Food Shopping," *Editor and Publisher*, September 29, 1979, p. 38.

5. "Youth Marketing," *Advertising Age*, April 28, 1980, pp. S1–S24.

6. Ibid.

7. Ibid.

8. Don L. James, "Youth, Media, and Advertising" (Austin, Texas: Bureau of Business Research, 1971).

9. George P. Moschis and Roy L. Moore, "Decision-Making among the Young: A Socialization Perspective," *Journal of Consumer Research* (September 1979): 101–112.

10. George P. Moschis and Roy L. Moore, "Purchasing Behavior of Adolescent Consumers" (Paper presented at the Annual Conference of the American Marketing Association, Chicago, 1980), pp. 89–92.

11. See, for example, George P. Moschis and Gilbert A. Churchill, Jr., "Consumer Socialization: A Theoretical and Empirical Analysis," *Journal of Marketing Research* (November 1978): 599–609, and Scott Ward and Daniel Wackman, "Family and Media Influence on Adolescent Consumer Learning," *American Behavioral Scientist* (January–February 1971): 415–427.

12. See, for example, Gilbert A. Churchill, Jr., and George P. Moschis, "Television and Interpersonal Influences on Adolescent Consumer Learning," *Journal of Consumer Research* (June 1979): 23–35, and George P. Moschis and Roy L. Moore, "An Analysis of the Acquisition of Some Consumer Competencies Among Adolescents," *Journal of Consumer Affairs* (Winter 1978): 277–291.

13. Alice E. Courtney and Thomas W. Whipple, *Sex Stereotyping in Advertising: An Annotated Bibliography* (Cambridge, Mass.: Marketing Science Institute, 1979).

14. Ibid.

15. George P. Moschis and Roy L. Moore, "Anticipatory Consumer Socialization" (unpublished paper, Georgia State University, 1980).

16. John B. Christiansen, "Television Role Models and Adolescent Occupational Goals," *Human Communication Research* (Summer 1979): 335–337.

17. Robert D. Hess, "Social Class and Ethnic Influence upon Socialization," in Paul Mussen, ed., *Manual of Child Psychology*, 3d ed. (New York: John Wiley & Sons, 1970), pp. 457–559.

Love's Baby Soft.
Because innocence is sexier than you think.

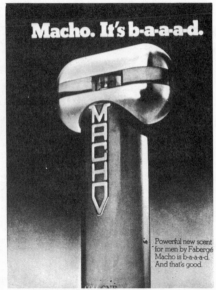

Macho. It's b-a-a-a-d.

Powerful new scent
for men by Fabergé
Macho is b-a-a-a-d.
And that's good.

Gentlemen prefer Hanes

These are only three of the many examples of sexist advertising that are pointed out in Jean Kilbourne's film "The Naked Truth: Advertising's Image of Women."

Sex Roles in Advertising

JEAN KILBOURNE

ADVERTISING AFFECTS ALL of us throughout our lives. Adolescents are particularly vulnerable, however, because they are new and inexperienced consumers and are the prime targets of many advertisements. They are in the process of learning their values and roles and developing their self-concepts. Most teenagers are sensitive to peer pressure and find it difficult to resist or even question the dominant cultural messages perpetuated and reinforced by the media. Mass communication has made possible a kind of national peer pressure that erodes private and individual values and standards. Margaret Mead once said that today our children are brought up by the mass media rather than by parents.

Advertisers are aware of their role and do not hesitate to take advantage of the insecurities and anxieties of young people, in the guise of offering solutions. A cigarette provides a symbol of independence. A pair of designer jeans conveys status. The right perfume or beer resolves doubts about femininity or masculinity. Since so many anxieties have to do with sexuality and intimacy and since advertising so often offers products as the answers and uses sex to sell, it is perhaps the concept of sex roles that is most deeply affected.

What do teenagers learn about sex roles from television commer-

* Jean Kilbourne is a media analyst, writer, and lecturer. She is the creator of two slide presentations, "The Naked Truth: Advertising's Image of Women" and "Under the Influence: The Pushing of Alcohol via Advertising," and a film, "Killing Us Softly."

cials? On the most obvious level, they learn the stereotypes. These stereotypes have existed for a long time and certainly have not been created or perpetuated solely by advertising. Sexism and sex-role stereotyping exist in every aspect of our society, and we receive these messages from birth. No messenger is more pervasive or persuasive, however, than advertising.

The stereotypes in television commercials have changed very little. Women are shown almost exclusively as sex objects or as demented housewives pathologically obsessed by cleanliness. Men are generally rugged authority figures, dominant and invulnerable. Men who are married or engaged in "women's work" are often portrayed as idiots and buffoons. These stereotypes, and to some extent their effects, have been well documented.

Young people are also affected by advertising in other more subtle ways—ways more indirect but perhaps more powerful than the stereotypes (which increasingly are being recognized and sometimes ridiculed). Advertising could be considered the propaganda of this society. It teaches us to be consumers, to value material things above all else, to feel that happiness can be bought, that there are instant solutions to life's complex problems, and that products can fulfill us and meet our deepest human needs. As a result, objects and things are given great importance and value, and people are often reified and objectified. This is particularly true for women but is increasingly true for men as well. Women, especially young women, are primarily depicted as sex objects and men as success objects. In both cases, the person becomes a thing, and his or her value depends upon the products used.

The sex object is a mannequin, a shell. Conventional beauty is her only attribute. She has no lines or wrinkles (which are, after all, signs of maturity, expression, and experience), no scars or blemishes; indeed, she has no pores. She is thin, generally tall and long legged, and above all young. All "beautiful" women in television commercials, regardless of product or audience, conform to this norm. Women are constantly exhorted to emulate this ideal, to feel ashamed and guilty if they fail, and to feel that their desirability and capacity for being loved are contingent upon physical perfection.

The image is artificial and can only be achieved artificially. Desperate to conform to an ideal and impossible standard, many women go to great lengths to manipulate and change their faces and bodies. More than a million dollars is spent every hour on cosmetics. A woman is conditioned to view her face as a mask and her body as an object, as things separate from and more important than her real self, constantly in need of alteration, improvement, and disguise. She is made to feel dissatisfied with and ashamed of herself, whether she tries to achieve "the look" or not. Objectified constantly by others, she learns to objectify herself.

Women are dismembered in commercials, their bodies separated into parts in need of change or improvement. If a woman has "acceptable" breasts, then she must also be sure that her legs are worth watching, her hips slim, her feet sexy, and that her buttocks look nude under her clothes ("like I'm not wearin' nothin' "). The mannequin has no depth, no totality. She is an aggregate of parts that have been made acceptable.

Girls and young women are primary targets of this message and are socialized to spend enormous amounts of time, energy, and money striving to achieve this ideal. They are made to feel very anxious and insecure about their appearance and their bodies. This preoccupation diverts energy and attention from more important pursuits and the development of their minds and spirits. Ironically the heavily advertised products, such as cosmetics and soft drinks, are even detrimental to physical attractiveness. There is very little emphasis in the media on good nutrition and exercise and other important aspects of health and vitality.

Most women learn a sense of inferiority and insecurity and of hostile competition with other women. Even the rare teenager who does approximate the ideal suffers. She may experience stunted development in other areas of life and damaged relationships with other women. The constant objectification can lead to callous disregard for others or to a fear that her entire value is contingent upon her appearance. The cultural worship of the adolescent female can lead to unrealistic expectations for the future and can contribute to lifelong rage against women by rejected men. The image harms us all, whether or not we approximate it briefly in our lives.

Young women are also discouraged from growing up and becoming adult. Growing older is the great taboo. Women are encouraged to remain little girls ("because innocence is sexier that you think"), to be passive and dependent, never to mature. The contradictory message, "sensual, but not too far from innocence," places women in a double bind. Somehow women are supposed to be both sexy and virginal, experienced and naive, seductive and chaste. The disparagement of maturity is insulting and frustrating to adult women, and the implication that little girls are seductive is dangerous to real children.

Young people also learn a great deal about sexual attitudes from the media and from advertising in particular. Advertising's approach to sex is pornographic; it reduces people to objects and deemphasizes human contact and individuality. This reduction of sexuality to a dirty joke and of people to objects is the real obscenity of the culture. Although the sexual sell, overt and subliminal, is at a fevered pitch in most commercials, there is at the same time a notable absence of sex as an important and profound human activity. Sex in commercials is narcissistic and autoerotic and exists apart from relationships. Identical models parade alone through the commercials, caressing their own soft skin, stroking and hugging their bodies, shaking their long silky manes, sensually bathing and applying powders and lotions, and then admiring themselves at length in the mirror. Commercials depict a world in which there is pervasive sexual innuendo but no love and in which passion is reserved solely for products.

The curious sterility is due mainly to the stereotypes, which reduce variation and individuality, mock the process of self-realization, and make empathy impossible. When the goal is to embody the stereotype, which is by definition shallow and uniform, depth, passion, and uniqueness are inevitably lost. Men lose, of course, as well as women. Although not as subject to the tyranny of the aesthetic ideal themselves, men are made to feel inadequate if their women—that is, their property—don't measure up ("My wife, I think I'll keep her"). Women are portrayed as sexually desirable only if they are young, thin, carefully polished and groomed, made up, depilated, sprayed, and scented —rendered quite unerotic, in fact—and men are conditioned to seek such partners and to feel disappointed if they fail.

The main goal of sex in advertising, as in pornography, is power over another, either by the physical dominance or preferred status of men or what is seen as the exploitative power of female beauty and female sexuality. Men conquer and women ensnare, always with the essential aid of a product.

Although men are allowed and encouraged to become adults, the acceptable images for males are limited and rigid too. Men are generally conditioned to be obsessed by status and success as measured in material terms and to look upon women as objects, as things to be acquired as further evidence of status. There is a great difference between the portrayal of single men and that of married men. Single men are generally independent and powerful. Married men are often presented as idiots, as if contaminated by their relationship with women. This is particularly true of those few men shown doing domestic chores or relating to children. The stereotypes of men have changed very little.

There have been some changes in the images of women. Indeed a "new woman" has emerged in commercials in recent years. She is generally presented as superwoman, who manages to do all the work at home and on the job (with the help of a product, not of her husband), or as the liberated woman, who owes her independence and self-esteem to the products she uses. These new images do not represent any real progress but rather create a myth of progress, an illusion that reduces complex sociopolitical problems to mundane personal ones, thereby trivializing the issues and diverting energy and attention from a search for genuine solutions.

Superwoman is perhaps the most damaging stereotype of all. Many young women now seem to feel that they can effortlessly combine marriage and a career. The myth of progress obscures the fact that the overwhelming majority of women are in low-status, low-paying jobs and are as far removed from superwoman's elite executive status as the majority of men have always been removed from her male counterpart. The definition of success is still entirely male. The successful woman is presented as climbing up the corporate ladder, seeking money and power. The working woman is expected to get ahead in this man's world, which requires strict adherence to male values, while always giving first priority to her role as wife and mother. In addition, the myth of superwoman places total responsibility for change on the individual woman and exempts men from the responsibilities and rewards of domestic life and child care.

The models for adulthood that commercials offer adolescents are extremely limited and contradictory. Women are supposed to be little girls or superwomen or both. Men are rigidly socialized to repress all feelings of vulnerability, thereby virtually guaranteeing that intimate relationships will be impossible. Motherhood is presented as essential for women and fatherhood as irrelevant for men. Sexuality becomes a commodity.

Resources, Chapter Eight

Bodec, Ben. "Fewer Teens, More Spending." *Marketing and Media Decisions* 16:4 (April 1981): 76–78, 116, 118.

Churchill, Gilbert A., and Moschis, George P. "Television and Interpersonal Influences on Adolescent Consumer Learning." *Journal of Consumer Research* 6:1 (June 1979): 23–35.

Kilbourne, Jean. *Images of Women in TV Commercials.* New York: Workman Publishing, 1977.

"Killing Us Softly: Advertising's Image of Women." A twenty-nine-minute, 16-mm film based on Jean Kilbourne's slide presentation. Produced and distributed by Cambridge Documentary Films, Inc., Box 385, Cambridge, Mass. 02139.

Meyer, Ed. "It's a Tough Challenge, but the Teen Market Has Its Rewards." *Advertising Age,* February 19, 1979, pp. 62–63.

Monat, Zucia. "Most 17-year-olds Are Not Skilled Consumers." *Christian Science Monitor,* October 7, 1979, p. 5.

Tan, Alexis S. "TV Beauty Ads and Role Expectations of Adolescent Female Viewers." *Journalism Quarterly* 56:2 (Summer 1979): 283–288.

Index

217